HOUSE OF PAIN

NOV - - 2013

FARMERS BRANCH MANSKE LIBRARY
13613 Webb Chapel
Farmers Branch, TX 75234-3756

D1260524

House of Pain

NEW AND SELECTED ESSAYS

Laurence Gonzales

The University of Arkansas Press
Fayetteville
2013

Copyright © 2013 by Laurence Gonzales

All rights reserved
Manufactured in the United States of America

ISBN-10: 1-55728-999-9
ISBN-13: 978-1-55728-999-5

17   16   15   14   13   5   4   3   2   1

Designed by Liz Lester

♾ The paper used in this publication meets the minimum requirements
of the American National Standard for Permanence of Paper
for Printed Library Materials Z39.48–1984.

LIBRARY OF CONGRESS CONTROL NUMBER: 2013945834

To the memory of Carolyn Florence Lorence
(June 29, 1947–April 23, 2013)

CONTENTS

PREFACE

When I was a child I was fascinated by my father's daring. He had come miraculously through the war, and now all his life seemed blessed with a magical quality, both rich and impervious, and he launched himself into it, laughing all the way. He married the beauty queen and had seven strapping sons. He became a respected professor and turned out hundreds of doctors and dentists from his student body at Northwestern University. It was something of a fairy tale, and I was part of it. Yet all along I felt that to be a real part of it, I had to be annealed in the fires as he had been. I felt that I needed some stamp of authenticity to participate fully in this life.

In a sense, my career as a writer has been a long quest for that authenticity. And these essays are a product of that quest. They eventually led me down the road to writing another book, *Deep Survival*. I folded all these experiences into that book and explored the question that had always taunted me: *who lives, who dies, and why?* Along the way, I learned that the quest for authenticity always involves risk and does not always end happily.

These essays represent my own formative years as a writer and have formed the basis of all my work that came afterward. They represent my attempt to face down danger and prove myself. And they later went on to become the foundation of my quest to understand what happens in that earthly bargain and why it happens the way it does.

HOUSE OF PAIN

MARION PRISON

Next to killing someone or trying to escape, the most serious offenses that a prisoner in the US Penitentiary at Marion, Illinois, can commit are drinking and being caught in possession of money.

There are many ways to make alcohol in USP-Marion, but the simplest is to take two small boxes of Kellogg's corn flakes and dump them into the toilet bowl in your cell. Let them fester for a week, and the result will get you drunk. Some inmates are more ambitious than that. From the prison log: "August 5, 1982: Approximately four gallons of brew found in cell of Ronnie Bruscino, 20168-148."

It is part of the magical transmutation of elements that occurs in the most maximum state of incarceration in America today: Marion Prison. After an extended period of being locked up with nothing to do, cut off from the sight of other human beings, the sounds and smells of normal life, you begin to see the world transform itself. Nothing is as it seems. One thing changes into another. If you stare at a typewriter for long enough with nothing else to occupy your mind, nothing else to stimulate your senses, the platen rods begin to look like shish kabob skewers. Then one day you find yourself with one of them in your hand, and it has been sharpened, and you have wrapped a sweatband around the blunt end for a better grip, and you are plunging the point into someone's chest. Jack Henry Abbott, convicted murderer and author of *In the Belly of the Beast*, wrote, "It is like cutting hot butter, no resistance at all."

The guards come and take you away. The administration orders the typewriters removed from the library. You are locked in your cell. You are left with nothing but the steel bunk, three walls, the air vent, the grille. But after you've stared at the air vent for months on end, it too begins to change. Instead of the metal frame and duct, you begin to see long, gleaming isosceles triangles. You get a four-inch bit of hacksaw blade that someone at Lewisburg Penitentiary swallowed before he was transferred here and expelled from his body upon arrival, a scrap of metal that has been passed from man to man, mouth to mouth, rectum to rectum, hand to hand, by the fleeting practiced prestidigitation of inmates making contact on the way to the shower or the visiting room. You spend weeks gently sawing at the edge of the air vent with this tiny bit of serrated metal, and each day you putty the cut you've made, using a mixture of Dial and Ivory soap, blended to match the flesh-colored paint that seems to obscure everything in this prison. And when you've finally sawed the shank of metal free from the edge of the vent, you spend another week (or two or three—you have time, nothing but time) on your hands and knees, patiently rubbing it against the concrete floor whenever the guards aren't looking, until it becomes pointed like that isosceles triangle you dreamed of. Then you work on it some more until it is sharp enough to shave with. It's almost art.

You ignite a book of matches and melt your toothbrush to make a handle for the pristine knife.

Then one day you find yourself plunging it into someone's chest. And the guards take the metal beds away and replace them with concrete slabs, and they throw you in the hole with nothing but a Bible and your underwear and a bed sheet. So you soak the Bible in the toilet until it is water-logged and weighs fifteen pounds, and you wrap it in your T-shirt, and when the guard comes to get you for your weekly shower, you swing it overhead like a bludgeon and fracture his skull.

All of these things have happened at USP-Marion.

An entry in the prison's log:

> April 2, 1980: While being processed for a U.S. District Court appearance, inmate Bryan, Joseph 15562-175 was found to be in possession of two (2) handcuff keys made from a "Doodle Art Pen." They were found hidden in the hollowed out bottom of his tennis shoe. The keys were made to fit the S & W handcuffs carried by the U.S. Marshall's Service. Bryan was in the Control Unit (H-Unit) at the time the incident occurred.

How does a Doodle Art Pen become a cuff key? These are the secrets of solitary confinement at Marion that no visitor can learn. A

MARION PRISON

judge from the US Circuit Court wrote, "On at least one occasion a prisoner had smuggled a homemade bomb into the courtroom via a 'keister cache' lodged in his rectum. When the bomb exploded, a correctional officer lost three fingers on his right hand."

As I walked the corridors of Marion one day, I stopped to greet a prisoner in his cell. "What's happening?" I asked.

"You want to know what's happening?" he asked in his abject outrage, his face flushed and splotchy. "Get in that cell next door for about ten years, you'll find out what's happening!"

At Marion, reality is kaleidoscopic. As I learned, a visitor does not visit USP-Marion, he is led through a warp that winds its twisting way among three dimensions the way a cavern winds through the earth. One dimension is inhabited by the prisoners, one is inhabited by the guards, and the third is inhabited by the prison officials—the warden, associate wardens, and so on down the line. Whether Marion makes you crazy or your own craziness gets you sent to Marion, once you arrive, peculiar things begin to happen, and they happen fast and all the time.

The Administration

USP-Marion is the modern-day replacement for Alcatraz. It is supposed to be so secure that the Bureau of Prisons (which provides administration for all federal prisons) invented a new level of classification for it: it's called Level Six, the only place of its kind at the time I visited there. Marion is the end of the line.

Marion sits on acres and acres of rolling manicured lawn. To reach it, I drove about fifteen miles east of Carbondale, Illinois, then followed the access road toward a sky-blue water tower. The tinted glass and clean lines of the cast-concrete gun towers make them look more like airport control towers than battlements. The low, louvered buildings of Marion were surrounded by a dancing silver aura that confused my eye as I approached. It was like the first brilliant reflected sunlight I've glimpsed driving toward the ocean. Then I rounded a curve. The scene snapped into focus: thousands of yards of razor wire, each individual razor blade picking up the sunlight and reflecting it back the way rippling water does. The light was a glittering energy barrier around the sand-colored concrete buildings. From the road, I could not yet tell that the modern prison factories were abandoned, the new cafeteria idle, the gymnasium as silent and empty as the chapel.

In the bright, air-conditioned anteroom beside the entrance to the warden's office, a secretary sat before a large plate-glass window. Behind her was a poster with the inscription: "Caution—Human Being. Handle with Care." Her window overlooked the freshly mowed expanse of lawn where a helicopter had landed on May 24, 1978. Barbara Oswald, a friend of one of the inmates, had hired a helicopter and then pulled a pistol and ordered the pilot to land inside the walls of USP-Marion. The pilot wrestled the gun from Oswald and shot her six times, killing her. He landed the helicopter on the grass. When he opened the door, Oswald's body tumbled out onto the green lawn right in front of this window.

"This is the prettiest spot to be in the fall and spring," the secretary told me. "There's a lot of dogwood and redbud that come out," she said, pointing at the tree line in the distance. Between us and the tree line, a hundred yards of silver razor wire curled up and over the fence like an ocean breaker.

On February 14, 1979, two inmates actually climbed over that barrier after wrapping their arms in newspaper, which would seem to confirm what the administration says: that the typical prisoner at Marion is a desperate and violent man, always on the verge of escape. To support that point of view, officials display homemade weapons—pen bombs and hacksaw blades and handcuff keys—evidence that those who are put in USP-Marion are a special breed.

John Clark, executive assistant to the warden, summed up administration policy this way: "It's a matter of who's going to run the prison, us or them."

"All of 'em are total sociopaths," said the acting warden, D. B. Bailes.

Marion officials stop just short of saying that there is such a thing as a born criminal, the notorious "criminal type" that went out of vogue among penologists and criminologists a hundred years ago.

Not many people are sent to Marion directly from court after being convicted. Most are sent there for "failure to adjust" to institutional life, which means that the prisoner has done something at Leavenworth or Lewisburg or Lompoc or some other federal prison that made those officials feel that he needed the more secure and repressive atmosphere of Marion to make him adjust. In addition, state prisoners who fail to adjust to state institutions may be sent to Marion. Precisely what it takes to get into Marion is the subject of controversy. A US magistrate in the Southern District of Illinois, in a recent decision involving transfers to Marion, cited a case called *Meachum v. Fano*, saying, "Therein, the Court held that prisoners may be transferred between or among institutions arbitrarily—for no reason at all."

It is equally difficult to say how a prisoner gets out of Marion.

When I saw it, the airy mess hall was equipped with a contemporary salad bar, red tile floors, and stainless-steel cafeteria equipment that gleamed in the noonday sun, which poured through the glass-brick skylight thirty feet above. Light-orange and yellow decor made it look as if it might have been a modern cafeteria in a hospital. Some of the tables that were set up in a small area of the dining hall had blue-and-white-checked tablecloths on them. The room was frankly inviting, and the food was more palatable than what I was served in my college dorm.

Only no one ate there. No one except a handful of men who had recently been singled out to leave Marion, having gone through a mysterious process that no one could explain—not prisoners or officials or guards—by which (the warden insisted) one can work his way out to the regular prison system.

I watched half a dozen prisoners line up for chow one day, dwarfed in that enormous echoing cafeteria. One of them, a highly educated man considered to be an escape artist, tried to explain how he had achieved his status in this elite group eating lunch in the mess hall. With a wry smile, he said, "Abreit Macht Frei."

There are many differences between a normal maximum-security prison (where you might be sent for murder or bank robbery) and Marion. One is cell time. A normal maximum-security prison operates this way: At 6:00 a.m. your cell door opens, and you run down to the mess hall for breakfast. You then go to work in a prison factory or on an outdoor work gang. All this time you are moving around freely, within the confines of the outer wall of the prison. You go to lunch in the mess hall. You have recreation in the yard or go to the gym to punch the heavy bag or lift weights. There's a 4:00 cell count, during which time you must be in your cell. You hit the chow line again in the evening. And at some point you are locked into your cell for the night.

At Marion, prisoners are locked in their cells twenty-three hours a day. One hour a day, one man at a time is removed for recreation. (The exception is the elite group mentioned above.) There is disagreement about precisely how and why this condition, known as lockdown, was put into effect at Marion, but it took place on October 28, 1983, in the atmosphere of general disruption that had been building since the summer and had culminated in the killing of two guards and one prisoner. The Marion lockdown is now the longest in two centuries of US prison history.

Asked who has been incarcerated at Marion to justify these conditions, the administration will list such criminal luminaries as Joe Stasi, the French Connection; Terrance Alden, the Bionic Bank Robber (so called because he could stand flat footed and jump right into a teller's cage); and Alton Coleman, a kidnapper who went on a six-state murder spree in 1984 and was eventually caught in Evanston, Illinois, a few blocks from my home. Before they reached Marion, numerous others had on their records cop killing, rape, murder, armed robbery, bank robbery, and multiple escapes. One quarter of the men at Marion have committed murder while in prison. The average sentence is forty-one years, while some are serving multiple life sentences. Marion houses numerous members of the white supremacist gang known as the Aryan Brotherhood, including the infamous Joseph Paul Franklin, who bombed a synagogue in Chattanooga, Tennessee.

One Marion inmate was serving a federal life sentence, to be followed by a state death penalty after his release.

The administration of Marion, as well as the Bureau of Prisons, maintains that the population of USP-Marion, being radically different from all other prison populations, merits such radical conditions as total lockdown and justifies the forty thousand dollars a year per man that it costs to maintain those conditions.

Clark and Bailes explained the official point of view to me as we sat on green leather couches in the gold-carpeted warden's office one sunny summer day. (Jerry Williford, the warden, was on leave.) Bailes was a tall, fit-looking man in a conservative gray suit, with a bald head, a big smile, and an easy manner. Clark, a former Catholic priest, was a large, bespectacled man, partly bald, with curly brown hair. He wore shirt-sleeves and a loose tie, his shirt open at the neck. He had an unflinching stare and did not laugh easily. Both prison officials had the look of hard-working, unpretentious businessmen. An architect's model of the prison was on a coffee table in the middle of the room. It had two main concourses—called East Corridor and North Corridor—from which the louvered concrete cellblocks extended like fingers.

"We don't know what causes crime," Bailes said. "We don't make any pretense at rehabilitation."

Clark said, "One of my theories about prisons is they're drama schools where people learn to act rehabilitated. They tried here for several years to operate more or less as a normal penitentiary when they didn't have a normal penitentiary population. They finally decided that just wasn't realistic."

I asked how long-term isolation affects prisoners.

"After so many years, they begin to break down," Bailes admitted. "But," he added, "the prisoners let you know when one of 'em is getting flaky," so that the affected inmate can be taken out for psychiatric treatment.

The primary emphasis was that these were desperate, dangerous men who would do anything to escape and who had no regard for human life, not even their own. Many prisoners have contraband already in their intestinal tracts when they arrive at Marion, having inserted it or swallowed it before leaving a less secure prison. Drugs, syringes, handcuff keys, and even hacksaws and Silicon carbide rods are routinely found, Bailes said. Most prisoners are now x-rayed before being allowed into Marion. Some are dry-celled: put into a cell with no running water, so that their feces may be inspected.

"But that's not foolproof," Bailes told me. "They'll re-swallow it." To detect contraband, Bailes prefers a method he calls the "finger wave." Physicians call it a digital rectal examination. "We don't have an alternative," Bailes said.

Richard Urbanik, one of Marion's two resident psychologists, introduced himself by saying, "I'm considered the most liberal person here." He confirmed Bailes's assessment of the population at Marion while admitting, "This would be a very harsh way to treat the normal prisoner." Urbanik called his 335 patients "the most vicious group of people in the United States" but disagreed with acting warden Bailes's opinion of their psychological problems. He claimed that the odds are "relatively low" that this type of inmate would suffer from a two-year lockdown. "The Marion prisoner is antisocial severe," Urbanik said. "The Marion prisoner is different. Different behaviorally. They don't feel anxiety. They don't have the capacity. That's been shown in many research studies. Psychopaths don't learn under punishment. I'm a psychologist. We look at behavior. We're not really worried about whether there's a mind."

Urbanik characterized the situation at Marion as "basically like your four-year-old being put on his bed for misbehaving." He said that immobilizing a prisoner in a six-by-nine-foot cell twenty-three hours a day does not affect him. The fact that the bureau sent him to Marion means that he is severely antisocial, and "his being antisocial buffers him against the normal effects, although," he added, "there hasn't been a lot of research into the effects of long-term incarceration."

Precisely what a Marion prisoner is and what he is not, precisely how much he can tolerate before the punishment serves to make him more violent instead of less so, are the subjects of heated debate and of at least one lawsuit that was recently settled in favor of the bureau. The official position of the Bureau of Prisons is this:

> It is the mission of the Unites States Penitentiary, Marion, Illinois, to provide for the safety of inmates, staff and the public through appropriately designed correctional programs and procedures for those inmates identified as the most difficult to manage. . . . Marion's success in controlling these dangerous and disruptive offenders at one location allows other facilities to continue to function as open, working institutions.

In the recently settled lawsuit (*Bruscino et al. v. Carlson, et al.*), a US magistrate called the methods at Marion "prudent," while characterizing complaints by prisoners about conditions there as "vicious and unjustified attacks."

The Staff

The prison log indicated that doors were frequently found mysteriously unlocked. Everywhere I went inside Marion I saw locks being changed. It's not like changing a dead bolt. Folger Adam locks have to be burned out with a cutting torch and new ones welded back into place. The halls of Marion smell like hot flux from all the welding. The heavy Folger Adam keys come with a silver cover that snaps into place when the key is not in use, because for some of the inmates, just one glance is enough: they can memorize the steps and then cut a copy out of anything—plastic, metal, wood, glass.

In the guard office at the end of each cellblock is a board with little cards on it. Each card has a prisoner's cell number and a note that might say "Killed Staff" or "Caution!" or "Bad Fight" or some other warning. One had a skull drawn on it.

The guards go around tapping the bars with rubber mallets once a week to check for any odd sounds and look for metal filings. Someone is always cutting his way out.

Nail clippers and Bic razors are kept on little numbered hooks in a locked case at the end of the range.

There is a wire litter for carrying wounded.

The attitude of the guards toward the prisoners is implicit in the language they use. Beating a prisoner is called "counseling." The inmates don't eat, they feed. When the stress of continuous solitary confinement becomes too much for an inmate and he does something rash—anything from refusing to go back into his cell after a shower to hitting a guard with his shackled hands—they say he "went off." As an unexploded bomb will finally go off if you agitate it enough.

The guards understand the stress. They suffer from it, too. It is possible to get the idea that the guards (who prefer to be called correction officers, in keeping with bureau policy) are hired by the pound and are nothing but big, ignorant bullies, but that, like most stereotypes, is not the entire picture. Not only do the guards understand the nature of stress— theirs and that of the prisoners—but they also have a deep and subtle understanding of their relationship with the inmates. Most of them expressed undisguised loathing for them.

One guard, who had been at Marion for fifteen years, said, "The only thing wrong with this system is that we don't have the death penalty." He was a controlled and good-humored man most of the time, but when he spoke of inmates, his whole body tensed. He trembled as he told me, "I hate inmates." One of his best friends was a guard named Merle Eugene Clutts. He was murdered by an inmate named Thomas Silverstein.

It wasn't always that way at Marion, said J. B. Killman, a guard who had been at Marion for seventeen years. "You never completely relax around inmates. But it used to be inmates would speak to you. We were on a first-name basis with them." He recalled a time when the staff and inmates lived in a kind of uneasy detente. "They had things to do then. There was leather craft. They'd have movies on Friday nights with hot buttered popcorn. Basketball. Outside entertainment would come in. Sixty people worked in the kitchen and dining room. It was a nice institution back then. It started to change in the late seventies when a different type inmate began to come here."

What Killman noticed was one of the periodic shifts in the practice of penology that has been taking place since the 1600s. Prisons go back and forth between rehabilitation and repression. In the 1930s, Alcatraz was the repressive model of a prison. It caused a scandal (as such prisons eventually do), and during the 1960s the United States tried rehabilitation. The pendulum swung back. Marion is the new repressive model. When it causes enough of a scandal, another rehabilitation model will replace it.

The guards know that the administration holds the view that everything that happens to a prisoner is his own fault. But they also know that they can control the behavior of inmates to an extent, too. Probably without being aware of it, they are masters of practical behavior-modification techniques. A guard can make an inmate go off, or he can help to defuse him before he goes off. A guard can overlook an infraction. (You can be thrown in the hole, for example, for having an extra pair of socks.) Or he can overlook the fact that your toilet doesn't work, he can make you live in your own waste. Of all the powers that anyone has in the world over us, few people have the broad discretionary powers of a prison guard. The guards know their own power, and like all people everywhere, some abuse it, some respect it.

They carry black Lifetime riot bludgeons, three-foot-long weighted hardwood bats with a round steel ball protruding from either end. The metal ball is there so that the bludgeon won't break ribs. The steel ball separates the ribs, tearing the intercostals, and then pops out. While the pain from it can be intense for weeks and months afterward, the bludgeon tends not to leave obvious marks. But if a guard really wants to hurt an inmate, he doesn't need to touch him. Under the right circumstances, he can take his life simply by letting one inmate out while another is handcuffed and helpless.

And yet the guards and prisoners are often nothing more than reflected images of one another. Often they come from the same backgrounds, and the factor deciding who becomes a prisoner and who becomes a guard is often blind luck. One former guard at Marion, speaking of his job at another prison, told me of a case in which one of the inmates turned out to be a boy he'd grown up with in a small town in southern Illinois. He caught the inmate with drugs and had to report him. "He was my best friend as we were growing up," the guard said. "We just took different roads in life. Because my friend was busted by me, he was beaten, raped, and turned into a punk for the rest of the inmates. I was told by my captain that I was a rotten son of a bitch for setting up a friend like that."

One of Marion's two prison chaplains, Gavin O'Conner, said, "Most prisons operate on the goodwill of the inmates."

Clark agreed. "At any time the inmates could take over because they've got you outnumbered."

Any guard who has been in a prison riot knows that. Several of the guards I talked to had been surrounded by prisoners at Marion, and they described it in the same terms I had heard used by men who had been surrounded by the enemy in war. In a typical prison (the way Marion was before the lockdown), the guards—one or two or three at a time—wade in among the unrestrained prisoners—dozens, sometimes hundreds—and simply hope that nothing happens. They avert fear by blocking it from their minds. Once the idea of fear enters, however, they are marked men.

One such marked man was David W. Hale, who had been a prison guard since he was eighteen years old. At the age of twenty-eight he left Marion. The administration, which was forced to ask Hale to resign when Hale admitted beating prisoners, says he was an officer with many problems. The stress got to him, they say. He began abusing his powers, mistreating prisoners, and refusing orders from his superiors. The US magistrate in the *Bruscino* case (which involved a long list of complaints by prisoners about conditions and practices at Marion) said, "The Court has serious reservations regarding the entirety of the testimony of former correctional officer David Hale."

Others, including former guards who knew Hale, claim that the administration was angry with him for what they called "spreading rumors to frighten other officers." Inmates, Hale claimed, were telling him that they were going to kill guards and take over the prison. Hale was on the yard one day before the lockdown, when he was surrounded by inmates. He called 222, the emergency number—"dialed deuces," as the guards say—but no one came. A guard of twenty years' experience stood and watched. It was at the discretion of the inmates that Hale lived to tell about it.

Hale and others have claimed that the Bureau of Prisons was intentionally trying to provoke an incident at Marion, which would provide an excuse for a protracted lockdown. That would, say the guards, serve the dual purpose of getting the administration a bigger budget and realizing the ultimate repressive model of a prison: total control.

When I met Hale, he was living on unemployment compensation with his wife and children in a frame house beside a pond, an hour's drive from Marion. Young and boyish, he seemed deeply disillusioned with what he had fully expected to be his career for life. "When I started working there," he said, "it was like any other penitentiary. The inmates were all out, they were working in the factories. Sure, there'd be stabbings, fights, and stuff, but that was to be expected. The staff was never involved. It was between inmates. And then [the former] warden [Harold] Miller started taking more and more stuff away from inmates. Like you're going to work longer hours, we're going to cut your pay. You're gonna have less time on outside recreation. And he just kept taking and kept taking until finally the inmates went on strike."

Hale said that the atmosphere at Marion in 1979 and 1980 was one of increasing terror and intense frustration for the guards. Prisoners assaulted guards almost daily, but the staff could not fight back. The administration did nothing to try to stop the disruptions and would not allow staff retaliation, even though, according to Hale, inmates were often shackled to their bunks or beaten for minor infractions of the rule.

Hale finally decided to take matters into his own hands. He felt that if the staff didn't respond to the aggression, the prison would go out of control, and there would be widespread killings of guards. Hale was going to beat an inmate who had assaulted a guard to demonstrate that these attacks would no longer be tolerated. The lieutenant stopped him, and Hale requested to be taken out of the cellblock at that point. The significance of his action was not lost on Hale's fellow officers: it was tantamount to desertion in the face of the enemy. It was career suicide.

Hale said, "I was so mad I was crying, because I knew what was going to happen, and nobody was going to listen to me. I said, 'Why don't you tell these officers that these inmates are going to take this place over and they're going to kill every fucking one of us? And you people don't care. We're like a bunch of meat on a hook you're dangling in front of them to see what they're going to do.'"

Roger Ditterline became a guard at Marion in 1980 after six years as a state trooper. He is now retired with total disability. He was one of three officers stabbed when Robert Hoffman was killed by an inmate named Clayton Fountain. He said, "There weren't any controls. When you have this many murderers, rapists, people doing hard time, antisocial characters, you try to keep a lid on them fairly tight, but it didn't seem to be that way." At that time the guards did not even have riot batons. "We were moving these guys all the time up there with their handcuffs locked in front of them. Now, that goes against everything I was ever taught in law enforcement."

One day before the lockdown, when prisoners were allowed to walk freely to the mess hall for meals, Ditterline found himself surrounded by seventy or eighty inmates when he and another officer were sent in to get a bowl of beans a prisoner had taken from the cafeteria to his cell in defiance of the rules. The prisoners could have killed the two guards, but they did not. Some say it is this very balance of terror and respect between guard and prisoner that makes a normal prison system work. The guards cannot brutalize prisoners too much, because they know that one day they may face being surrounded by those same prisoners and be judged on the spot. When that even strain between guard and prisoner goes out of balance, the system breaks down, and riots or takeovers result. Ditterline, Hale, and other Marion guards believe that the administration and the Bureau of Prisons may have intentionally allowed Marion to go out of balance.

Ditterline said, "It seemed like the administration was trying to get something to happen, and we couldn't figure out why."

Ditterline and Hale said that under Warden Miller, changes in the rules seemed capricious and designed to frustrate prisoner and guard alike. One day the guards would be ordered to remove all sugar packets from the cells. The next day it would be salt. One day razors were issued, the next day they were prohibited. "It was crazy," Ditterline said.

During the winter months, when the wind blew through the lou-vered windows along the ranges, the administration would allow inmates to hang blankets on their cell bars to stop the wind. The inmates would get used to that for three or four weeks, and then a memo would come from the warden's office: immediately confiscate all blankets hanging up. Although the guards may have seen a conspiracy, it could just as easily have been the typical workings of a bureaucracy.

Jim Hale is another former guard at Marion (no relation to David Hale). The day after the killing of officers Clutts and Hoffman, he claims that he began carrying a knife for his own protection because he felt the administration was not sufficiently concerned about safety. He was forced to resign when a fellow officer reported him. It is illegal for a guard to carry any weapons other than those issued by the prison, such as the riot batons (or guns in the towers).

When I visited Jim Hale, he was living in a motel room on the out-skirts of Marion, Illinois, in a room not much larger than a prison cell. The shades were pulled tight against the white-hot light reflecting off the highway outside, and the room was dense and dark with his belong-ings. The air was still and thick. Clothes, combat boots, dishes, and mag-azines were everywhere. He had an unusually large number of knives. A Bowie knife on top of the television and a machete propped up by the door. A Gerber boot knife was on the nightstand. The closet shelves were stacked high with junk food, and Hale and I sat on the bed while we talked. He was a large, soft man in his twenties and was wearing an undershirt. His pale arms were tattooed.

"The administration was just waiting and hoping for somebody to get killed so they could lock it down," he said.

"Why?" I asked.

"I don't know," Jim Hale said. "I can't really say much about that. Harold Miller has a reputation throughout the bureau. You hear people talk about him: when they want a place locked down, they send Harold Miller there. And it gets locked down. When he left Marion [shortly after the lockdown began], he went to Lewisburg. Within two weeks after he got to Lewisburg, they locked the place down because they had a work strike."

Referring to the day when two guards were killed at Marion, Hale said, "The associate warden, a guy named Ken Stewart, told the crew that was working H-Unit [the hole] that night to go ahead and run it like it was normal routine. Take these guys to Rec, put them in the showers. Now that doesn't make a lick of sense. They should have locked that unit down—it doesn't have to be the whole joint, just that unit [i.e., cell-block]. Lock that unit down and shake it down. It wasn't locked down, it wasn't shook down. Okay, Tommy Silverstein killed a guard that morning. That made him a big shot, the way the cons think. Well, here's Clay Fountain sitting upstairs [in the same cellblock]. And he's a rabid little bastard if there ever was one. There's no way in hell he's going to let Tommy Silverstein have all the glory for killing a guard. If he got the chance that night, he was going to have to have some of that glory. Well, he got his chance. Bob Hoffman was killed because of it."

Later I asked John Clark why Fountain had to kill a guard. He said, "To keep the body count up, I guess."

"Then why weren't normal practices followed?" I asked. "Why weren't the cells searched after the first murder of the day?"

"That's the first time I've ever heard that even mentioned," Clark said.

Jerry Powless was the officer escorting Fountain when Fountain stuck his hands into another inmate's cell. Fountain spun around with one cuff off and a knife in his hand. Before he could get to Hoffman, however, he had to face Powless and Ditterline. He plunged the knife into Powless's chest, and Ditterline stepped between Powless and Fountain.

When Ditterline told me about this, his voice dropped almost to a whisper, and tears came to his eyes. "I remember blocking a couple of the blows, but he nailed me a couple of times, and I fell backward. I was kicking at him, trying to keep him at bay as best I could." Fountain rushed past Ditterline and Powless to attack Hoffman, fatally stabbing him.

"And you know who the first person through that front grille was?" Ditterline asked. "Hoffman's boy. His son. He saw his father die."

Hoffman's son, also a guard, just happened to be the first person to respond when David Hale dialed deuces. When Clay Fountain saw him come in to help his father, he hollered out, "Come on! I've never gotten a father-son combination before." And then Fountain did a little victory dance down the range, laughing, amid cheers from the other inmates.

The Inmates

When a person has passed through five grilles, he can say he's been in Marion, and he can look back out to the front door and see what effect all that steel has on sunlight. The world he knew—the bright, new, air-conditioned front vestibule, which with its magnetometer and guard looks like an airport terminal—is dimmed and shattered into an alien logarithmic cross-hatching on the mirror-polished floor. But even there he is still not really in Marion. He is protected from it by his mind, which keeps alive the images of what he just left outside.

On the other hand, if he were to stay in Marion for a long time and had to move past those grilles, it would be difficult to remember what was out there, the white parking lot glittering with red and blue and tan automobiles—models he has never seen, which will come into and go out of style before he is released—and beyond that, the Crab Orchard National Wildlife Refuge, with more than forty thousand acres of forest and lake, deer and opossum, fox and quail.

When a prisoner goes off at Marion, he is taken from the East

Corridor "normal" population to the North Corridor "special housing"; he passes those grilles on his way into solitary confinement. You have to wonder if the designers planned it this way: A man going to the hole can actually see outside, almost into the parking lot.

I saw a young black man being dragged to the hole, shackled hand and foot. He was moved along by three guards. One held the handcuff chain behind his back to jerk him flat on his face at a moment's notice, while two others held their clubs at the ready to strike him down if he made a move. As the prisoner passed the divided shafts of sunlight on the gleaming yellow linoleum, he strained to look out beyond the grilles. After long enough inside Marion, the inmates simply call everything out there "the street."

"Being in the hole twenty-three hours a day for two and three years is a son of a bitch," said Garrett Trapnell, who is serving a life sentence for hijacking an airliner. "Some men are over in H-Unit today, and the only way they're ever going to see a skirt or ride in a car or eat at McDonald's is by killing somebody. So in our society, here, there's no punishment for murder. For murder you get rewarded. I've seen guys talking: 'I wanna see a girl, man! I wanna smell the world, I wanna see the grass, I wanna ride in a car. How am I gonna do that? I'm gonna kill this motherfucker.' An automatic trip—it's court time."

Dr. Frank J. Rundle, a psychiatrist who visited Marion, described "security conditions of a degree I have seen nowhere in ten years of visiting prisons around the United States." He added, "If more humane conditions are not soon restored there will be a catastrophe."

Joseph G. Cannon, a professor in the administration of justice at the University of Missouri in St. Louis, wrote, "I have worked in and around prisons and jails for the greater part of my life (now in my sixtieth year) and I have never seen procedures so extreme and so seemingly designed to degrade and aggravate the prisoners. . . . If the present procedures at this prison are permitted to continue, violence will be the consequence."

Craig Haney, a social psychologist specializing in prisons, said, "Unless the draconian and Orwellian conditions that now prevail [at Marion] are significantly abated, I believe that major outbreaks of violence will result."

What they mean is that one prisoner who escapes could pull a lever and let out eighteen prisoners on a range. Those eighteen could overwhelm the three to five guards at the end of the range and then let out an additional fifty or so prisoners. Those fifty could overwhelm guards on another cellblock, and so on, until the entire prison was in the hands of the inmates. What they are saying is that even the tightest security must slip up once in a while, and then, if you haven't already developed the goodwill of the prisoners, you'll have a prison takeover on your hands. Marion could be the next Santa Fe. At that prison, inmates murdered thirty-three guards in a thirty-six-hour siege in 1980. Some guards were tortured with electric drills before being killed.

———————

I walked along the ranges, passing cell after cell. Hot moist waves of air moved through the flesh-colored bars like a vaporous animal sweat. Faint scent of burning paint and the resin binder of a grinding wheel. Someone was changing a lock on the corridor. The smoke drifted to us and mixed with the sublimated sweat that poured off both guards and prisoners and rolled down the hall like a fog.

In some of the cells, inmates had been allowed to fashion ducts out of laundry-bag plastic to direct air from the vent toward the bunk; these looked like giant condoms protruding from the walls. Each six-by-nine-foot cell had a vent and a bunk, a combination sink and toilet, and a cardboard locker about three feet wide and eighteen inches deep. The cells faced out onto the range and onto a concrete wall with louvered windows. If the louvers were opened (at the guards' discretion), the prisoners could see across to the next louvered concrete cellblock. The prisoners could not see one another. They carried on conversations by shouting up and down the ranges.

Sometimes the inmates would not even look up to see who was there as I passed. At other times they would loom up out of the darkness, tattooed and apparitional and white, like rare fish surfacing from the ocean depths. A skull and death's head mask came up out of one cell, and I read beneath the blue hallucinations the words *weiss macht*, German for "white power."

Then I saw that it was tattooed on a man's stomach, and I shifted my eyes to see his face. He might have been in his middle thirties. His head was shaved, his well-developed upper body was an atlas of tattoos. He had so many tattoos that it appeared that his clear, pale skin was turning blue from within, the last stages of some disfiguring disease. He looked up from a copy of Edward Abbey's novel *The Monkey Wrench Gang* and stared out at me. Swastikas had been hammered into his skin here and there, single-needle work, skulls and images of the Grim Reaper squirming on rippling white flesh. Deep mass of scar tissue on his left arm near the elbow. I asked what had caused it. He said he'd removed a tattoo. I asked why.

"I thought it might cause me some trouble in here," he said.

"What did it say?"

"Oh, nothing. Just some initials."

"What initials?" I asked.

"A. B.," he said.

I walked away. I didn't get it until I had seen two or three men adorned as he was. Then it hit me: Aryan Brotherhood.

Some inmates came right up to the bars talking, as if I had been there all along. They did not touch the bars. They behaved, in fact, as if the bars were not there, passing papers through the bars, shaking hands with a casual, graceful ease that could have come only with long practice. An eight-and-a-half-by-eleven-inch sheet of paper was deftly folded with the fingers of one hand, then passed through the bars and unfolded again as if by magic.

Henry B. Johnson, a mild-mannered, clean-shaven black man wearing black horn-rimmed glasses and a forest green knit ski cap, came up out of the darkness of his cell, chattering softly in a long enunciated drawl, and didn't stop talking until I walked away. " . . . Leavenworth, Atlanta, Terry Haute, Lewisburg, El Reno, I done twenty years flat. They say I robbed a Safeway, a stickup, armed robbery, right? I originally started my time in the state of Virginia, then transferred to the federal system. I came here, moved to El Reno, El Reno to Leavenworth, Leavenworth to Atlanta, Atlanta back up here, to Terry Haute, back to Atlanta, Atlanta to Lewisburg, Lewisburg back here, Otisville to Lewisburg, and back. Now, the flux of the situation that I like to bring to hand is this here: the reason that the prisoners are locked down in this facility has nothing to do with the prisoners per se. It's the economics of the thing, the politics. You know anything about politics? Here's what I'm saying: what took place in the Control Unit—which is the last stop in this particular facility, right?—has no bearing on the population in this particular facility, right? It was an isolated incident. Now it's my understanding that the alleged officers that they claimed was murdered in the Control Unit should have been dealt with at that end. Since then, the past twenty-one months, we've been locked in our cells twenty-three hours a day, right? And a long period of incarceration without proper medical diet breeds psychosis. You know what psychosis is? It makes one become predatory, compulsive—his behavior is other than normal. So what I'm saying is if they plan to relieviate the situation, try to get things back into control, they should open the facility up. In my particular case, right now, I'm seven years overdue for being released. I come in when I was eighteen. I'm thirty-nine now."

Paper is the currency of prison; it was paper that got them into this fix, and paper, they hope, will get them out. An administration memo can grant a privilege or take it away. Almost all the prisoners I spoke to showed me something on paper—a writ, a lawsuit, a plea, a letter, a shot (citation for infraction of a rule), even a poem.

Clark sneered at the legal actions brought by prisoners. "It's part of the way they structure their time," he said. It is also their only hope.

On the other hand, the librarian told me of inmates who simply request one legal volume after another—"sequence readers," he called them—one a day, until they've run through every volume on the shelves. He has to answer every request, or they'll file a suit saying they're denied legal counsel. As a result, with an inmate population of only 335, he processed ten thousand requests for books in 1984.

A lawsuit is no trivial matter. I visited one room in the prison stacked hip high with some forty thousand pages of documents involved in *Bruscino*. The case contended that the harsh conditions of USP-Marion violate a wide range of constitutional rights. The room was dark, abandoned looking, with a paper wasp pelting its body in vain against the bright metal mesh of a single window up near the ceiling. The long tables where researchers had sat, the high yellow ceilings, the dust, all contributed to the impression that this was what remained of a vanished civilization. "The only option they have at this time to change their self-imposed plight," said the magistrate in that case, "is to manipulate the judicial system for their benefit. This Court will not be a party to such manipulation." And, he added, "Conditions at USP-Marion, singularly or totally, are constitutional."

As I walked the ranges, I saw one man sitting on the toilet, staring out. We might have been shadows on a scrim. The only privacy in prison is the privacy you create by refusing to see.

Another inmate sat bolt upright on the edge of his bunk with his face just inches from the television set, staring with rapt attention at the close-up face of a soap opera heroine. Channel 10 is a closed circuit on which the prison broadcasts religious services and, now and then, the Jane Fonda workout tape first thing in the morning. It was once a favorite, but after two years of solitary confinement, the inmates have become inured even to that. Prison authorities decide who can have a television set or a radio or any possession for that matter. A list of approved articles is distributed. Anything not specifically approved is forbidden. In the hole, there is nothing.

A big, white, freckled kid with red hair cut marine style squinted, pacing angrily in his cell. He looked as if he were about to hit someone, only no one was in there but him. When I approached, he spun on me accusingly, his fists balled. "There's no sense in me talkin' to you," he said. He had an eye tattooed in the center of his hairless chest. He was almost shouting. "I've been here for *five years!*"

Another man rushed the bars, saying, "Yeah, don't believe anything they tell you. They're just covering their own asses. I was roughed up in Lewisburg and protested. I fought back. I was charged with assault and sent here." Behind him on his shelf was a copy of *Art through the Ages.* Some prisoners are allowed to have books sent to them from outside. "Now what sound man is going to attack ten officers?" he asked.

Michael Price had *Weiss Bruder* tattooed across his stomach and a little swastika needled into the tender flesh just outside his right eye. Elsewhere on his body: a skull, a Grim Reaper, and the word *dago.*

Glen West said he'd committed robberies, escaped from prison, and taken policemen hostage since his career of crime began. "I'm not saying I don't belong in here," he told me as I passed his cell. "I don't care where they put me. But isn't it funny that the Bureau of Prisons hires nothing but perfect people? None of them make mistakes." He couldn't read when he was first put in prison. He taught himself during the rehabilitation fad.

He handed me some papers. They magically folded on his side of the bars, passed through, and unfolded again in the air before me. It was a trick as neat and unconscious as a cowboy rolling a cigarette with one hand. I read the BP-DIR-9 form, "Request for Administrative Remedy," which has two parts, one labeled Part A—inmate request—and the larger labeled Part B—response. In the top portion West had written:

> I have been told by both the Warden and now the counselor that even though we have a cabinet in our cell which can be used as a table to eat our meals on they won't allow us to. We are being told to either eat out of our laps or off the floor. This simply because they think the cell looks neater if the cabinet is where we can't use it. We can't eat out of our lap like a sea otter because often the trays have food or water all over the bottom of them. Besides to say eat out of your lap because we like the way the cabinet looks over there is ridiculous. Why not just give us a bowl and we can eat off the floor like a dog.

The warden wrote back, "This is in response to your request for administrative remedy receipted 5/31/85, in which you request to be allowed to use your storage locker to eat off of. Lockers presently issued to inmates are designed for storage of personal property, also a shelf for televisions. Shelves are presently being considered for placement in each cell which will serve the purpose for eating, writing, etc. Accordingly, your request is denied."

It's the sort of treatment that is so difficult to define, so gentle is the method, like the Chinese water torture or the death of ten thousand cuts. Each cut is so clean that you never feel a thing. Psychiatrists fear it will drive men to violence, make men go off, and one day make Marion as famous for carnage as Santa Fe.

One day at Marion I watched an inmate go off. (The administration calls it "acting out.") He was a black man in his mid-thirties. He'd been let out of his cell for his sixty minutes of indoor recreation, and he was walking up and down the range in his bare feet, cackling and howling, refusing to be locked up again. He didn't realize he was more locked up than most of us will ever know. Freedom to him was an hour out on the range: A yellow-painted steel screen at the far end covered a ventilation shaft. A sliding grille of prison bars blocked his way out past me and the guards. Still he wouldn't go back into his cell— I guess freedom is a relative thing—and no one was about to go in there and talk to him until the riot squad came. So he was allowed to hoot and carry on until he wore himself out. Then the SORT team came and did a forced cell move on him: held him down and carried him away. SORT stands for Strategic Operations Response Team. Inmates call it the Goon Squad. When the SORT team comes to get you, all your possessions are removed and taken to the second floor of the hospital, where they're stored in an abandoned ward.

After the guards were killed, inmates say, guards beat prisoners for revenge. Mike Sizemore, a young white man, was one of the alleged victims. He told me his version of the events: "Shortly after the lockdown they moved us early one morning. I was dressed in shorts, T-shirt, and shower shoes, nothing else. And this was the middle of November and all the windows were wide open and they were writing up shots left and right." A prisoner is never given explanations, such as why he's being moved, or to where, or why he's being made to stand nearly naked in a November breeze. "I asked if they could close the windows," Sizemore said, "and the guy jabbed me through the bars with his stick and told me to shut up."

The next day the SORT team came for him.

While they were moving him, someone "hit me in the back of the neck and knocked me to the floor. And then it started. It was a long way to the hole. They beat me up all the way, throwing me into the walls. They still didn't handcuff me, but I saw no point in fighting back. I'm not a man who will let a man smack me in the face and not do anything. But they were all dressed out [in riot gear], and I couldn't have hurt them if I tried." When they got him to H-Unit, the guards punched him around some more, Sizemore said, and asked why Clutts and Hoffman had been murdered. Later a physician's assistant happened to be passing his cell, and Sizemore asked to see a doctor. He was told he could not see one.

The US Seventh Circuit Court of Appeals ruled in the *Bruscino* case that such charges by prisoners were untrue and without foundation in fact.

———————

By a mysterious paradox of the system, if you go off frequently enough, unless you kill or maim someone, the guards finally back off and leave you alone. Describing "the process of dissolution" that takes place after long incarceration, Jack Henry Abbott in his book *In the Belly of the Beast* wrote, "The pigs can sense it and they pass the word. They place you on the pay-him-no-mind list. You are allowed to roam the prison and do and say anything you care to and the guards overlook it, ignore you as if you were not even there. Only if you commit an act of violence do they pounce and drag you to the hole."

Danny Atteberry, known as Schemo to his friends, is a white inmate with long black hair hanging past his shoulders. He paced his cell, bobbing and smiling and laughing. He had set his steel bunk on end in an attempt to make the most of the fifty-four square feet of floor space. Atteberry had hung his clothes on the steel bedframe and rolled up the mattress in a corner. Like so many inmates I saw, Atteberry was doing his paperwork when I walked up to his cell— preparing or reading or researching various legal documents. Tom Krajenta, unit manager and immediate superior of all the guards on the unit, stood behind me, facing Atteberry, as we talked. I asked Atteberry why his cell was arranged the way it was.

"I'm living in the bathroom, in the shitter," he said. He laughed: a-hilk! "I mean this is where I've got to live. There ain't nothing I can do, I'm in here twenty-three hours a day. And so I'm gonna live however I want. Now, they're putting guys in the hole if they don't set their bed up here, if they don't put their TV back." A-hilk! A-hilk!

"So how come you're not in the hole?" I asked.

"I generally stay in the hole. I've gotten like twenty shots in the last eighteen months for calling them turds and shit eaters and maggots and for putting up a sign on my locker that says fuck authority. They take me away from my constitutional rights and put me in the hole."

"So how come you're not in the hole right now with your bunk up on end like that?" I asked.

Atteberry got a wild grin on his face and edged closer to the bars. "Because they're treating me real nice. They don't want to put me in the hole for some reason. I don't know." A-hilk! A-hilk!

I turned to Krajenta and asked why Atteberry wasn't in the hole.

"In this unit the regulation as far as the actual furnishing— we just don't enforce it. The other unit manager or I have the discretion to say if you don't have your bed down you're going to go to the hole, but I haven't done that in this unit because I don't have any problems in this unit."

"I'm the only one that fucks up," Atteberry added. A-hilk!

"How do you feel about being called a turd by Atteberry?" I asked Krajenta.

"I just totally disregard anything that comes out of his mouth."

I asked Atteberry what he'd done to get into prison in the first place.

"I was a youngster. I've been here seventeen years. I went down when I was twenty-two on a robbery charge. After that I escaped and caught a robbery and assault on a police on escape. And then after that I took hostages and stabbed nurses in a prison takeover in 1974 in Walla Walla, Washington."

I asked him how long he might be in prison, and he said he didn't know.

I went down into I-Unit, a cellblock containing seventy-two strip cells, what used to be called Oriental cells at Alcatraz, with nothing in them but a toilet and a bunk. B-Range of I-Unit contains the boxcar cells, which have closed fronts to cut off sound and ventilation. There are the bars, as on a regular cell, and then a few feet in front of that— just far enough so that the prisoner can't reach—is a second set of bars covered with Plexiglas. A door can be closed so that the inmate's screams are muffled, so that airflow is cut off, so that he can't throw food or feces out of his cell. As I walked down the range, I could hear the man in the last cell hollering, "Hey! Lemme speak to you for a moment! Hey, newspaper boy! Open the door! Open the door!"

"The door's open," I told him.

"Oh," he said, as if he'd just noticed.

I went through the door and stood in the small space between the two sets of bars.

"My name is Abdul Salam, aka Clark." A piece of paper materialized on my side of the bars. It said he was once Jesse James Clark but had become Muhammad Mustafa Abdulla. He was an enormous black man, perhaps 250 pounds. Very little of it was fat. In the middle of his stomach a great scar bloomed like a pale flower from the dark flesh of his navel. Smaller scars adorned his arms and upper body. "Now, tell all the women that they gonna send me to Springfield," he said.

"Can we take your picture?" I asked Abdulla.

He hollered up at the ceiling, "Hey, Price-Bey! Hey, Price-Bey!"

A voice drifted down from D-Range above us: "I heard dat."

"You gonna let 'em take a picture of you, man?"

"Yeah, I am!"

"Okay," he said. Abdulla's cell was littered with clothes and bits of torn-up paper. The walls and ceiling had been smeared with something dark. He showed us his prayer rug and Koran. He insisted on putting on his shirt and shoes before having his photograph taken, saying he was a religious man, and he held his worn, green-bound Koran and posed deliberately for each shot. One of his sneakers was laced halfway up and untied. The other was completely unlaced. As he moved his tremendous bulk in that cramped and littered space, he lurched and staggered, though he never quite hit the walls or the bars. Even for Abdulla, the bars seemed not to be there.

"Hey, Clark," Abdulla said to the warden's assistant. "I know ya'll sending me to Springfield for a medical, for a mental, and you know I don't have no mental problems. You ought to send me back to DC."

"I'm not sending you anywhere," Clark said.

Abdulla suggested this caption for his picture: "I want you to put in there that I am trying to get back to DC and that any Muslim that desire to contact me that it's cool and I'm tryin' to do right but Marion is holding me here as a contract prisoner and don't want to turn me loose."

"Tell me about that scar on your stomach," I said.

"Naaah!" Abdulla said modestly. "I don't want to talk about that. You know, because that involved me getting shot and then I shot somebody else, that's all. But lemme tell you: They keep my door closed twenty-four hours a day. I been on lockup in this place right here for three months."

He kept on talking as the associate warden and I walked back up the range. Jesse James Clark was taken away the following week to the hospital facility at Springfield, Missouri, for a psychiatric examination.

While I-Unit is known as the most disruptive and rowdy in the prison, D-Unit, which the guards call Dog-Unit, is just the opposite. No radios or televisions are allowed on I-Unit. They are allowed on D-Unit, yet it's surprising how quiet D-Unit is. I never heard music as loud as you might hear on any bus or subway. D-Unit felt almost monastic.

Only forty-five men lived on Dog-Unit, although it could hold seventy-two. One of them was Frank Lewis, a soft-spoken thirty-year-old black man, who looked weary and contrite. He had robbed a bank with someone in New York in 1977, and when I asked him to tell me about it, he said, "I'm not proud of it." He smiled slightly when I asked him to tell me if anything good came from being in Marion. "It makes you think much more. Think about your life and how things are fucked up—how you fucked up. And you start saying, 'Wait a minute, I've got to do something about this.' Most of the guys here are in the hole. I've been around. I've been to plenty of institutions, and this one here is tight. It's very tight." He said he didn't mind Dog-Unit because it was quieter. "There's a great deal of maturity over here, guys can somewhat deal with it."

I asked Lewis to compare Marion with Leavenworth, which is where he was serving his sentence before being transferred to Marion.

"Ah, no comparison. At Leavenworth there's much more freedom. You can move around. There's a lot of programs, and you can pretty well occupy yourself. Here there's nothing, so if you can't read, you can't write, and you have no discipline, you're in trouble. It's dangerous in the sense that a lot of guys don't have any money, been down awhile, they've lost contact with their girlfriends, and a guy reaches a level of frustration. So it does present a large amount of danger. In fact that's why I'm over here, because the guys can handle it." Dog-Unit is designated for those the administration identifies as gang leaders.

I asked him if the robbery involved any violence. .

"Well, a gun was used, and the threat was there."

"How long did you get?" I asked.

"I got twenty-five years," he said, "because it was the second time."

"So what got you to Marion?" I asked.

"I got in a fight with some officers," he said. "Or a struggling match anyway. But it doesn't take anything major to come here."

It takes something major to get out.

I visited John Greschner in the hole, which has many names: H-Unit (we were on A-Range), the Control Unit, disciplinary segregation, solitary, strip cell, Oriental cell. Whatever you call it, Greschner put it this way: "There's nothing in there but me." Even when on H-Unit, an inmate is let out of his cell for his hour of recreation, but he is merely put in a larger cell for that hour.

Greschner stood in the exercise cage as I spoke to him, an elongated steel-mesh box along the range of eighteen cells. In the box were an exercise bike, a chinning bar, and nothing else. If he requested a jump rope, I was told, the guards would give him one. Then again, maybe they wouldn't. Prison authorities gave me their point of view on a few of Greschner's activities since he was sent to Marion in 1976:

> November 18, 1979: At approximately 3:30 p.m. on "A" range of "H" Unit Greschner, John 2550-135 attacked and stabbed Logan, John Henry 87870-132 with a sharpened weapon fashioned from a round metal rod. Logan received approximately twelve wounds to the chest and upper part of the body. The wounds required that Logan be transported to Marion Hospital for treatment. April 28, 1980: Inmates John Greschner, Reg. No. 02550-135, and Clayton Fountain, Reg. No. 89129-132, escaped from their cells in the Control Unit by way of the air vent system in the rear of their cells. Using the air vent system, they gained access to the pipespace in the Control Unit and attempted to escape from that area. Squads of officers had to go into the pipespace using riot batons, plastic shields and tear gas guns to force the inmates to leave the pipespace.

When I saw Greschner, he was very pale and sweating from exercise. He had black hair and a goatee. His shirt was off, and he was holding it around the back of his neck to absorb the sweat. He pointed across the range at his cell. "I'm down here for insolence and use of morphine or heroin."

"How do you get morphine in here?" I asked.

"Well, that's what I was trying to explain to them, how do I get morphine in here? You know, they've got it locked down. I don't have any contact with anybody in the streets, I don't have any visits, I don't have anything." Balancing on the balls of his feet, he smiled and shrugged as we struggled to see each other through the steel mesh. Like the bars, it seemed designed to frustrate human contact. The bars and screens seemed always to be just at eye level and spaced so that you could never quite see anyone with both eyes at once. Like everything else at Marion, the effect was disorienting.

"But this is no good here," Greschner said. "They lay people on these shelves for years and years. As a matter of fact, they've got a new shrink here. He's been placed in this unit since the killing of the guards and the allegations by the prisoners that people deteriorate down here—long-term isolation, sensory deprivation. There is no TV, no radio, and if they consider you're disruptive, even if you're in the cell and you can't get out of the cell, they will run in and jump you with a Goon Squad and beat that ass and tie you to a bunk. So they brought a shrink in here, and the first time I seen him I asked him, 'You know there's a lot of things been happening here and you've been getting a lot of testimony [in *Bruscino*] by psychiatrists that these units are harmful. They aren't doing any good. Also, a personal friend of mine named Silverstein, who ya'll got for killin' one of these guards, was down here for years on end, and they knew that was going to happen with that guard because he told them it was going to happen with that guard if they didn't get that guard off his back. And I was there when he told the unit manager that after months and months and months and months of the harassment from that guard, Clutts, finally he says, 'I can't take it anymore. If you don't get this guy off my fuckin' back, I'm gonna have to do it.' He told J. T. Holland that. That was the Control Unit manager. They never did it. I went to Leavenworth. Six months later I hear they got Silverstein for killing Clutts."

As Greschner talked, he became more animated, pointing his finger at the flesh-colored steel mesh that separated us. "Now, I have no problems with a guard doing his job. That's what he's here for, to make sure we ain't sawing windows out and all that. But when you start poking at a motherfucker and start fucking with a motherfucker all the time, you know, putting shit in his food, fucking with his rack, harassing him, shaking his shit down—you go in and you find pictures of your old lady, or your mom, with boot prints on 'em. Then you go to his superior and say, 'Hey, look, check this out, look what he's doing in there,' and they don't do nothing, finally, it reaches the point where you're either going to take it or you're going to do something.

"Now, I'm trying to explain this to this shrink. I told him, 'Yeah, I did almost nine years in solitary confinement, I went down to Leavenworth, yeah, I'm annoyed and fucked up, man, and . . . I'm doin' okay . . . but I'm fucked up and having a hard time navigating, man. I been away from people so long, you walk up and I don't know you, I'm kind of annoyed with you. . . .' You know what I'm saying?"

"Yeah," I said.

"And consequently, I'm down here for four months, and I get in a little old beef with this dude, man, I get in a killing. Now I'm back here. They gimme a double life sentence. And I'm saying, 'What do you think of that? What do you think of the detrimental effects of a unit like this?' And he says, 'You know what, Greschner? You just gimme good reason to keep you locked up in here forever.'"

Being in the hospital was like being on the bottom of a swimming pool, an indistinct green coolness after the oven of the cellblocks. The physician's assistant in charge of rectal searches carried a radio and a set of keys like a guard. He said, "I have yet to see a beating here."

The dentist, a civilian drawing lieutenant colonel's pay, said, "I've got the needle, the ultimate persuader." And he laughed.

I took the armored elevator to the second floor, a ward that used to house inmates but is now deserted except for one guard and one prisoner behind a steel door for his own protection while he's testifying. Federal witness protection. He squinted out through a slit at us. A walking dead man.

At the end of the corridor were two large hospital wards now piled high with upturned hospital beds, discarded IV stands, old duffel bags, and the belongings of prisoners who were being kept in strip cells.

I asked the fat, boyish guard, "What do you two talk about up here?"

"I avoid talking to most of these convicts," he said.

"Don't you talk to him at all?"

"When I have to."

"Why?"

"You start off talking about apples, and pretty soon you're talking about oranges. The next thing you know you're talking about tangerines," he said. He turned the key and sent me on my way in the steel elevator.

I went out of the hospital and down the corridor and back out through the magnetometer and into the world. The parking lot, the cars, seemed dazzling and fantastic after days inside USP-Marion. As I stood on the brink of the Crab Orchard Wildlife Refuge, I thought how cruel it seemed to deprive someone of all this. Then I remembered one prisoner I'd asked what he thought his punishment should have been for all he'd done.

"What do you think they ought to do to you?" I said.

"By the code that I live, I would have done something. I expected it. I'm not in here unjustly. I stabbed the officer, and that's what I'm in here for. Wasn't nothing unjust about that. It was just something that happened at the time. I couldn't get around it. I have my own code of ethics I live by on the streets. I don't live by society's laws, so when society catches up with me, I got to be punished. I accept that. It ain't no big deal. I accept what's coming to me according to the society."

"Would you try to escape?"

He looked up suddenly and angrily, as if to see whether or not my question was serious. "Would I try to escape? Of course."

WORLD TRADE CENTER

No one had to tell people to use the term *Ground Zero*. It had been waiting, buried in our language, since before Hiroshima. It emerged on its own when the right time came. Of course, *Ground Zero* is the term nuclear scientists invented during the Manhattan Project to refer to the point at which the atom bomb exploded; everything else was measured outward from there, as everything was now being measured outward from a heap of twisted steel located at three addresses in lower Manhattan that used to be right about at Cedar Street just west of Broadway.

The steel won't be there much longer, but the name will stick: *Ground Zero*. Even the police commissioner used it in his interviews on television, and each time it came out of his mouth, he reacted as if he hadn't expected himself to say it, but he couldn't figure out where else he might be standing. Certainly not at the World Trade Center. That didn't exist any longer.

So there I was, at Ground Zero, watching a twenty-story yellow crane lift a bucket with three men in it and lower them like a sacrifice to an angry god into smoke that rose a thousand feet into a paper blue sky. The men in their bucket disappeared into the cloud, and in a while, the crane's boom lifted a girder out of the chaos and set it on a flatbed truck. It rumbled away through the people lined up on Broadway, who pointed their cameras at the two-inch-thick steel, which was twisted back on itself in a way that threw the very solidity of our world into question.

The scene was like a state funeral: thousands filed past, pressed in so tight that it became difficult to walk. I was jammed against a preservation architect named Mary, who was calmly trying to get home to

125 Cedar Street, which had faced the World Trade Center. She laughed as we talked, saying, "Isn't it strange? I preserve historic buildings!" And she pointed out some local landmarks for me, saying that it looked as if they'd survive. Then she engaged a policeman, earnestly entreating him to let her go home.

Somewhere else in town, the daughter of the architect who designed the World Trade Center telephoned her father, and he sadly told her, "I can't fix it this time." A block away, the antenna that had stood atop the North Tower jutted skyward like a javelin from the cemetery of Trinity Church.

———————

One morning I saw a couple on the subway with that thousand-yard stare. They were all over town, those people, but especially on the trains, because no one could stand to sit still. They were in their twenties and stood holding onto each other as the train rattled downtown. They said nothing. Their hands did not move over each other's bodies, as they must have only days before. They didn't look at each other and smile that secret smile that makes us look away. I saw none of the normal whispered giggling, the titillation of contact, which we're so used to seeing in public places. They'd been the envy of a care-worn world, which spread around their delicious lives, their catalog clothes and financial sector jobs. As recently as Monday, many of them could scarcely believe their luck—God, they were running the world. And what a view! Daylight brought the Statue of Liberty, a goddess of plenty just outside their windows. Nighttime they spent planning vacations in Tuscany and selecting cool names out of handbooks for new parents.

Now they had those Hansel and Gretel eyes, as if they hadn't slept for days. They were so young to be shipwrecked. The fact of their touching was no longer embarrassing, it was painful to watch. Their groping connection gave no comfort as they reached for something that wasn't there. And those were the lucky ones, the ones not interred at Ground Zero. After Hiroshima, the Japanese called it "do-nothing sickness," the apathy that settles in the post-traumatic haze.

I didn't have to follow them, because we were both getting off at the Brooklyn Bridge. I climbed the stairs behind the couple. They stopped on the wide concrete deck of the converging streets, and she collapsed against him, saying, "I don't think I want to go. I don't think I can see it."

"That's all right," he said, holding her. "We don't have to."

"But I want to!" she cried.

And that was the paradox—to see and not to see—as everyone poured around them and down along the avenue. A man leaned against a scaffolding beside a building and wept openly, and a stranger passing by simply stopped and put his arm around him and leaned in close to say something. None of us knew if we could stand to see it, but we all had that almost voyeuristic urge to look and not to look.

Uptown and downtown I saw people lurching headlong down the street, telephones pressed to their ears, weeping, screaming, "How can it happen! How can I go on!" I saw a man in his twenties collapse against a fence at City Hall and fall to the ground, screaming, as a silent couple stood beside him, holding each other, watching helplessly, lost in their own thoughts.

Gary was a laborer with the Local 79 Union in Manhattan. He worked at 120 Broadway, which had a clear view of the World Trade Center across One Liberty Plaza. He was on the thirty-sixth floor that morning when he heard the first plane hit. He and an executive looked out the window and saw the black smoke. "That's bad," Gary said. He thought a transformer must have exploded.

They grabbed a digital video camera and "a bunch of binoculars. You know, everybody has binoculars. They like to look out on the city and watch things," Gary told me as we stood at Ground Zero. I'd found him as we all found one another, by the simple act of being there to bear witness. I was looking, but like everyone else, I wasn't quite sure what I was seeing: The heart of a sandstorm, pure sunlight dimmed by flaming plastic, the cataclysm of new mountain ranges heaved up overnight, smoke rising higher than the helicopters or the circling gulls. We had no model for this. The senses could not compass it. And so we looked a little longer, and it made less and less sense the longer we looked.

Gary materialized beside me wearing a Fire Department T-shirt and a backward baseball cap. He looked as if he hadn't slept in a week. He stood gaping at the pile, eyes rimmed in red as if he'd been crying— who hadn't? He was a solid man in his thirties, built like an athlete, tapering down to solid boots, and he appeared to have been gutted somehow, a silhouette of a once-strong man, lots of white showing all around his irises.

I'd started our conversation the way everyone did: Where were you? Each person seemed like a hand grenade with the pin pulled, just a touch and he'd explode with information. It just came pouring out, as if Gary had been holding it in for days. He couldn't seem to stop talking. He paced the street, gesticulating, and I followed him down to Nassau, where we had a piece of pizza and a Coke.

They had gone to the roof, Gary and a number of others, and were watching, trying to figure out what could have made such a hole in the building, all that smoke pouring out. At first it was just a silver wall, an object, an obelisk with a black wash of watercolor. It wasn't real.

Then people began to come out the windows just above the hole, and he made the connection: "Oh shit," he recalled. "There are people in there. And they're burning alive."

I saw nothing weepy or sentimental about Gary's story. He told it straight, and as he did so, he'd look me right in the eye, like he was looking into my soul, and the pain I saw in him was physical, like an athlete with a broken ankle, a guy who knows how to handle pain.

"There was a woman in a red dress," he said. "For some reason I'll never forget her. And she came out the window on the North Tower about the ninetieth floor and grabbed onto that cladding outside and was just hanging there, screaming and screaming and screaming. We were so close we could hear them all screaming as they came out. Man, it was crazy. I watched her with my binoculars like she was *this close*, I could practically tell you the color of those people's eyes up there. I'll never forget it. And then they started coming down like helicopters. They'd grab hold of that cladding on the outside and then the fire inside would heat it up until they'd just let go, they couldn't hold on any longer, it was too hot." He gestured with both hands, as if jerking them away from a stove.

"There was a stage down there in the plaza where they have music. It's a wooden stage, and the people would land on it, and it would shatter and there'd be body parts flying. I mean, the people just exploded."

At ground level, the Fire Department had rushed two tour commanders, twenty battalion chiefs, and five fire-rescue companies to the scene. One fire fighter was killed when a jumper landed on him. Mychal Judge, the department chaplain, knelt beside the crushed fireman to administer the last rites, and then he was hit by falling debris. It killed him instantly as the others, more than two hundred firefighters in all, rushed in. None of them would ever find out what started the fire.

Meanwhile, above, one woman appeared at a high window holding a baby out into the air, as if to let him breathe. The baby's arms were thrown out in what must have been an instinctive reaction to height. Just a few stories above where the first plane went in, perhaps ninety stories above the ground, a man was clawing his way over a woman to get out the window. Dozens were working their way out, gripping the aluminum cladding that made the drab steel building look silver in the sun. Perhaps in the rush of adrenaline they thought that they could shimmy down or just hold on for long enough to be rescued. They had all moved to the outside of the building, trying to get away from the flames, and those who had the strength were clinging there. Smoke poured out around them.

By that time, a number of people had gathered on the roof with Gary, he couldn't say how many. They all watched with binoculars as a young man in a business suit climbed out with an incongruous sort of calm determination. "He wedged himself between the tracks on the outside of the building," Gary told me. The man began shimmying down from the seventieth floor in a mountain climber's series of moves, as if he'd done something like that before. He had a plan, he had a method, and he had the adrenaline and the strength. He was going to chimney down.

Gary got a very sad look on his face as he described him. "Aw, he almost made it, too. He got down to about thirty from the seventieth floor, and he was just wedged in there, you could practically see how muscular and strong this guy was, like he'd practiced this move before, and he shimmied and shimmied, and we all had our binoculars trained on him and we were cheering him on: Come on, man! Come on, you can make it! But when he got to about thirty, you could just see him begin to tire out and get exhausted, and then he finally just let go with both hands like that." Gary gestured again with his hands, pushing the building away. "And he went like a helicopter, down and down. Then I couldn't watch anymore."

Finally, the towers began to collapse, and Gary and his group left the roof and went down. But when they reached the lobby, the streets were impassable with smoke and flying debris. Cars were exploding everywhere. High above on the ninety-eighth floor, a carpenter who was installing venetian blinds watched his partner get blown through them and out into thin air. A streetlight exploded, and the flying glass killed someone passing by. All the world's rules seemed suspended.

"It was insane," Gary told me. "People were running and screaming. There were bodies everywhere and shoes everywhere, high heels and loafers, I don't know, it was just weird. Everything was covered in dust, and people were trying to drive out, like cab drivers, man, they were just running people down," and here he made a sound, *ka-bump*, like someone running over something soft.

By that time, nearly 150 people had gathered in the lobby of Gary's building and were trying to figure out where they could go. Then the building's locksmith, an older man, who had worked at 120 Broadway all his life and knew every part of it, showed up and directed them all to the tunnels beneath the building. And in his dirty jeans, the old man led Gary and the executives down the stairs and through the subterranean maze.

"We all followed the locksmith down into the tunnels," Gary said. "Because he knew the way and he had the keys. He told me to help keep the people calm, so I was trying to do that, just telling them that everything was going to be okay, and he was going ahead, leading the way and opening the doors. It was just a miracle I happened to run into him, because all them doors are locked down there, and he just opened them one by one and we went on through."

They crossed beneath an entire city block and emerged in a bank on Nassau Street, where they climbed out to find a surreal scene.

"It was black as night out there. You couldn't see a thing." The building had been made of box-steel girders embedded in poured concrete and insulation, but the girders had been stripped clean, and the concrete had been turned to powder and blown into the air by the force of the collapse. Now all that material came drifting down like gray snow. The nighttime lasted another forty-five minutes, Gary said, and then the sky began to clear. "When the F-16s started coming over, everybody thought it was another plane and hit the dirt, but a cop there told us it was the national guard."

Gary returned to the scene to volunteer with the Fire Department workers. They were trying to reach their comrades, who had been buried, along with those who jumped, under almost two million tons of wreckage. Now Gary returned day after day like so many others, to stare, to somehow achieve the bitter victory of believing the evidence of his own senses.

Just behind us, Moshe Alfassi stood in his shop's open doorway and stared in shock. He had moved here from Israel twelve years earlier to open Chelsea Jeans, which faced the towers from just across Broadway. Its plate-glass window had exploded in the collapse, and now his entire stock of clothing was covered with an inch of gray dust. He told me that for a year and a half, his manager had never failed to open the store at 9:00 a.m. But on September 11, 2001, he missed his ferry from Jersey City, which docks at the World Trade Center at 8:45.

As I wandered through the city, I heard dozens of stories like that, little miracles of coincidence and timing. Katherine Illachinski, at seventy years of age, couldn't run or even walk down all the stairs from the ninety-first floor, and yet she had the sense to get in the elevator when the first jet hit the tower next door just above her level. She did not wait in denial as so many did. She was in Two World Trade Center, the South Tower, but even from next door, the fire was so hot that it drove her from her office. When she reached the forty-fourth floor, where people change for the elevator to the ground, the lobby was so crowded that she took the stairs. She was smart enough to ignore the announcement on the public address system that told everyone to return to their offices. Quite naturally, many others did as they were told. As Illachinski was nearing the street level, the second jet hit her building, but because of her head start, she managed to get out and away.

I could only wonder, then, at the stories I'd never hear, the messenger who happened to go into the building, the visitor who happened into the observation floor, or perhaps the lady who had brought her baby that day and found herself holding him out the window as the office was incinerated behind her and her friends were falling to the street below.

In the coming days and nights, the snowplows came and scraped the winter-gray snowdrifts away. Then the street sweepers brushed and washed it down, and the shopkeepers sprayed with their pressure hoses, and the people came and looked. One Liberty Plaza, a black building directly across from Ground Zero, was covered with gray dust to a height of fifteen stories. I found scorched interoffice memos hanging in the trees.

———————

For me it began at about 7:43 a.m. on the morning of September 11 as I was driving in my car in a suburb of Chicago. I heard on the radio that a "twin-engine airplane" had collided with the World Trade Center. I had seen airplanes get in the way of buildings before. I thought to myself: Some moron with more money than brains drove his Beechcraft Baron into the World Trade Center. I hope no one in the building got hurt.

I went straight home and turned on the television, not even sure it was big enough news to warrant live coverage. As I flicked the remote, the silver tower appeared with a gaping hole in it and black smoke pouring out. And it was on every channel. Chicago is an hour earlier than New York, so it was about eight o'clock, and I felt a cold rush of fear: That's no light twin, I thought. That hole looked like it was ten or fifteen stories tall. I couldn't conceive of an airliner hitting the building. They're all on flight plans, on radar, talking to air traffic controllers. I've flown in New York's airspace and know how tightly they control us. In fact, I had flown right past the World Trade Center in a small plane and right over the Verazanno Narrows Bridge, so I knew exactly what it would take to get that badly off course. And on a clear day like today, it would be impossible not to see those buildings. It was obvious that something grave, very grave, had taken place—wait, it was taking place. For even as I watched, another plane had come out of nowhere and hit the other tower.

It was like seeing a miracle: a bird, banking hard, descended into the mirrored surface of a pond and vanished without a ripple. The trembling silver building seemed to have swallowed it whole. But a second later, the opposite wall vomited orange flame and greasy black smoke, as the South Tower exploded in a cataclysm of debris.

I don't know how many times in history millions of people have all had the same thought at the same instant, but that was surely one of them: at that moment we all understood that the collisions had been deliberate.

Then I saw someone jump from the first tower, but my mind refused to believe it. I told myself that it must be debris. For nearly an hour, CNN executives ordered the second impact replayed over and over, as if they couldn't believe it either. Then the South Tower collapsed. It was like watching a great fuse spewing smoke as it burned down to the ground. I felt as if we'd all been sitting peacefully right on top of a bomb, its twin silver fuses raised to the sky, just waiting for someone to light them.

I did as we all did and phoned everyone I knew. That first day, I even rushed to my daughter Amelia's school to take her home. I'm not sure why. I just had to have her near me.

Then it was a long slide into an unreal world in which I sat with my jaw dropped, sleeping little and waking with a sigh of relief: thank God that's over, and wanting to tell someone that I'd just had the most awful nightmare in which people were jumping out of the World Trade Center. Then I'd wake a bit more into an even more terrible nightmare: it's all true.

On the second morning, September 12, I rose and saw what must have been the reason that the terrorists had chosen the date they chose. It was still dark when I went outside: the sickle moon formed a curved exclamation point with Venus, the brightest object in the morning sky, making a striking Islamic flag for all to see. It was such a clear morning and such an obvious reason for the choice of September 11 that I was alarmed that no intelligence agency or news anchor had mentioned it. (What else, I wondered, didn't they know about Islam?) My brother called from Minneapolis to say that he'd seen it, too, and commented, "Madmen are more like poets than generals. When I saw it, it was almost directly overhead, and it was just so obvious."

I recalled working in Washington with the Center for Strategic and

International Studies (CSIS) in the mid-1980s. While writing an essay on terrorism, I heard that they played war games at CSIS, making up scenarios and playing them out. They knew then that Iran was training people to fly fully loaded airliners into buildings. They had scenarios much worse than that, too, some of them easier to carry out. I spoke to a former expert in terrorism from special forces, who said that in the early eighties, his group had known that all it would take "is someone evil enough and smart enough to bring off this kind of destruction. Our society is so open, there's no way to prevent it."

After two days of gaping at the television screen, I got up, rented a car, and drove (no planes or trains were running) to the East Coast, stopping only for gas. When I reached Lenox, Massachusetts, where my friend the photographer Jonas Dovydenas lives, I discovered that American Flight 11 had turned south toward the North Tower practically right over his house. Clearly, the pilot had found the Hudson and followed it south, an obvious landmark that would lead him to the World Trade Center. Navigating to and ramming into the World Trade Center is no mean feat of pilotage. The second plane almost missed, and even after banking sharply at the last minute, managed to hit only its southern edge instead of colliding with it dead center.

Jonas and I reached lower Manhattan to find the streets chaotic, thousands of people milling, looking, dozens of police at every intersection, trucks rumbling, sirens squawking, as cop cars edged through traffic. The cops inside had to show ID to the national guard, who stood blocking every street that led to Ground Zero. We could see their HMMWVs roaring around with whip aerials and spotlights, while smoke and dust drifted over everything. The whole city smelled of burnt insulation, and near the towers, the noise was deafening—of demolition and reconstruction and of the clanking, groaning motion of the great makeshift machine that had been set in motion to try to control the post-traumatic circus of humanity surging around the blast site. That vast sea of motion and emotion seemed to sweep everything into its vortex, and all we could do was wander up and down, trying to find ourselves, as if we'd all somehow been lost in the wreckage, too.

The images on television gave no real sense of it. As we followed Broadway south, looking west, we tried like everyone else to see, but we weren't even sure what we ought to be looking for. We'd crossed through the looking glass of the television and were part of the picture now. Here, we could smell it and feel it. Now and then a couple with bulging suitcases would be escorted out from behind the pile by a police officer, people who'd been allowed to go home long enough to ransack their apartments for a few belongings. I saw them all over town, riding subways and crossing streets or hailing cabs. The collapse took the heart out of Manhattan's youth, for it was largely young people who worked in that financial center. As we moved, police and national guardsmen screamed at us to keep going. Some would rush us, warning that we'd be put in handcuffs if we took pictures. I showed one my press credentials, and he said, "I don't give a shit if you're the pope." Behind him, a band had set up on folding chairs beside 195 Broadway and was playing "America the Beautiful."

The first suggestion that something was wrong was the black wall of a building. It took a moment to register: that wasn't some architect's design, that was an entire office building that looked like melted chocolate. A cloud of white smoke behind it rose a thousand feet into the air.

At Liberty Street we saw the jagged silver latticework that had been the base of one of the towers. It stuck out of the ground like a page torn from history. All around it were heavy steel beams, wrenched and twisted into shapes that seemed impossible. The world had blown itself up and lay in furiously burning heaps. Each passing block provided another view, and by the time we'd passed St. John and reached Cedar Street, the scope of the devastation had begun to sink in. The pile created by the collapse of two 110-story buildings and one 47-story building rose nine stories at its high point and covered sixteen acres. Yellow and red two-hundred-ton boom cranes angled over it. The building on the northwest side of the Trade Center complex had a great javelin of girders stuck in its side twenty stories up. It looked like a mythical lightning bolt throw there by an angry god. As we watched, hot spots in the debris flared up as oxygen hit them, and a white and brown amoeba of smoke rolled over the fire fighters, rose on the breeze, and obscured the scene from view.

The last standing wall of the World Trade Center was a ten-story naked steel sculpture. The original aluminum cladding still winked in the sunlight. It had a solemn, cathedral quality to it, light pouring through a gaping hole in its middle, a serpent of smoke squirming upward, giving it the look of an ancient world long vanished. Only the yellow crane and the men in the bucket betrayed the modern moment. One element of the pile, something sticking up on the eastern perimeter, had been festooned with American flags.

Here in this plaza the generators rumbled, feeding power to the mobile cell phone antennas rigged on telescoping masts. Office lights burned on Cedar Street, and a single neon sign glowed red from the second-story window over the southeast corner of the pile. Gray flags of window curtains waved from broken glass high up the sides of dusty facades. Bent beams as big around as men came lurching past on flatbeds heading south on Broadway. The fire fighters in the box affixed another girder to the cable, which now lifted it out of the smoke and set it on another flatbed. Backhoes gobbled piles of slash, sending smaller gouts of dust into the air, then dumped their buckets into waiting trucks. That last hanging wall of the World Trade Center teetered above the tiny men, who had to scramble over the piles of wreckage and operate the machinery in its shadow. It leaned out from the pile toward the southwest, showing which way the forces had gone.

Look. Look again: articles of clothing, blouses, suit coats, underwear, hung from the aluminum cladding.

As I watched, two men in hard hats with "Coast Guard" sewn onto the backs of their blue jumpsuits walked in toward the ruins, past Plaza Nails and Steve's Pizza, which occupied part of a four-story brick building that stood undamaged in the lee of Ground Zero. I wondered what the coast guard was doing there, but then again, everyone had come, army, OSI, secret service, sanitation, Health Department, not to mention AT&T, Verizon, MCI, Sprint, Con Ed, insurance adjusters, engineers, architects, every union in town. The South Florida Urban Search and Rescue Disaster Response Team's semi-trailer was parked against the aluminum cladding and the roasted black steel. Police and fire fighters from all over the nation came, with every manner of craftsman and laborer in tow, and in their wake, a million others with a million urgent reasons to *do something*. The madhouse of bureaucratic structures was as twisted and vast as the collapsed buildings themselves. I saw cops showing ID to national guard, national guard showing ID to secret service, and secret service showing ID to cops in a mad Orwellian circle of bureaucratic one-upsmanship. Even the newsmen were interviewing each other. (Media from everywhere in the world had arrived. I'd stood in line at police headquarters for two hours between a woman from Thailand and a man from Germany to get my press credentials and learned that more than two thousand had been issued by the time I arrived.)

As I watched people on the pile in baby-blue Tyvek suits with their purple respirators and camo-green goggles, I couldn't help thinking that fortunes and careers were being made right before my eyes, as the uncountable river of money, which was pouring in from every source imaginable, promised to create perhaps the longest hog trough in history for anyone who wished to feed at it.

Street sweepers rumbled by every half hour, spraying down the dust, as trucks went in and out from the pile, laden with debris, "Keep NYC Clean—Don't Litter" stenciled on their sides.

———————

For two days I wandered the area, looking at the destruction from every angle, somehow thinking that if only I got into the right position, it would click into focus and make sense. But it remained just out of reach. The main press area had been set up on Greenwich Avenue with a view of the wreck, and while the public was hustled past, we could stand there and stare as long as we liked at what had come to be called the Pile. The location was Ground Zero. The thing they dismantled they called the Pile. Yet somehow, the way the buildings framed it made the Pile seem like a giant image on a ten-story television screen, something out of Times Square. The authorities seemed almost ashamed that we could sit there and gape at it. The Cartesian grid of our world had fallen into such a jumble that it seemed an affront to the most fundamental principles of order. And what could have been more ordered and orderly than the World Trade Center, the graph-paper grid that we took as proof of our indelible economic triumph?

The building had no face, in fact, until people began jumping out of it (one couple was seen holding hands during their long fall). So perhaps the hostile reaction of police when someone pointed a camera had to do with the people who were still inside, the knowledge that they were even now being pulled out bit by bit. The number of people missing had risen steadily, appallingly, by the hundreds each day, as the bureaucracy caught up with the dreadful thing itself, that series of images, which we shared more fully as a people than the explosion of the space shuttle, the assassination of John F. Kennedy, and perhaps even the crucifixion of Christ. Everyone had seen it in some form. It was everywhere and unavoidable. The graph of numbers that appeared in the news rose for more than a week, and then held at about sixty-three hundred, as reports filtered in that it might go back down, owing to some people having been counted twice. It settled at last at something under three thousand. (According to news accounts published years later, 2,753 people died, of which only 1,629 had been identified by 2011.) In all likelihood, we'll never really know how many died, at least not with the precision that we hold so dear.

Instead, the graph exploded into signs that were taped up everywhere across the city, on light posts and buildings and even parked vehicles: color Xeroxes of faces, brief descriptions of the people and where they were last seen. Then a plea, always the same, call us day or night.

The faces were mostly young, guys holding their sweethearts or women in wedding dresses, smiling. I saw pictures of parties, happy faces in crowds of confident, successful people. The good life that was. There will always be a hole in history, right where so many of their generation vanished without a trace.

I had covered disasters off and on all my life, and I knew: catastrophe draws out people who have stories to tell. Day Eight I met a woman who was mingling with the press among the satellite trucks jammed up on Greenwich Avenue just above Chambers Street. We were sprawled around watching the Pile. Nina had come all the way from Michigan, drawn here like so many who could not explain it. She had light brown hair, blue eyes, and a pretty face. She was almost bubbly with good cheer as she told me about her husband, who had been crushed by a cement truck and killed a year before almost to the day. She hadn't been able to rest since then. She said perhaps this mayhem might release her from her sorrow. She was amazingly cheerful and talkative and even called me later on my cell phone "just to get together and hang out with you guys," she said. When I left Manhattan, Nina was still there, wandering around the Pile, talking to anyone who would talk, as if New York had transformed itself into some vast group therapy meeting.

Many had been called, they said, by Christ. Dan Sudnick was a plumber-fitter-burner from Cleveland, who like me had been watching it on television when he simply stood up, told his wife he'd been called, and piled his van with tools before heading out. "I'm a born-again Christian," he said. "And I just felt that the Lord was calling me." I asked him what he'd seen in there, and he said, "I don't know that I have a word for it. It was a mess." Then he gave me a tract on accepting Jesus into my life as my personal savior and went back into the Pile.

I met two Baptists who had driven all day and all night with ten others in two vans from their organization in Kentucky to cook meals for the rescue workers. One of them, Jay, read aloud from the Bible at the site each day, screaming out the word of Jesus Christ at the top of his lungs as people streamed around and tried to pretend that he wasn't there. When I first saw him, I ignored him, too, perhaps embarrassed by his behavior. But the next day I saw him again and introduced myself. He was with his partner, Asa, and while Jay went on with his reading, competing with the din of machinery, Asa told me about his missionary work. He'd spent eight years in Africa and five in France. He was a handsome man in his thirties who wore a reddish-brown beard and carried a Bible. He was soft-spoken and amiable. He said he'd seen terrible poverty and oppression all over the world. That was in addition to the suffering he'd seen in the United States, where his group provided services after disasters. He'd been in Algeria when a helicopter gunship blew terrorists out of a cave. "If they'd known that we wanted to convert them," he told me, smiling gently, "of course, we'd have been dead on the spot."

I met a Latin American-looking man, who was dressed like a

rescue worker—respirator, blaze-orange vest, protective gear, gloves, fire-fighter pants, and headgear. He was about to be interviewed by a Colombian television station. The man told me that he was an architect with Tishman, working safety for the fire fighters. He'd go in first to see if it was safe and then lead them in. We were talking in front of a TV satellite truck in the midst of dozens of such vehicles in front of the Pile. Beside us, a number of construction workers in hard hats had congregated at the door to a large Verizon truck.

The man, who was accompanied by his wife, said that he and the fire fighters that morning had found forty dead bodies in one of four bomb shelters beneath the World Trade Center. While they were there, they'd heard noises and tapping—people were alive in one of the other bomb shelters—and they were going back in soon to try to break through and pull them out. Natalia Cruz, a TV reporter from Colombia, was about to put him on the air, live, with what appeared to be the scoop of the week, when the group of construction workers turned in unison and slapped handcuffs on the man in the respirator. As they presented us with their detective shields, one of them said, "I'm a police officer. Don't listen to anything he says. He's completely bogus." His IDs were fake, his gear was stolen, and the police had been looking for him. They took his wife away in handcuffs, too.

Bob Gayer had been one of the first inside the Pile after the collapse. He'd worked as a volunteer, but now his work was done. Like so many, he felt compelled to return again and again, unable to rest anywhere else. I spoke to numerous people who said they had tried to go home but kept coming back, and so there they were, red eyed and exhausted, unable to do anything these days except tell their stories over and over. Gayer had by chance had a number of disposable cameras with him when he arrived on the scene in his SUV, and as a result, he had four folders of photographs, which he was showing to anyone who would stop and look. He had snapped pictures of the towers coming down and had run for his life, then run back in to help when the smoke cleared. Working with fire fighters and two doctors he had picked up on the way, along with a deputy police commissioner, he had entered the underground parking structure to look for survivors. "It was pitch dark in there," he told me, "so I had flashlights all over me. I had a flashlight up

my ass, and I was scared to death that I'd never come out of there alive."
They found no survivors. Instead they found cars with their windows
smashed, their lights turned on, their batteries dead. "Obviously, the
people in that garage had turned on the car lights so they could see, but
I have to assume they got out." They found one person alive down there.
He was looting a jewelry store and was arrested by the deputy police
commissioner. Gayer said the looter was a corrections officer.

I wandered over to the east side of the Pile, where I saw a red-
headed police woman leaning against a fence in front of City Hall. She
had that strange look I'd seen on so many faces, an odd paradox of
giddiness and stress, like the adrenaline had run her way past exhaustion to a place where she couldn't feel anything at all. So I asked her if
she had worked inside the Pile. She said she had, that and sorting at
Fresh Kills, which was the dump on Staten Island where all the debris
was being taken and where volunteers were bagging body parts. She
said, "We got a leg with a boot on it," and then she laughed like she
couldn't believe she'd just said that. I asked if she was going back in,
and she pursed her lips and shook her head slowly back and forth.

Later on, Jonas and I walked down the West Side Highway, which
was flanked by mountains of supplies on skids. Enormous stacks of
bottled water and soda were held together by clear plastic wrap. Many
of the cases had burst open and were spilling into the street. Boxes and
boxes of food and clothing had been tossed off of trucks until the ridge-
lines of supplies ran for blocks. The effect was as if we walked through
a canyon of plenty. True, we are a self-absorbed culture, and we luxuriate
in what our money can buy, but when the earth opens up beneath someone, no matter how distant, we pour out that same wealth to any and
all without stopping to count the cost. A young national guardsman,
looking lost, wandered up to me carrying two large boxes of Mounds
bars and peanut M&Ms, saying, "Candy? Candy? Want some candy, sir?"
Then he wandered into the crowd, offering it to everyone he passed. This
truly was where the buck had stopped.

I saw people working their way down the street among the stacks,
taking whatever they wanted, from respirators to those little packs of
human dog chow they serve on Southwest Airlines, mountains of
which had been sent from some mysterious central warehouse and

dumped out here on the street. In that moment, when no one could figure out what to do about the terrible things we'd seen, our hearts went out to others, and we did the only thing we knew how to do: we gave and gave. Everywhere the drive was on for donations of any sort. But it was a cruel trick, because we gave to ourselves in this mad circle of consumerism run amok, a transaction in which nothing really changed hands. Only the rats would make out like bandits and the bandits would make out like rats. At last, in a final inversion of logic, the drive became a drive to stop the drive. Mayor Giuliani had to appear on television and make a plea for people to stop coming, stop donating. "We have everything we need," he said. Even the blood drive became a drive to stop people from giving blood. No one needed a transfusion. Everyone was dead.

For three days and three nights, Gary from the building at 120 Broadway had worked with the teams of fire fighters. He returned home from time to time, thinking he'd sleep, but he only walked the floor, afraid to fall asleep. "I kept seeing that lady in the red dress," he told me, "screaming and screaming." Although he assured me that he had caught some winks, his eyes were as big as golf balls. Each time he went home, he'd turn around and get back on the train and come back to the site. He could find little else to do.

I met many like that. I stood with them among the tall buildings that seemed to lean against a paper-blue sky now. Those buildings no longer seemed as solid as they once had, because we'd all witnessed their undoing, and it had seemed so effortless, so simple. We knew now that they were just as fragile as we were.

A janitor from a nearby bank had watched it all on John Street, where he'd run to get his wife. They stood and saw the second plane hit. "I heard a scream and saw a lady jumping out," he told me. "Then all these bodies started falling. I don't know whether they jumped or were blown out, but I don't never want to see nothin' like that again." His wife made him get on the train back to Brooklyn before the towers collapsed. Now as the yellow backhoes clawed at the wreckage, he had come to bear witness with that vague look that says he couldn't quite believe it, that he expected to wake soon, and that things would once more be as they had been.

As I said goodbye to Gary, we were standing about two blocks from the Pile, eating a slice of pizza and drinking Cokes. "Now, every time I see a bird go by, I think of those people helicoptering down," he told me sadly. He was getting set to go back in and help, he said, but by now he knew that he had little left to do. They'd stopped the bucket brigade, lines of men with five-gallon plastic tubs who had been trying to find survivors and not to disturb the large pieces, which might have injured someone. Now the red and yellow cranes were in there lifting girders.

———————

There had been talk of it all week in hushed tones, and Wednesday afternoon, eight days after the attack, it hit me as I entered the Fulton Street subway station. Everyone around me had looked up, mouth breathing, eyes wide, as if we'd all been startled by a loud noise, though the station was quiet. Then in unison we grabbed for something to put over our faces—handkerchiefs, shirt tails, respirators. It was no longer the smell of uncollected garbage or burning insulation. Police urged us to hurry onto the cars, but it didn't matter. No one wanted to linger.

WIRE WALKER

I was sitting in a tent that served as a dressing room watching Ayin De
Sela, the wire walker of the Pickle Family Circus, limber up before a
show. We had been talking, and now she lay silent on a mat, folding
and unfolding herself like a marionette. She stood and stretched. She
twisted and writhed. She undulated and flowed like mercury and then
gently lifted her toe to her ear with her left hand, immaculate and
motionless. Except for the tympanic beating of her abdomen, I could
imagine that she was not real. She was small and still and beautiful,
and her eyes were Mexican blue, a color that could look at once like
the sea and the next moment like the sky. It could look, as well, like
the inside of the Virgin Mary's garments in a Catholic church.

Ayin let her foot down. It touched the blue floor of the tent and
planted itself as if never to be moved again. She bent at the waist and
placed her palms on the floor, and they, too, seemed to extend roots
into the very earth. Her long, straight golden hair fell and formed a
tent around her. She straightened to her full height, just under five feet,
and took a deep breath. Her hair fell down, tumbled, arranged itself
in shining cataracts. Then in a few lightning moves, like prestidigitation, she took off all her clothes, and all the air was sucked out of the
room. Even the saxophone that had been playing somewhere in the
distance beyond the tent stopped, the way birds will stop all at once
when a new creature, a new danger, appears in the forest. She stood
for a moment in contemplation, Venus, appearing in a shell upon the
sun-freaked sea. The moment seemed to last forever with Ayin before
me in nothing but her fresh olive skin sprent with blisters of sweat
across the scaphoid shape of her breasts, a line of downy darkness trailing from her navel like a smudge from an artist's charcoal. It was over

much too quickly, nothing, a non-event, a young woman deciding what to wear. Then she slipped into another skin of gold and continued stretching as if nothing had happened. The saxophone player went on with his licks, and the drummer kicked in, and the world went back on pitch once more.

———————

I sat in the audience on aluminum bleachers just after noon one hot October day in Tucson. The clowns had come and sprayed us with water, and the tumblers had tumbled, and then Lorenzo Pisoni, a child-demon with an angel's face painted to look like a devil, stood before us and flipped his thin, muscular body into the air and cracked it like a whip. He was more agile than seemed humanly possible, and he smiled mockingly throughout the whole affair, as if to say, "Kids, don't try this at home."

In a few minutes the jugglers performed. Four of them faced one another across a chasm so wide it might as well have been the state of Arizona. They started slowly but eventually juggled sixteen clubs among themselves, tossing them back and forth so fast that they made a white and creaming wave overhead. I had learned juggling when I was in high school, and I had worked the pins with these jugglers for several days to understand what they were doing. The jugglers' eyes didn't exactly meet, because they were watching the motion of the wave created with the white clubs. The trick was to watch the invisible force that kept the clubs moving. It was real, and it was dangerous, and I could see how when one juggler just missed a throw, the catcher would recover and adjust the rhythm, and then the whole thing would go on. This was what this circus was all about, showing not something perfect but something real.

The Pickle Family Circus is the first American circus of its kind in the modern era, a one-ring, European-style traveling show. It is almost the antithesis of the three-ring extravaganza that most of us in the United States think of as the circus. This circus is small, for example, and all the performers are human. It's much more exciting to see real people doing amazing things than amazing people doing unreal things. In the Ringling Brothers Barnum & Bailey Circus, everything is BIGGER THAN LIFE!!!! Everything is impossible. With the Pickles, everything is natural, human. And it is all very possible. And extremely close. Things break. People feel pain.

A few hundred people at a time can see a Pickles show. The audience is seated in three sections of bleachers and crowded onto the grass around a single ring made of a piece of blue rubberized canvas with a pad underneath, surrounded by a raised, red plastic curb to soften the leaps and falls. The top of the arena is open to the sun, and only a red, blue, and yellow canvas wall separates the audience from the outside world. This is a circus you could roll up and put in your backpack.

Between the acrobats and the aerialists came the clowns, the famous Pickle Family Circus clowns, known for inspired characterizations and genuine theatrical qualities not often found in the traditional white-faced clown. One of the Pickles' most famous clowns, Bill Irwin, performed with the circus from 1975 to 1980, then won a Guggenheim Fellowship and a MacArthur Fellowship in 1984. Geoff Hoyle, recognized throughout the world for his one-man shows, was a central character with the Pickles from 1975 to 1981.

In 1990, Joan Mankin, known professionally as Queenie Moon, was not only the premier clown and ringmistress of the circus but also a serious and accomplished juggler. Although trained as an actress, Mankin discovered a few years ago that she enjoyed clowning and that she was very good at it. Her Queenie Moon takes a mocking, knowing, self-deprecating stance that seals an immediate bond with her audience. Throughout her performance, it was evident that no matter what sort of silliness was under way, beneath those waves that played out on the surface swam a deep and barbed intelligence like a manta ray.

Jens Larson emerged from the plastic walls to do the Roman rings. His skill and strength were Olympian. But he also did his routine high enough to make it dangerous and close enough to us so that we could smell him and see the powder smoking off his hands as he changed his grip in the hot lights. He was a mere human, and he had to hold on tight and do well, or else he would fall. The aerialist in the Big Top shows us how unlike him we are. Larson was showing us how like him we are: *This is you*, his performance said. *This is your life. Hold on tight, do your best, and be very careful.*

Then and only then, when all this circus business was done with, did Ayin come out to walk the wire. For the wire is the ultimate test. While Larson reminded us that the Roman rings are life, Ayin elevated that to a new level—no, no, no, wait: This, most of all, more than anything, is your life: You can't hold on. There is nothing to hold on to. You are on a strand of silver high above the crowd, and everyone is watching, waiting for you to fall.

Her balance was almost too good. She sat on the wire, her legs stretched out before her, and then stood from that position, a sea-shell-shaped fan clasped in her right hand. Her movement was as solid as that of a gyroscope on a piano wire. Her power was as formidable as that of a lion let loose in the ring. She wore her skin of gold with her golden hair caught up in a shimmering ponytail, and she wore ballet shoes and walked the wire en pointe, doing arabesques and pliés. Every now and then she turned from her mask-like concentration to smile at the audience, but it was clear that the smile, unlike the act, was an adornment.

Ayin disappeared through the Dizzy Rig, a colored canvas backdrop, and returned to the ring in another costume. She had performed those lightning moves again, that prestidigitation, and now she was scarcely recognizable as the same person. She became just another tumbler in the general commotion of the circus. During a misstep in the wild action of rolling and leaping and flying through the air, Ayin came down hard and landed wrong, the pain creasing her face as if she'd stepped on a scorpion. She cursed under her breath: *Damn! I meant not to do that.* Then she caught herself, put on her professional face, and finished the routine in a blinding fog of pain.

She stumbled as she went back through the Dizzy Rig, and then the pain became too much: she began to weep. Ayin's sister Miriam, who was only twelve but had been in the circus longer, came over to comfort her. Ayin sat on the floor of the blue tent, rubbing her ankle and grimacing. "I don't think I'm going to come back next year," she said.

"Why?" I asked.

"Because it's too hard."

In many ways, Ayin's story is the story of the Pickle Family Circus itself: the old ideals are proving difficult to sustain. The Pickle Family Circus grew out of the San Francisco Mime Troupe, which was part of the California performance-and-politics movement in the sixties. Most of the Pickles' members in some way adhere to the values and ethics that reflect that radical, anti-capitalist, West Coast lineage. Ayin's parents were, by her own description, hippies. Many of the performers have had college educations, have careers waiting for them or some other potential for a more traditional role and status in life. But role, status, salary, prestige, none of this could ever compare with the raw, demanding, immediate reality of the circus.

The Pickle Family Circus was never intended to make a profit: it is here for the good of humankind. In fact, it is run by a foundation and funded by donations and grants from such giant agencies as the California Arts Council, the James Irvine Foundation, and the National Endowment for the Arts. Although the Pickles are in the big leagues of the arts, they continue to suffer from a lack of money owing to their long-standing unwillingness to compromise their principles for what they see as the vicissitudes of the marketplace. They sell their tickets cheap. They use sales to raise money for what they consider to be worthy causes, most often in the local area where they are performing. They have traded their shot at the big-money venues for the small schoolyards of the nation, where they believe they can do some good. No one knows how long the Pickles can keep this up before they are simply hungry and homeless like the people they're trying to help.

When I saw them, their normal crew of thirty-five or so was down to fewer than thirty. For the first time in its history, this circus had scheduled a six-month hiatus, during which the cofounders and the foundations' directors would put their heads together with others to try to come up with a compromise that would bring in money while sustaining the principles as the founders saw them. Writing proposals for grants was getting old. The Cirque du Soleil makes loads of money, they thought. So why not the Pickles?

The difference was a philosophical one. The people who ran Cirque du Soleil didn't mind making money. They saw money as at least part of the point of creating a show in the first place. The Pickles saw money as a necessary evil. The Pickles faced deeper, if simpler, dilemmas. Their best performers ultimately moved on, if for nothing more than the opportunity to sleep in a bed instead of on the ground. At the Pickle Family Circus everyone works all day and sometimes all night. When they aren't setting up the tents and the main ring, they're tearing them down. When they aren't doing that, they're performing. When they aren't performing, they're rehearsing. And if they get any sleep at all, it is outside, in a pup tent, with an outhouse serving their other needs.

One afternoon I watched Ayin do her makeup as she sat cross-legged on the floor of the Mad Moid, as they call the costume tent. Using a broken fragment of mirror to view her countenance, she worked out of a fishing tackle box that contained all of her brushes and blushes, her lipsticks and powders. She looked up at me with a hopeless and beautiful smile. "We're homeless people!" she said in a rising voice that suggested the futility of all her efforts.

As we sat there on the floor of the Mad Moid, Ayin told me that she wanted to go to France and study at the Châlons-sur-Marne circus school. Another of her sisters, Sky, nineteen, was already there. Ayin said that although working with the Pickles was an extremely important experience and had helped turn her into a professional performer, she had no time to practice. Her life seemed a constant race against time and entropy. She looked on the point of tears. As she often was.

Outside the open flap of the blue tent, I could see Lorenzo Pisoni running like a gazelle. Someone was chasing him with a paper plate full of whipped cream, the traditional pie-in-the-face. It was his thirteenth birthday. Lorenzo was born into the circus. His father, Larry Pisoni, helped to found the Pickle Family Circus in 1974 with Peggy Snider (Lorenzo's mother and a Bennington College graduate) and Cecil MacKinnon (MFA from New York University). A photograph shows Lorenzo as a baby in the arms of Bill Irwin, the scowling and ominous-looking Guggenheim Fellow clown. Lorenzo wears a button that says, I'M LORENZO. I BELONG TO THE CIRCUS.

Some people are born into the circus. Others are drawn there, as if by forces they cannot explain. Three of the six De Sela sisters became circus performers, although their father was a schoolteacher.

"We had a really strange childhood," Ayin said. "We traveled around Mexico in a school bus. My parents were in love with Mexico. My father gave up his American citizenship when they tried to draft him, and then we just lived in Mexico. I was born in Mexico. And my father always used to do these funny things. Like he'd say, 'And now she will jump through the hoop of death!'" Ayin smiled, remembering her first performances as a child. "And I would jump."

Ayin and her sisters were born into the circus, but first they had to realize that their life was a circus, and then they had to go and join it. Lorenzo knew at the outset: Life is a circus. The circus is life. The magic happens when the audience sits down and, for a fleeting moment, understands. Accepts. And then lastly, believes.

"I think it's going to rain," Ayin said. We were still sitting cross-legged, face-to-face, like Plains Indians on the floor of the Mad Moid. Ayin had on her war paint.

"Don't say that," said Rosalidnda Rojas, a lovely Puerto Rican acrobat and hand balancer. Another show was coming up in a couple of hours, and rain could ruin it. The Mad Moid tent was pitched on the grounds of a school. It was a Saturday. Hundreds of kids and their parents were turning out for a big Arizona-style barbecue with the Pickle Family Circus as the center of attention, the entertainment. But Ayin's keen animal senses sucked in the rain from high above in the stratosphere. "Well," she said forlornly. "I hope it does rain." She was sullen, pouting. "I don't want to do tonight." But even as she spoke, she stood to test her ankle to see if she could make the show.

The Pickle Family Circus doesn't believe in risk for the sake of risk. Its acts are grounded in reality, and the reality of life is that we all fall down now and then. We shouldn't be sentenced to death for our human frailty. That is one of the many philosophical differences between the Pickles and the big commercial operations. The large circus draws people in by suggesting that its performers are superhuman and that if they aren't, they may die right before your very eyes. Their acts are described as death defying, and we are encouraged to look for their flaws, not to participate in a celebration of their art and skill.

The Pickles perform a series of engineering and technological tricks.

The acts involve real human beings interacting in uncommon ways. The fact that they're mortal and not omnipotent is a gift of revelation to the audience. We see the performance, not the specter of death. We see all human potential expanding before our eyes. Possibilities reveal themselves: *Hey, people can do these things—and we're people, too!* The audience comes away feeling connected to the action, not belittled by it.

Although I had been walking the slackrope since high school, Ayin told me when I first met her that she would teach me how to walk the wire if I wanted to try. So one afternoon, when I found her practicing, I took off my shoes and socks and climbed to the plywood platform with her. No larger than a dinner plate, the platform was scarcely a place of refuge. The first time I put my foot on the wire, I could tell that it was alive. I felt the singing of the strings in the ball of my naked foot, and I waited until my calf muscles found the pitch. Behind me, the drummer was practicing that same figure over and over: chick-a-boom, chick-a-boom, chick-a-boom. I understood that the wire would not stop its singing to accommodate my weight. It was going to keep right on trembling, and if I wanted to make it across the twenty-two feet of steel stretching before me in the sunlight, I was going to have to get in tune with the wire's restless animation. I stepped out into the air. There for a moment, we were one, the wire and I. And then I fell.

The crew set the wire low for practice, with plenty of pads underneath. The point of the exercise wasn't to risk injury. It was to balance the forces of nature with the forces within us and bring the two into harmony. Since the will of steel won't change, that meant changing myself. And that meant having a self left to change after I fell. I fell many times. But with Ayin's encouragement, I worked all afternoon, and ultimately I did get it.

It was late, and Ayin had gone off somewhere, leaving me to practice, walking and falling and walking and falling. When she returned, she watched me make the twenty-two feet from platform to platform and clapped and smiled. Then I got down, and she climbed up. She worked out on the wire. For her it was ten feet wide. She tested her ankle to see if she could manage the evening show. She was framed by mountains, and when she went up en pointe, it was as if she stood atop the gray sculpture of rock in the background. "Want to see some stag jumps?" she called down to me in her little girl's voice that could not conceal her pride. She leaped off the wire like an antelope, feet high behind her, and she seemed to hang in the air for a moment. Gravity stopped for her the way traffic stops for a line of baby ducks. Then, as if on her command, the laws of physics resumed, and she came down precisely on the wire. I calculated that during the year and a half she'd been with the circus, she had walked more than a thousand miles on the wire.

When she had finished her practice session, I asked if she would do the evening performance. "Yeah," she said. "I wish I didn't have to." She looked up at the sky, which had been simmering all day and now seemed to have reached a rolling boil. "I wish it would rain."

A few minutes later, we were back in the Moid, and I began to believe that Ayin controlled not just gravity but all of nature. As she sat on the floor, scraping the soles of her wire-walking shoes with a metal rasp in preparation for the show, we both began to hear the steady ticking of rain on the blue-and-red roof, and she smiled a secret smile as if to say, *See? I did it.* Suddenly, the drumming of the rain on the canvas increased, and lightning split the sky with a cymbal crash of thunder. A tremendous wind came up and punched through the tent like a fist. I heard Ayin scream, and then the tent came down around us, and we leaped out through the open fly as the poles collapsed. A cyclonic storm was whirling out of the mountains and taking us away. A show was on, but whose show was it?

Out on the grass behind the main ring of the circus, clowns were running and yelling. Thunder cracked through the chittering of voices, and fifty yards away I could see the amoeba-like shapes of the little tents lean away with the wind and begin to take flight, as people ran in every direction, carrying suitcases and chairs and sacks of juggling clubs.

I helped Ayin gather up her things, and we went racing among the running people and threw everything into garbage bags, trucks, vans, and the kitchen trailer, while lightning flickered in the east over the mountains. Then came the pealing sound of a crack that at first we thought was thunder, until the great wall that separated the circus ring from the backstage area came down, tearing metal and crushing the

Dizzy Rig, and then the whole circus collapsed into a flat expanse of colored plastic. It was the ultimate clown act: everything went wrong all at once with a finality that could not have been invented. All across the area, structures of nylon and canvas were folding up in the face of the mighty wind. Before we had finished carrying everything to the trucks, the Pickle Family Circus was four acres of devastation, and night was falling around us in accompaniment to a thunderous driving rain.

———————

The next morning the sun shone all around Tucson, but the circus was still flat. Ayin's ankle was worse than ever, grossly swollen. She had a black silk scarf wrapped around her neck and wore a black sweater, and she was glum about the prospect of doing anything stirring and beautiful that day.

"You're sad," I said to her. "Why?"

"Because I have to do today," she answered. Then she added perfunctorily, as if she were repeating something someone had told her, "It's up to me if I don't want to push it." But we both knew—at least at that moment, at 8:30 in the morning after a storm blew down the Pickle Family Circus—that Ayin really had no choice in the matter. The performers arrived and began pulling the debris up off the wet ground to see how, like a puzzle thrown from its box, it might all fit together again.

"It's hard," Ayin said, meaning life in the Pickle Family Circus, this old-time, from-the-heart, work-like-a-dog circus. "It's so hard."

I could smell coffee brewing in the kitchen trailer behind Ayin, who sighed and stood and stripped off her sweater and picked up a big push broom and began to sweep the standing water off the blue floor of the Moid. I thought of Emmett Kelly's legendary sad-clown act of sweeping up the spotlight circle until it closed in upon itself and vanished to a point of light, and then the whole tent, the whole world, would be dark. So Ayin seemed to sweep the sunlight away with her sadness.

It was only two hours before the Dizzy Rig was up again. Soon the backdrop was lifted into place, its structure repaired with a splint of wood. Then even the Moid was up again, and the personal tents were put back together, and I could hear the saxophone player beginning to warm up on the bandstand. The sun had risen high enough to dry out the grass, and I saw a silver-gray hot-air balloon hanging motionless over the mountains in the distance. The crowd was arriving as the band began to play. The day was going to be very hot. Ayin was now sitting on the wire, balancing without thinking, just draping herself there in her idle insouciant beauty, as if she were sitting on a park bench. An aerialist came over and suggested that she leave out the toe work to save her ankle. "That would be a dinky act," Ayin said. From her seated position, she rose to her feet as if pulled to her full height by a celestial rope, a marionette drawn up from above. Then she danced lightly across the wire, her face relaxed as if in sleep. I watched her arms wave smoothly, rhythmically, back and forth above her. She was gliding like a bird in soaring flight, tilting with the fluctuations of the wind. Behind her a juggler was tossing clubs in a pouring white cascade, and the saxophone played arpeggios, which sounded like the juggling of golden thimbles in the air. Then an accordion started up from behind the Dizzy Rig. Lorenzo stepped out into the ring and looked at the sky for a moment in concentration, then did a backflip as if it were just a nervous tic or something he does while thinking about something else.

"How is it?" I asked Ayin.

"It's pain," she said, slipping across the wire, backlit by the immense gray mountains, sliding and dancing and turning on one foot as the whole machinery of the circus gained momentum for another show. "It's just pain."

BLUE MEMPHIS

Driving from the Memphis airport to the Peabody Hotel, I happened to pass Sun Studio. I hadn't expected to see it so soon. Without thinking, I changed lanes and turned into the parking lot accompanied by a chorus of angry horns. I'd written the name on a list of civic shrines I wished to visit, but I'd had no idea, in fact, where it was located: yet here it was, with "SUN" written in neon above the picture window, a small beaten-down white frame building set amid hospitals and housing projects beside a barren lot now engulfed in the furious ravening of weeds, which bloomed in crazed profusion with tiny white flowers. Cairns of cracked concrete were set here and there in a squirming sea of rebar hydras. This then was the cradle of civilization as we now know it, the place where "Rocket 88" was recorded, considered the first white rock and roll, and then "Mystery Train," Elvis Presley's first record, an old Mississippi Delta blues song, which had been reanimated with upright bass fiddle and the syncopated whacking of a drum kit.

A tour of the studio was already under way. Chris, a recent émigré from Poland, a thin young man with hooded eyes, was explaining about the song "Bloo Zeud Zshoes" to a small crowd of tourists assembled inside the studio, twelve or fifteen fans, one of them confined to a wheelchair, an aging rocker in T-shirt and sneakers.

"I mention name Johnny Cash," intoned Chris. "Here recorded Johnny Cash a song, 'I Walk a Line.'" Chris pressed the play button on a reel-to-reel tape deck at his side and played a few bars of the song. The studio was no larger than a living room, covered wall and ceiling in old acoustic tiles, floriated with water stains, a dismal and unpretentious place, where Jerry Lee Lewis recorded the largest-selling rock-and-roll record in history, "Great Balls of Fire," which sold eight million copies at a time when Elvis's biggest record had sold only six million. Thirty years later in this very same room, U2 recorded a Dylan-Bono composition, "Love Rescue Me," for its *Rattle and Hum* album.

Chris went on about Roy Orbison, saying, "He didn't do nothing special here, wan song, 'Ooobie Doobie,' beeg hit he recorded here." And he played the tape while the visitors let their jaws go slack in gaping reverential solemnity: "Ooobie-doobie, Ooobie-doobie."

Behind Chris lay the heart of the recording studio, the control room. We could see it through the soundproof glass. A band entered from the parking lot behind the building, where I had parked my car beside a great green steel coffin labeled "grease only." Now this quintet milled about in the control booth, talking soundlessly with Gary Hardy, the owner of Sun Studio, a man in his forties with long reddish-brown hair and a drooping moustache, who gesticulated, laughing wildly, as the band of twenty-year-olds with buzz cuts and goatees fixed him with disdainful looks of disbelief at his outrageous squareness.

Chris stood beneath a huge grainy black-and-white enlargement of what must have been a 35-millimeter photograph. It depicted Elvis seated at a spinet piano. Jerry Lee Lewis, Carl Perkins, and Johnny Cash stood behind him. Elvis had been caught in the act of turning around, beautiful and boy-like, hands on the keys, as he gazed up with a dreamy smile at the trio. The picture hadn't been very sharp when it was small, and now it was huge and spectral as if it still expanded from the Big Bang, its light reaching us after traveling a billion years. Chris said, "Carl Peer-kins, he was doing here his session. Elvis was hang around here with his fraands and sits at this piano—not *this* piano but piano much like thees wan. Is part of session from 1956." And he began the tape once more. Through the glass I could see Gary's arms shoot up to the ceiling as he laughed madly, and I saw the band shrink back, their eyes wide.

Our group shuffled out of Sun Studio onto Union Street, where a tour bus farted diesel smoke and traffic roared past. I stopped in next door to eat a cheeseburger at Gary's Sun Studio Cafe. Elvis, Jerry Lee, and the others were to my generation what old Civil War soldiers had been to my father's, and I wanted to be able to tell my grandchildren that I had been here, that I had done that cheeseburger thing at the Sun Studio Cafe in Memphis back in the nineties before the turn of the century. The room was decorated with rare photographs from Sun Studio's history and had a jukebox that I could have listened to for days. I knew that the little black specks on the French fries weren't pepper, but I ate them anyway. The cheeseburger wasn't bad.

It feels cool to be in Memphis.

I checked in at the Peabody Hotel. Where else? The Mississippi Delta is said to extend, unfolding in looping and serpentine coils, from the Lobby of the Peabody Hotel to Catfish Row in Vicksburg, the last important Confederate stronghold on the Mississippi during the War (there is always and only one war down here). Eric Clapton was already checked in when I arrived. After a quick workout and sauna in the basement health club, I changed and went down to meet Jim Jaworowicz, who had helped to open such renowned blues clubs as B. B. King's and the House of Blues.

The lobby of the Peabody was decorated in a riot of railway-station architecture and whorehouse , cut glass and artfully agonized metal, opulent marble, stone fountains, and carpets from far-off lands. The lobby was swaying with people in plumes of smoke and laughter and overpowered by clouds of noxious drugstore perfume. Southern whiskey was being poured in the bar with beer chasers under flowered cutwork and candelabra, all electrified and pulsing in beveled tavern mirrors with a frieze of reflected liquor bottles and the cackle of bland, confused optimism, as orange-suited bellmen pushed carts piled high with luggage back and to, and lines formed at the cashier's cage like a Tahoe casino at the blossoming of midnight.

People had gathered in ranks around the balconies and all across the main floor, pushing and jamming in close to stare with solemn zeal at something that would come down a red carpet laid out from the elevator to the fountain. I thought they must be waiting to see Eric Clapton, except that they all seemed to be over the age of sixty. After considerable anticipation, an antebellum Negro dressed in livery like an iron jockey tapped his cane at the elevator door, causing several trained ducks to walk out. The congregation cheered and squealed as the ducks traversed the length of the red carpet, climbed a carpeted stair to the travertine fountain, topped by a floral arrangement, wilted and gargantuan, and began swimming around beneath naked Cistine angels that were micturating from invisible pores.

Already applause was general within the chamber by the time Eric Clapton came on. Jimmy Vaughn had persisted in a thermite glow at the geometric center of this amoebic vault of pulsing air. Behind him, smoke had streamed up into the sucking vacuum of the lights, which erected a heaving tent of vapors cut with crimson stakes, a throbbing medusa of undulating beams, as if he were held in the prison of his own energy. His backup singers poured forth a Zulu sound, a mocking entreaty of voices, a tribe descending in darkness on rapid footbeats, coming to kill us. We were in the Memphis Pyramid, third-largest pyramid in the world, this cathedral of girders, the startling new civic basketball arena, whose exterior is surfaced with mirrors so bright that at high noon it can be seen from the space shuttle. Now it was filled wall-to-wall with a shaded spirit world of creatures in folding chairs. Yet amid this Egyptian catatonia drifted the boys selling beer, who seemed not to have noticed the transformation, the women in business suits talking on cell phones in their box seats, and the people in general eating pork-shoulder-on-a-bun and crimson hot dogs.

Eric walked on looking at his feet, dressed in white T-shirt and white pants, his hair almost flattop short, a tall and frail man with the nervous, modest aspect of someone who's been asked to make a small mechanical repair before the concert could begin. Then he sat down with two other guitarists and played the encyclopedia of blues for two hours without a break. Spokes of smoky light radiated from him like an astral diadem. We seemed suspended in a matrix of beams like pelagic creatures caught in a celestial net, spindle, and mote. We crawled the sea floor in this apocalyptic canister of brilliance, this shadow world where obscure and cryptic dramas were played out by silhouettes on far balconies, while twenty thousand people screamed and clapped, plunged in twilight, to hear a dozen do their work.

Eric ran through the songs of Bessie Smith, Freddy King, Albert King, Eddie Boyd, Muddy Waters, Big Mesio, Otis Rush, Robert Johnson, Willie Dixon, and when he was done and left the stage, the people wouldn't go home until he had done it all once again. He returned with Jimmy Vaughn and his Tupelo singers. A splendid arc of searchlights crawled squid-like across our faces like the fingers of a thousand gods, probing this palpitating city of the dead. It was as if the great hills had awakened to give back the richness that had once completed the earth.

After the concert, Jim Jaworowicz and I retired to B. B. King's on Beale Street to hear some blues. Memphis is, after all, the city of the blues, and the blues is an expression of melancholy. To visit Memphis is to grapple with the blues, to spin the gyroscope of the soul that stands us upright on the wire of our life. Here in this city with its Coptic obsession of 150 years, named after an ancient city dedicated to the Egyptian god of the arts, the town council held a parade down Beale Street in honor of Booker T. and the MG's. Not Martin Luther King, not Saint Patrick, not Christ, but Booker T. and the MG's. Cadillacs that day crept astride a marching band, which played "Green Onions." That's what kind of a city Memphis is. Blues Fest in May is a month-long celebration of the music that coronetist W. C. Handy is said to have invented here. A statue of him watches over Beale Street. The power of music is a civic power.

Jim and I went from concert to club at midnight on a Wednesday, and the room, which was jammed with people when we arrived, grew more intense as the night made its slow dissolve. A house band called the King Bees played, as Jim led me through the throng to the owner's private box seats on a balcony above the stage. The petty hierarchy of the nightclub back rooms, enforced by cadres of minimum-wage weight lifters with ponytails, a zealous and unofficial secret police, swinging with elliptical lunacy from snarling threats to fawning servitude at the blink of an eye. One moment Jim and I were the object of their malice, the next we were seated behind locked doors, protected and served by them. One brought a platter of steaming tender catfish, deep fried dill pickles, and potatoes, while the other served beer and Coke.

Jim Jaworowicz has his own business buying and selling rock-and-roll memorabilia. When Elvis's estate purchased Colonel Tom Parker's collection, Jim was hired to sit at Graceland for eighteen months going through four houses full of artifacts and documents, cataloging and evaluating it. He became interested in rock and roll in 1966 when he was young and impressionable and a family member took him to Memphis to see Elvis's house, after which they went to a Beatles concert. The Ku Klux Klan was demonstrating outside the theater, because John Lennon had said that the Beatles were more popular than Jesus Christ. When Jim worked at Graceland, he found among the Colonel's effects telegrams that the Beatles had sent to Elvis that day. They wanted to come to Graceland and say hello, but Elvis wasn't home.

Little Jimmy King came up to the balcony and reached between me and Jim. "Can I have one of your pickles?" he asked, popping a fried dill pickle into his mouth. Little Jimmy King was feral and beautiful, with wet curly hair and gleaming skin, deeply black. He was gaunt and shining and noble, bobbing anxiously behind us as if he had just robbed somebody, furtive, glancing all around while he fingered tidbits into his mouth with delicate ursine tentacles.

Little Jimmy King wasn't really a King at all. His name was Gales. His brother Eric Gales had a well-known blues band. But when Jimmy was just a kid, Albert King took him in. Jimmy calls the late Albert King "my grandfather." Now taking one last pickle from the platter, Jimmy slid off into darkness. A bodyguard held the door for him as he vanished into the heaving herd.

Below on the dance floor, I could see Al Green's bass player come in, shaking hands with musicians all around. A moment later several members of Eric's band came in from the concert, and everyone was shaking hands, embracing, screwing the caps off of beer bottles down by the stage. The nightclub's co-owner Tommy materialized out of the darkness beside me and sat at our table. "This is *not* blues," he proclaimed of the King Bees. Ruby Wilson, a local soul singer, was gurgling out a tune from her huge taut belly. "This is *Memphis* music. Rhythm and blues. It's got to be *fun*." He had attended the Clapton concert and offered the opinion that it was dull. He liked the "uptown" blues with the shuffle beat that Jimmy Vaughn had played.

Below now Little Jimmy King stepped into the spotlight, and the crowd, recognizing him, went into hysterics. Little Jimmy King played left-handed and backward, with the guitar strung upside-down, and he looked like a burning statue rooted to the spot, as if he'd just been removed from the kiln and was still smoking. Then all at once he leaped and shook his long curls, grinning and grimacing and performing some sort of wild cunnilingus on the guitar, which was shaped like the point of an ice axe. His music was the electric scream of feedback.

Introducing his brother, Eric, Little Jimmy King said, "The last time you saw two left-handed guitar players on this stage was me and my grandfather Albert King, and tonight it's me and my baby brother." And then the electricity backed up and ran right through him, and he screamed and leaped about. His skin was almost purple in the stage lights. Now and then he shook out his right hand as if it had caught fire, and then he and Eric Gales would sweep into another song with undiminished savagery at a volume so loud that the drummer put in earplugs. From my vantage on the balcony just above him I could see Jimmy's eyes as he threw his head back, shrewd and desperate, cunning and lively and longing for something tender to come to him that most likely would not come. Because his need was too big.

It was sometime after two in the morning when I slipped out into the suppurating darkness of Beale Street. I heard the far-off complaint of a freight train. Beale Street is a scant two blocks of cobbled streets and ancient facades, some held upright by a spiderwork of girders, a place where anyone can play the blues. As in New Orleans, beer in plastic cups was sold from outdoor vendors. As in Austin, often the best bands were playing for tips.

As I walked back up Beale Street, Little Jimmy King was still shackled to that burnt-out stage by the black cord of his guitar, pacing back and forth, glistening and mad like a captured beast. I stood for another moment, listening to the sadness he expelled from the sharp and lance-like instrument in malevolent, incomprehensible bursts, wearisome and harrowing. I heard him remonstrate with the crowd now, saying,

BLUE MEMPHIS

73

"And if the music's too loud, you got a hole in your soul!" He was right. The music was too loud. And I do have a hole in my soul.

In 1818 Andrew Jackson negotiated a treaty with the Chickasaw Indians to vacate this spot. The very next year he entered into a land-developing agreement with John Overton and James Winchester. Within a few months, they had laid out the original town lots of Memphis, Tennessee. The town was named during a craze of interest in Egyptian culture spurred by the accidental archeological discoveries that attended the French invasion of Egypt during the close of the eighteenth century. It says here the blues came out of Negro work songs and chain gang hollers, but I don't believe that. I believe that the blues came out of the Mississippi River. It came at night in the shape of a fog, and it infected the population indiscriminately, black and white alike.

Sunday morning a melancholy church was testing its tones against a windless sky alight with birds. A boat went up river with a foundry racket. I walked the streets and found the World News stand on Union Street. The man behind the counter said, "You know, people who just buy a little paper or two? They make it real hard for an honest man to stay in business sometimes." And then he and his partner laughed and laughed. I thought they were crazy, but they were just quoting from *Mystery Train,* the Jim Jarmusch film about Memphis.

I drove to the Fourway Grill for breakfast. It was in a part of town where it seemed that the houses would have fallen over if they had not been leaning against each other. I was the only person in the restaurant who was not African American, and when I walked into the quiet little room, a room that would have been at ease in 1957, all heads turned from the television set on the bar to follow my progress. Irene Cleves had been the owner of the place for forty-seven years, and it appeared these were her original customers. Brother James Salton exhorted the faithful on Channel 30, WLMT, from the pulpit of his program, entitled *Jesus Makes You Well.* A woman in a white apron came out from the kitchen, where great aluminum cauldrons of greens were beginning to boil, and she stood over me and stared without saying anything.

"I'd like to have breakfast," I said.

"Well, then you gone have to set down somewheres," she said, wiping her hands on a sacking towel. "I can't serve you standin' up like that." And she turned away and crossed back to the kitchen in a cloud of steam.

I crossed a floor made of red- and salmon-colored rock fragments set in concrete, and I settled into a booth. The walls were painted brown and green, and the paint had bubbled with age, mirrors decorated the walls, and billed caps hung on hat hooks. On the gray Formica tables were bottles of green peppers in vinegar. Heat ducts, wide and truck-like, imposed from above, festooned with soot and cobwebs set in kitchen grease. Above the bar were photographs of family members in military uniforms beside the Immortal Americans poster in a dimestore frame and captioned "Builders of Racial Good Will."

The same woman who had greeted me served me ham steak with the bone in it and marrow inside the bone, alongside white rice and red-eye gravy. The ham was crisp and salty, almost like bacon, and the gravy over rice was rich and delicious. I ate slowly, savoring each bite. I was in the company of ancient people in threadbare clothes who held up triangles of toasted white bread like Eucharist in solemn contemplation of Brother James Salton's message.

I drove right by Graceland mansion the first time. I couldn't go in. I found it on a street called Elvis Presley Boulevard, a squat beehive of limestone with Corinthian columns and dozens of busses going in and out, trapped in a zoneless district of commercial, industrial, and residential buildings, all of which seemed to have been thrown together amid a blizzard of glittering tinfoil flags, which announced the used car lots and the strip malls that had sprung up in a mitosis of wires and hopped-up advertising signs all bedecked in cryptic glyphs. As I drove past Krispy Kreme Doughnuts, the facade of arcades quickly broke down to jack pine and Johnson grass, the very same way it had when I passed through the western town on the Warner Brothers lot in Los Angeles. I turned off the main road onto a small lane of clapboard warrens with lean-to carports where unsprung horseless buggies balanced on precarious footings of cinderblock, and magnolia trees rose out of collapsed skirts of their own decaying leaves in disordered yards of rank holly bush and honeysuckle. Creosoted pilings ran a disordered loom of phone cable back and to across the sky. Burst black steel mailboxes stood in irregular ranks on poles, and ladders leaned against trees in a mute eternal optimism, as if by some miracle one or the other might not inevitably fall under the weight of time. A Lincoln town car with no front wheels. A neglected dwelling had collapsed, and now the lot led in a short distance over the broken back of the house across overgrown thicket lashed together with vines, beset by shedding poplars and phone wires and wildgrown bushes to a primordial forest that seemed never to have been touched by human tenancy. Great tree limbs had been snapped down in an ice storm early that year and gave the scene a look still more forlorn. The road dead-ended in railroad tracks where a freight train clattered south with open boxcar grates. I pulled into the blacktop parking lot by the sign that said "Full Gospel Tabernacle—Rev. Green" and parked beside a church of painted white cinderblock.

I crossed to a raker in denim, bent to his raking among the stumps, past the vine-crawling collapsed split-rail fence amid fallen leaves. No sidewalks: culvert and ditches of frog eggs waiting to hatch at the first rain and fill the air with peeping. He was a gaunt and ghostly neighbor with stringy red hair and an accent so thick I could scarcely grasp his meaning, out there alone with a rake on two acres of lawn that were ankle deep in leaves. I asked when the service was.

"Eh?" he asked. He was young, but he had a mouthful of discolored pearls that looked as if they would drop out into his hand if he coughed.

"When is the church service? Over there," and I pointed.

"Whenever that lot fills up with cars, that's when they be having they service," he said. I asked if he knew *about what time* the lot was apt to fill up with cars, and he shrugged and smiled congenially, revealing lacerated gums. He told me to knock on the door of the outbuilding in back of the church and ask for James, but don't disturb the Reverend's kin in the big white house under the spreading oak.

An asphalt drive led me back. A voice came through the bolted door: "Who is it?" I wanted to know when the service was, I said. "The Reverend speaks at noon," he hollered, and I heard retreating footsteps.

I said thank you and walked back to the front, a right spire, thin and peeling white paint. A woodpile ready for winter. Such provisional dwellings. And down the block one perfect brand-new house, which in optimistic lunacy displayed a white wooden sign that read "Homes of Distinction" and was festooned with yellow mums.

My friend Wayne Jackson, trumpet player for the Memphis Horns, had told me to go to Al Green's church. "Now everybody in this town works for Federal Express. But if there's anything left of Memphis, it's right there," he said. The Full Gospel Tabernacle is a bomb shelter of Cubist leaning that was the plague of architecture in the 1960s. Parallelograms and startling angles fitted with blue stained-glass panels that were crazed with an abstract reticulum of lead solder. It sits on a hill of sedge gently sloping with a stand of oak and pine behind. As I entered I was confronted by the spectacle of Al Green, dancing and screaming amid a choir of white-suited singers on tiers of heavenly stairs behind him. A Hammond B-3 organ pumped out the tremolo rhythm, along with bass, guitar, drums. Asian, white, black, and mysterious races filled the church. People came from all over to hear Al Green. After all, he had sold thirty million records in the five years of his career, from 1971 to 1976. The Reverend Green was grinning, he was happy, as he walked around the church, shaking hands, kissing people, asking where they were from, and placing a microphone before them to receive the answers—Seattle, Switzerland, Scotland, Nova Scotia. Banners printed by computer hung on the walls proclaiming, "Order My Steps in Your Word."

A painting on the brick wall behind me depicted a city suffering terrible car wrecks, graphically showing the bloody wounds of the victims. In the background, a DC-10 crashed headlong into a skyscraper, while all around white-robed figures flew up toward a Christ who floated among the clouds. On another wall: the passion of Christ rendered on black velvet.

"Idd'n it wonderful?" Al Green asked with a seductive smile. "We're so fortunate to have Sister Ann singing with us today. Idd'n it wonderful?" And then he slipped into "Amazing Grace," gliding up into a powerful falsetto that rattled the room and made the hair stand up on the back on my neck.

October 25, 1974, while the Reverend Al Green was taking a shower in his home, his former girlfriend Mary Woodson, whom the Reverend had called "a beautiful, gorgeous person," entered his apartment and poured a pot of boiling grits on him. She then shot herself dead. In 1981 his wife Shirley obtained a court injunction to keep Al Green away from her, at the same time suing for divorce on the grounds of "brutal beatings."

Sunlight fell through stained glass onto the potted flowers on the altar behind him. And when he broke into an operatic contralto the crowd came to its feet and exploded in compassion, applauding. Everyone was clapping and singing. The Reverend Al Green was grinning, punctuating his performance with the question, "Idd'n it wonderful?"

———————

A forty-five-minute wait for barbecue at Corky's, the best wet barbecue in Memphis. The place was huge and rough-hewn and crowded with loud people and the cymbal crash of dinnerware. Across from our booth, four young men sat talking quietly, and when their barbecue came, they bowed their heads in prayer. I couldn't help staring. My companion laughed, saying, "Haven't you seen that before? You see that a lot in Memphis."

———————

Our tour guide's name was Toshiba. I don't think she was Japanese. I stood in the dark interior of the old mansion next to a mother with a black eye and a baby. It was so quiet that we could hear the security guard (his name tag said "Jimbo") sucking on a hard candy. I realized with a jolt that I had been here before. In the 1970s, when I worked for *Playboy* magazine. Hugh Hefner's mansion in Chicago had looked like this, the moldy smell of green shag carpeting, the stale human spoor, the melancholy illusions created by too many mirrors in odd places, a monument to the sad darkness of perpetual loneliness, the introspective bad taste propelled by too much money. Near the end Elvis looked like Napoleon with his capes and his haunted expression, and I suddenly understood that Elvis didn't have a friend in the world by then. No one was on his side. No one looked out for him. For those around him, nothing on earth could have been more auspicious than his death. The estate had made $15 million a year when he was alive. Now it made $75 million a year.

His father kept an office in Graceland. In that office a television played a videotape of Elvis returning from Germany after mustering out of the army. It showed a frightened boy with his hair looking accidentally absurd, wringing his hands and grimacing, painfully shy, as he cut his alluring hooded eyes furtively left and right, and he said, "Someone asked me this morning what did I miss about Memphis, and I said, uh, 'Everything.'"

We passed through the great illuminated corridor that contained his gun and badge collection, the mutant fantasy of a childhood forsaken but not yet ended, the desperate expression of rage and solitude. The state of Colorado had made him a member of the organized Crime Strike Force. He was a badge-carrying special assistant of the Bureau of Narcotics and Dangerous Drugs when he died from chronic overuse of same.

I walked outside, where a sad little kidney-shaped swimming pool was luring withered leaves down out of the oaks and poplars. Broken lawn furniture with stained seats and rotting cushions was set about the pebbled concrete apron. A sign creaked back and forth in the wind, beseeching, "Do Not Throw Coins in the Pool." I could see the people who lived next door in a bland and unremarkable middle-class home. They were out gardening, mowing their lawn, kicking up clouds of dusty clay soil, which settled on the laundry they'd hung out to dry. Their fence was Elvis's fence, and Elvis's horses still rubbed their behinds against its tired wooden posts.

I feel as if the gift he gave me was a poisoned apple. This persistent sadness, which I first learned to feel when I was ten years old, imitating "All Shook Up" and "Don't Be Cruel." Memphis is a city of sadness, celebrating sadness all the time, with monuments to sadness and mystery trains and a river of sadness that flows right through it. Elvis is loved so much because he, more deeply than anyone else, was unable to love himself.

I waited on Main Street for the trolley. Far away and silent, the streetcar came toward me, teetering and uncertain. It came like a red and yellow spider aspiring across a green reticulation of wires and girders and the raw steel rails sunk in bubbly asphalt. As it heaved into view, it shrieked and rattled and slowed with a rumble until, shaking all over, it seemed to collapse on the spot and crash to a stop with the door sliding open on creaking tracks and with a final sound of metal uncoupling.

I climbed on board and dropped my fifty cents. Yellow-painted wooden chocks hung on worn ropes from the thumb-polished fare box, and a red fire extinguisher was lodged beneath like a bomb. A great bronze wheel as if to steer a whaling ship. A black and grease-worn wooden handle for setting the electrical current. A human hand made of like material set us in motion. Waddling along, it passed dew-green parks and the corniced concrete works of banks and horse carriages and peanut shops. A surprising number of billboards announced: "Abortion: America's #1 killer."

When I reached the Lorraine Motel I could see how clear James Earl Ray's vantage had been from the rooming house on Main Street. He'd had an unobstructed shot across the railroad tracks to room 306 on the balcony there, where Martin Luther King had stepped outside to greet some people in the parking lot below. In 1976 I had gone to Brushy Mountain, Tennessee, the state maximum security prison, and I had managed to get inside to interview James Earl Ray. Ray had escaped a few days earlier and had only just been caught after three days at large in the woods. When I met with him he looked thin and undomesticated, smiling sheepishly. His arms and face and chest were covered with scratches from running through the brambles and hiding under leaves and branches, where the dogs had found him. After several days of tape recording our conversations together in that a tiny oven-stinking cell, with the tremendous murmuring of human voices echoing all around the steel corridors like a chorus of devils, I knew in my heart that Ray was a pathological liar, that nothing he had told me could be believed, and that he and he alone had killed King with a single shot from a deer rifle, because he believed in his hopelessly backward mind that people would make him a national hero for ridding them of the leader of that cursed integration movement. And when I saw the little motel where he did it, saw how simple it had been, how cruel and simple, in this unassuming place, I was suddenly overcome. I thought I was going to faint. I sat down on a low concrete wall outside the Lorraine Motel and wept.

Between 1882 and 1968 4,743 lynchings took place in the United States according to the Tuskegee Institute—probably a lot, lot more by their estimation. Certainly two of the eeriest places in the world today are the Lorraine Motel and the old brick rooming house across the tracks, now overgrown with weeds. Not even the decorator's art that has filled the defunct motel with the polished displays and indirect lighting and background music of the National Civil Rights Museum can cover up the smell of blood and savagery that Ray engendered here when he blew Dr. King's jaw away with a Remington pump action Model 760 Gamemaster fitted with a Redfield 2 x 7 scope. It is an atrocity, a bitter sadness, that Memphis will never transcend. The place will always bear the burden of his deed. There will always be a stream of melancholy issuing from south Main Street and coloring the water uptown where people shout, still too loud, "Are you ready to party? Are you having a GOOD TIME?!" Always in the city of Memphis there is the insistent moaning of a freight train running in the background along the river.

I stopped in to meet my friend Wayne Jackson for lunch at Huey's (the best hamburger in Memphis). Wayne was a trumpet player and with his partner, Andrew Love, had founded the Memphis Horns. They played with Elvis. They played the Monterey Pop Festival with Otis Redding, backed up by Booker T. and the MG's. Aretha Franklin, Peter Gabriel, the Doobie Brothers, Jimmy Buffett, U2—they have three hundred gold records. Wayne told me, "I worked like a nigger on a jack hammer all my life." Andrew Love is black, and Wayne loves him like a brother. He uses the N-word humorously, as does Andrew. "And now I want Andrew to have a nice fishing camp where he can get away from his little white asshole partner. And me? I just want to get enough money together to get a nice house and open a little beer joint on the Gulf Coast around Pensacola."

In December of 1967, Wayne and Andrew were supposed to get on a plane with Otis but stayed behind in Memphis to put the horn tracks on his new single, "Dock of the Bay." The plane was making its approach to Chicago during a big winter storm. "Otis was afraid," Wayne told me, "and when he was afraid, he liked to get up in the cockpit and see everything that was going on. They found him in the cockpit with a big crease in his forehead." Wayne was quiet for a moment and then said, "Sam and Dave would leave the stage absolutely on fire, and Otis was able to walk out and melt that. He was the king."

"What did you do?" I asked.

"I went and got ready and went to work," he said.

We sat in Huey's festive atmosphere eating hamburgers and drinking Cokes. "You knew Elvis," I said. "If Otis was the king, what was Elvis?"

"Elvis. Oh, Elvis," Wayne said dreamily. "Elvis would fuck anything that moved," Wayne said without hesitation. "He was sad. His wife Priscilla left him and his mother died, and then he had no friends." Wayne and some other musicians took karate lessons with Elvis for a while. "He was so fucked up on downers that he had to be held up to make his karate kicks in class. And one night I saw him turn on his girlfriend, Linda." Linda had been told to wait while Elvis took his karate lesson. When Elvis was finished, he burst into the room where she waited, snapped his fingers at her, and jerked his thumb over his shoulder. "You," he barked. "Let's go!"

Wayne looked sad. "It scared me," he said. "The rage just scared me. I thought: Boy, she's really in for it. I felt really bad for Linda, having to go home with him that night."

I went jogging with a friend along the Mississippi River. Hawks drifted in soaring meditation of this alluvial fan, as we ran through a honeysuckle meadow by the river's slack mud lips. Down through sedge and whisper weed, across slim and transverse channels fitted with moldering log bridges, in the wake of downtown, like some huge and rusted eastbound ship. We passed alongside a thrown-up community of houses so alike as to give the impression of an army base. Five miles in we passed a couple in palsied embrace, her long black legs lifted to heaven in the late sun; they seemed to be rowing as his feet dug into the grass for purchase, her skirt spread capelike beneath them in a copse of trees stained with the slow ecstatic sleep of autumn.

We ran on through the joinery of a tree-shadowed thicket, through ivy, fern, and grapevine, down to the sun-splashed gloom of a far woods by brown and idle waters, which partook of stagnant torment in this somber dusk, leaves flickering as they scuttled by in dry autumnal whisperings. We emerged in a glade, some accidental prairie of warring grassland species, and ran back through the neighborhoods of Mud Island and up over the bridge and back to the city.

Now I came to the great reach, the Mississippi, stately, soundless, inchoate, worried and mottled gray in sunlight and breeze, tantalizing like a great height, and the high far matrix of the old black steel bridge, its spandrels ruling the sky in skeins of mitered rectitude. Cutting the pink haze as the brass sun flocked the trees of Mud Island. A lone dumpster tilted toward the water on this angled embankment. A mile across. Old logs lay on the bricks unpeeled; old scabs of asphalt bind the cobbles in their glue, bottles still in their rotted paper bags, exploding with time like secret mines among the bricks. Plastic lighters and condoms. Now a flock of bats at sundown surged across Riverside Drive toward town. The sun settled into a murky fluff of trees as fog grew and spread like a lost crystal virus. Link Belt hanging guts of cables over a ruined alley by the new construction festooned with davits and ladders and smelling cave-wet and crypt-cool, this new-poured Portland cement. A fungus of trees infests the crucible of the sun's heart. The emaciated stingy spires of radio relay towers transect the sundown. Night in Memphis.

I drove to the eastern edge of town, tuning to WEVL, FM 90, where one minute "Old Dooey's Goodies" played a rare and sadly beautiful rockabilly selection, and the next minute a scientist talked about analyzing the spectra of quasars. Out on Southern Avenue by the Coca-Cola bottling plant, I found a country restaurant called Buntyn's, a Memphis institution these forty-seven years. It looked like a country grocery store hard by the railroad tracks with benches out front for the old men to sit beneath the tattered canvas awning and watch the trains come snorting and stamping up like angry horses on the tracks across the street, against a frieze of brick and frame and old shingle houses, held in a coppice of autumn-tainted trees behind a white rail fence.

Fluorescent tubes hung unadorned in dusty ranks beneath a beaten tin ceiling that was working loose a cadaverous skin of old and yellowed paint. Beaded boards scummed with old varnish and naked smoke-streaked light bulbs stamped like coins in the dogged shadows of far dark corridors from which warm-looking women in loose clothing fled bearing trays of steaming food and pie and flagons of coffee. On the chalk board it said, "Gizzards and rice $3.95" and "Yams and cucumbers."

One of the women approached me, large and warm and free in her flour-sack apron and smelling of yeast. "Corn bread or rolls?" she asked, and when I hesitated, she concluded, "I'll mix you up, okay?" and hurried back to the kitchen under the timeless turning fans, past the men in threadbare coveralls and battered seed caps, who were wolfing down mashed potatoes at the counter. She brought me sweet and tender barbecue chicken, creamy mashed potatoes, and pickled beets. Hot cherry cobbler with my coffee. Even the food in Memphis carries a sadness with it.

I walked out into the road and watched the sun move across the trees. I thought I was beginning to understand that barbecue sauce and the river and the blues all shared a mystical affinity. I was working on a unified field theory of the blues. The blues, this captious, ranting, frank, unending wail beset by flourishes of whickering and despondent pleas and desolate anguish, a pandemonium of notes expelled in outrage. The barbecue sauce and the blues then are made of the same sweet sand, the slow and lonely substance that seems to seep out of the river air at night and lie in the treetops like a red fog in the cotton that we breathe. It settles like strontium in the calcium of our bones.

Great black eagles turned in flight over the gray froth of cotton fields, coasting on thermals, as grave as cut iron sculptures hung against these tallow clouds. Bright rookeries of hawks, white and still as paper kites, hung on the trees. The ghost shapes of the forest overwhelmed by kudzu like inchoate monsters developing out of an original protoplasm. Some shapes were stark and real, elephants or dinosaurs. Others, especially at twilight, were indistinct and just vaguely menacing.

I met my friend Larry Brown, a Mississippi novelist, at his house just outside of Oxford, and we drove the back roads in his pickup truck, wandering in checkered sunlight past Delay, Mississippi, and on toward his childhood fishing hole in a wrecked stand of cedars and watched the forest in its windless repose. Great pines lay fallen in the dark water. All around us the forest trembled with late afternoon warmth. Sunlight fell in silty spans among fingerling bass. Crickets went piping. Larry said he'd drained and dredged the pond and stocked it with bass and brim and catfish. He walked back to the truck bed and rummaged in the junk there—a rusted spanner, paper sacks of concrete that had hardened and burst in the rain—and he retrieved an old rusted rod and reel, and we took turns flicking the Rapalla lure out among chalices of sunlight.

I drove into Oxford and visited the cultural shrines, Faulkner's home and Square Books. Oxford is an outpost of Memphis. The University of Mississippi has the world's largest blues record collection, thirty-five thousand volumes. City Grocery is the favored restaurant (featuring crawfish quesadillas). Next door is the Southside Gallery of folk art. The best writers in the nation come to Square Books to read, three or four each week. George Porter, the bass player from the Meters, was playing Proud Larry's bar that night. John Grisham, the perennial best-selling author, was making Oxford his home.

One night Larry and I went to Taylor Catfish just down the road in Taylor, Mississippi, for the most authentic southern catfish dinner around. Battered wooden picnic tables crowded together in an open warehouse-like room with smoke hanging in the air. Families with children came in together, the father inevitably swinging a bottle of cheap bourbon.

Another night I had inland gumbo at the house of my friends Beckett and Mary Hartwell Howorth. Beckett calls his gumbo "ditch food" because it is made of crawfish, andouille sausage, and chicken.

The HoKa is a coffee shop and movie theater, a cultural nexus in Oxford, a bare-board room vexed with posters and bumper stickers with a theater in back made of burlap curtains and folding chairs. The decor is a latter-day hippie pipe dream of exploded tinfoil ductwork and India-print shawls hanging from the ceiling in a matrix of cobwebs and grease among rusted water pipes. Blinking Italian Christmas-tree lights. Linoleum and painted plywood and the illuminated crypts of ice cream freezers. Ron "Ronzo" Shapiro, the owner and founder of HoKa, says, "Yeah, Memphis. I have this love-hate thing with Memphis. Sometimes it really rocks. I came down here originally chasing a girl who lived in Memphis. It didn't work out." He excused himself and vanished into the back room, where he was about to show *The Adventures of Priscilla, Queen of the Desert.* The HoKa is probably the only place within five hundred miles where a movie like that could be seen.

I ate pork barbecue out of a big red truck parked in a mall parking lot—and it was damned good. But not quite as good as at the Handy Andy, a grocery-store barbecue place that looks like a gas station and serves the best fried pies I've ever had. I grew up in Texas, so I know something about fried pies.

That night I drove back to Memphis along obscure lanes, accompanied by the cyclops shapes of kudzu monsters. The sky was so huge. The forest so dark and moist. My heart began to fill with the same darkness that filled the hollows of this land. The road was deserted. And suddenly I pulled off in a hail of gravel and stopped the car and stepped out into the enormous night between the asphalt two-lane and the great black forest under stars so bright and wild that they transformed the gravel shoulder into a phosphorescent littoral against the sea of black. I know this place, I told myself. This is the place where Hansel and Gretel gave up. This is the forest of darkness. Red mud. Green kudzu. Luminous white pine. Sallow bark. Antimony bloom of silver beech. The pinchbeck twig of willow. These are the pallid birches bent under the weight of piebald clouds. The stars were stones in mica streams of ether, and as I watched, chance unhinged a meteor. A nebula of cold flame burst the bonds of its adhesion to the sky and was caught and hived in the earth's gravitation, leaving huge and jagged fragments dripping fire across the heavens as they fell.

I got back into the car and turned on my lights and drove out into the night. I crossed a bridge and fell into a world of scoured whiteness that seemed to abrogate the forest world.

The phone rang. Pete answered it and said, "Yeah. Yeah. Yeah," and then pushed himself up heavily from his creaking and beaten swivel chair with the cracked gray plastic upholstery and crossed his paint-peeling office to the window. He threw open the steel-framed, beaded-glass casement, and a gust of warm air poured in on us with the morning noise from Front Street, riffling a few papers on his big steel desk.

Pete stuck his face out and whistled down to the cotton-classing students who were smoking on the sidewalk, "Hey, where's Buck?" Someone answered indistinctly from below, and Pete crossed back and picked up the phone again and said, "Buck is gone to England," and then hung up.

Buck Dunavant, one of Pete's students, was the son of Billy Dunavant, the largest cotton merchant in the United States. His dad had called from somewhere in China to ask if Buck could miss a week of school in order to meet him in London to shoot some pheasant. They'd return together on the company jet, and Buck would be back in time for class on Monday.

Now Pete, a big man with gray hair and a wide soft face, which time and alcohol had reticulated with a fine weaving of blue and red veins, greeted another student, Coors Arthur, who wandered in complaining of a headache induced by a wild weekend. Pete peered at his computer screen over steel spectacles. He wore a blue dress shirt open at the collar, tieless, a white lab coat, and khaki pants. Coors leaned over Pete's desk to see the commodity prices on the screen. "How's it doing?" he asked.

"That thing's strong as goat guts," Pete said. "I hope you're long."

"I'm out," Coors said and left.

Pete walked out into the classing room between the block-long rows of black workbenches set at an angle like drafting tables on the bare plank floor. Shreds of cotton migrated in swirls and eddies in his wake. The tables were lit with rows and rows of classing lights hung in metal diffusion boxes that could propagate a shadowless white light ideal for representing the true color of cotton. Before World War Two the best classing rooms had skylights, and a good northern exposure was prized, because direct sunlight made the cotton look blue. "A company called Green," Pete explained to me, "now rents its cotton room to artists, because the light is perfect for painting." No one used natural light to class cotton anymore, he said, idly picking up a sample of cotton and pulling it like taffy, pulling and pulling, gently ripping it over and over as he talked. Years ago, when he was starting out, some mornings the classers would come to the room and the sky would be overcast, and they'd call "bad light" and go home. Or it would be too sunny, and they'd call "high blue" and have to quit. Now they routinely worked on into the night in the autumn when the cotton is coming up strong from the fields of Mississippi and Arkansas. Through this little row of ancient buildings on Front Street, Pete explained, passed the biggest cotton market in America. As he spoke, he worked the swatch in his fingers to a fine and uniform shred, called a staple. It looked like the tip of a wide artist's brush. He held the sample in his fingers, studied it casually, and set it on the black table, announcing, "That's an inch and three thirty-seconds." How could he tell? "Forty-seven years of experience," he said. That's what he was trying to teach the students who were smoking in the street below, to pull staple accurately, as well as to know strict low cotton from good middling cotton.

Down in Mississippi, Larry Brown and I had driven among cotton, which lay like dirty snow in the fields. Back in Memphis, I saw the samples in wide cardboard flats on black tables in rooms as big as sail lofts under lights so white they made everything look like a dusty Andrew Wyeth painting. That's where they classified the samples as to color and texture and moisture and such other esoteric qualities as the mills of the East could discern at a glance for the purpose of making J. Crew shirts and Levis jeans.

A month after my visit, the Cotton Exchange classing school on Front Street closed its doors for good. True, Roades College would be offering a class, somewhere out in the eastern area of Memphis, but moving off of Front Street marked the end of an era for the scions of the cotton industry, as well as poor boys just up out of the fields who wanted the better way of life that classing cotton offered. And not long after that, all manufacturing of clothes fled to the troubled spots of the world in Mauritius, Cambodia, the Philippines, Indonesia, Mexico . . .

I went down the stairs and out the door and watched the mid-morning traffic and the Mississippi River like a slab of tin fretted by the sooty harp of a fire escape in the shadowy space between two buildings across Front Street. I crossed and walked down to the river, hard by Exchange Street, where on the morning of April 29, 1900, John Luther "Casey" Jones pulled out of the long-vanished railway station there, driving engine number 382, and the next morning at Vaughn, Mississippi, he died for his troubles when he met head-on a freight train that had been parked there on the tracks.

I scrambled down the grassy bluff past the spot where the ferry boat *Sultana* had rolled over with a loss of more than 1,500 souls, most of them returning Union POWs. She was built to carry 376 but had more than 2,300 on board when she exploded and burned in April of 1865. I crossed the cobbles, great irregular man-cast stones, worn smooth and cracked by interval and vegetation, wharf and weedland here, cobbled with buried bottles by the soft and idle sucking of the brown water on baked mud turned to mucilage. Broken glass and flowering thistle and the bloom of sunlight on rufescent masonry and the high green span of the interstate leaping in surreal fusion like a headlong transom across the swarming daylight blue. Beyond, the mirrored pyramid, quadrate, cruelly illuminated, rose above the ancient heap of a Lone Star brewery.

I walked on, looking back at the horngabled city of Memphis, high and light filled, bound in iron: well-wrought walls of ancient stonesmiths. A stronghold of rooftrees and towers, this kingly dominion, undereaten now by centuries, scoured by storms, hacked in battle, held in earthgrip on these banks like the wrack of a race of giant wrights.

Here beneath my feet a thin creek had forged through the city's underkeeps and burst out beneath those paving stones, engendering a fecund tangle of thorns and leaves and purple flowers and even the whinnying cry of a single frog at its miniscule banks. For decades the Mississippi, that wriest river, had been trying to veer off into Texas, but generations of army corps engineers had fought it with concrete and made it a mile-wide ditch, dredging and filling like a group of fleas attempting to tow an elephant. But as I walked, more and more natural springs burst forth from beneath the city. Water would fetch off the foundation of those meadhalls all, B. B. King's and the like. And not the throngs of cheerful people walking up and down or the grim zeal of the engineers bent against the task would ever arrest its mute and steady catabolism.

Trees in a grave's grip of desolate mud. The riven land collapsed in gullies. Grand but miniature canyons. The slow explosion of paving bricks marked the sucking hypogeal channels. I passed by boats and barges lashed to ancient mooring rings on cables and discolored sisal hawsers and rusted anchor chains. Coiling rubber hoses snaked in and out of the water like red sea serpents in green river bilge. A barren gift shop afloat on the stifling tide. Paddle-wheel boats sat at anchor like great white clapboard houses trimmed in red and fitted with a complex filigree of painted iron. A buzzing window air conditioner cooled a pilothouse.

I watched night come on. The lights on the river lay in elliptic shreds like torn and glowing streamers. Bats jerked across the sky in shadowed congregations. The canticle feedback of an electric guitar drifted down from Beale Street as the failing sun set up futile grottoes of glare against the darkness. On Mud Island streetlights reeled out a fragile superstructure like a luminous spider web to hold up the dissipating metropolis. At night, when the air is cool, a fog transpires out of the warm blood of the river and rises to the road we travel. What drives this river on drives all this life and makes it murky. The blues is like the Tao. The blues that can be told is not the true blues.

EMPTY AMERICA

One: Terra Incognito

We came into that land from the rich and concupiscent Midwest with its green and rolling fields. The smell of cut hay and fresh manure drifted up through the air vents, as Jonas and I took long turns flying an airplane whose interior was so tight that it felt sometimes as if we reclined side by side in twin coffins.

Over Nebraska, the land grew severe, and as we rattled on through a barometric monocline at 8,500 feet above mean sea level, it rose to meet us. We climbed to 10,500, and a harder emptiness beckoned. Vast spaces like a whirling vortex. Though we were yet on its farthest edge, we could feel its inexorable pull. Who would go looking for true wilderness in the United States outside the boundaries of national parks and designated wild areas with names and regulations? And where would he find a true and lawless frontier? Look in the front of a big Rand McNally Road Atlas, where it shows the whole United States caged in a web of interstate highways. It looks like a sad old bear, snared in a reinforced concrete net. Even the spaces between the interstates are crazed with a cyclone fence of two-lane blacktop. But as you draw your finger out west to about the 120th meridian, there's one spot at about the 42nd parallel where it looks as if the bear could get a whole paw through. I-84 veers up toward Portland, and I-80 dives toward San Francisco, leaving a great swath nearly untouched. It was there we had set our compass: the last empty place in the contiguous United States. Though we felt increasingly lost, hour after hour as the land rose, we were intent on becoming more lost still, climbing and climbing, until at last we were dodging peaks that leaped above our altitude.

The air felt like hard waves beneath a speedboat, as the mountains thrust it up to hammer on our hull.

On day two, we came into the Great Basin after an overnight in Cheyenne and saw a desolation so complete that neither eye nor airplane could measure it. Higher and higher we climbed into skies marked only by the smoke from range fires, and yet we could see nothing man-made from pole to pole. Oh, a few scratchings, overblown by dust or overgrown by sage. But the airplane does not lie: *Praeter solitudinum, nihil video.*

Looking for a way in, then, we had selected the only dirt road we could see and dove at it. Down and down, hitting 230 miles an hour, I leveled off ten feet above it, where we could feel the ground effect like the rapids of an invisible river. The world meshed like gears around us. I had to concentrate not to get lost in staring and let a wingtip touch the earth. That would hurt. The blur of the world flashed past as I hugged the dusty two-track, which vaulted over rises in the land and dipped back into draws. We call that nap-of-the-earth flying, and by the height of the bushes down its middle, we could see no way to set the plane down on that road. It was hardly a road anymore.

We had wanted to land on a road. It is, after all, such a quintessential American symbol: the Open Road. Nowhere else is the road so much a part of who we are. But we flew on beyond the place where the bad road got worse and then ended altogether, where not even the most passionate follower of Neal Cassady would venture.

Just west of a reef of rock beyond the Black Rock Desert, we found our portal to the heart of Nowhere. We spotted the first few white patches from a distance of fifty miles, so brilliant that we thought they must be water. Then we dove down to investigate and saw what appeared to be dry lakes. We surveyed several and selected one between Jungo and Sulfur. For landing and takeoff, a quarter mile would have done nicely, and half a mile would have been extravagant. This nameless place was about nine miles long and clear of obstacles except for a double row of greasewood bushes cutting across it at an angle. But since most of the official information that we'd been given about landing sites was fatally wrong, we inspected it carefully. Again and again, we flew over it, looking for some sign. If it was sand or loose dust, we'd bury our wheels going ninety, the plane would flip end over end, and, well, that would be bad.

When you're a man and have worked with another man for thirty years, as Jonas and I have, you don't need to say much when you're working. You know what he's going to do and mostly you know why, and sometimes you even know what he's thinking. You just pull tight and push hard. As we made our third pass, angling up into the air and circling around like a crop duster, we were both thinking the same thing: what can we see that will transform this lake of deadly sand or dust into a hard, dry landing place? We came in, by my estimate, less than a foot off the surface. Jonas slowed the plane as we skimmed along. This was a two-man job, for he had to avoid crashing, while I looked for the conclusive proof that said we could land, a sign that we'd bet our lives on.

Craning my neck to look straight down, I saw at last the evidence I sought. "Cracks," I said. "I see cracks."

He put the gear down and dropped the flaps, and as the airplane settled, we felt the wheels touch something smooth and hard as concrete. We both let out our breath as we rolled out toward the line of man-high bushes. I turned around and saw a tower of white dust gaining on us.

It was a hot and windy afternoon as we tossed our gear out and stepped down from the plane. We stood alone on that alkali hard pack, flat as a griddle, bright as snow. And suddenly we were both seized by the same giddy reaction: we'd done it. We had set down in the middle of Nowhere, a place where no one else could go, right in the heart of America. Estimated population density: .04 persons per square mile, me and Jonas and about fifty square miles of lakebed. The number was probably even smaller, for beyond the lake we saw nothing but creosote bush, sage, and cheatgrass. No rules, no fences, nothing in every direction. We were as free as we were going to get in this life.

As I set to work making camp, we had enough daylight left for Jonas to take the plane up and shoot some photographs with the camera he had mounted on the tail of his Falco airplane. I watched him taxi far down the lake and then make the takeoff run toward me, dragging a huge column of alkali dust behind him. He took off right over me, then pulled hard into the sky and rocked his wings goodbye.

Then I was really alone. One bag of water, six beers in fast-melting ice, and few provisions. As the clatter of his engine faded into the dry gulches toward the north, total silence fell. The vast dome of the sky seemed to settle down upon the earth like a bell jar, and I a speck of gristle inside it, hoping he'd return. I had wanted to be alone in the last empty place in America and had but one thought now: be careful what you wish for.

I had a hard time finding even a single rock, but I located a small one, which I used to drive stakes to hold our tarp. It was like trying to drive nails into iron, and the hollow *tink!* it made as I struck the steel put me in mind of a Martian landscape. I kindled a fire of greasewood that was protected by razorous thorns.

Sunset brought out dust devils as I scanned the sky, calculating in my mind how much fuel the airplane had left. When at last I saw the tiny dot on the ridge and heard its faint mechanical hammering, I felt the way Robinson Crusoe must have felt when he saw that footprint on the beach. Jonas dove triumphantly and buzzed the campsite, not ten feet off the ground, then popped up, rolled the plane, and settled in a plume of white dust.

We sat on the tarp with the cooler between us. The wind picked up and the light faded, animating the oddly shaped bushes into almost human forms. The dust devils danced around, harrying and jostling them, and the leaping fire and crying wind made it seem as if we prepared for a ritual sacrifice. As the last streaks of light withdrew behind the mountains, a smothering darkness closed around us, palpable as black felt. The empty land stretched away from the fire's nervous light, and the night wind snapped the tarp, as we sat and watched Cassiopeia rise across the misty wheel of the Milky Way, which bridged the heavens, pole to pole.

I walked half a mile out onto that featureless tableland, then turned back to view our campsite from afar. The ghostly bushes seemed to writhe in agony by the firelight like hunchbacked trolls. The wind made the flames roar like a smelter and drove orange cinders dancing across the dry lake, leaping and vaulting in wild arcs, bearing their mad and antic light down the long reef of the night until the demonic parade dimmed and vanished in the distance.

Deep in the night, we saw satellites course overhead from south to north. A trio of silent falling stars lit up the purple sky. With such luminescent creatures migrating around us, it felt as if we sat marooned at the bottom of a sea. Mars and Jupiter towed a hollow moon up through a far deck of stratocumulus. Holes in the clouds sent spotlights down across the playa and made a death's head of the moon, until it breached the wall of cloud, luring mountains out of dark. The Milky Way faded, and a trillion worlds winked out. The desert glowed all night with an eerie chemical light.

At dawn the alkali moon hung in the western sky, as pale as if it had been chipped off the dry lake, brethren to that place. Walking out across the miles of nothing, I cast a shadow all the way to the distant hills. We found an old abandoned campsite, with a threadbare parachute for shelter, two La-Z-Boy armchairs, a fifty-five-gallon drum cut in half for a fire, and an orange shag rug for the comfort of home. It was a mystery how they'd gotten there. Archeologists find arrowheads. We found rusted military cartridge casings and unexploded Chinese firecrackers. Those who took the trouble to get there did so because it was a last place of justice, where the only rules are the ones you carry inside of you. So if you wanted to express yourself with a machine gun or settle a grudge, here was the ideal place, where only you and God were in on the deal.

On the way back to the plane, we stumbled on a shrunken boot, the toe curled up, filled with mud dried to concrete. It had a riding heel. Where was the man? The horse? The other boot? It put me in mind of grisly deeds that land must have seen.

The land looks so simple, flat and white, like a canvas on which nothing had ever been painted. At first you think you get it. But a wiser man named Dutch once advised taking a closer look. "There's a mile of wire in a screen door," he said.

Two: Where The Road Ends

For more than a quarter century, I've been searching for the heart of Nowhere. Oh, sure, I could have myself dropped into Tibet or Africa, but I love America, sweet land of liberty: of thee I sing. So it was that we moved toward the emptiest spot in the lower forty-eight. Was it true, I wanted to know, as Gertrude Stein had said in 1936, that "in the United States, there is more space where nobody is than where anybody is"? And just exactly where does the road go after it has ended? Does a road, like a person, have a soul that goes on, invisible, after death?

Once Susan Boswell, president of Cartographic Technologies in Brattleboro, Vermont, set out to find the spot farthest from any publicly maintained road. It turned out to be the Thorofare Ranger Station in the southeast corner of Yellowstone. And the distance was twenty miles. On the other hand, Jonas and I actually visited places that are a good deal farther from what any SUV-driving housewife would call a "publicly maintained road." There are roads there, yes, like there are tracks on the moon. We drove some of them, too, and nearly destroyed our rented Ford Excursion. A lot depends on how you define your terms.

I asked an archeologist with the Bureau of Land Management how they maintain those roads. He laughed. "We maintain them by driving them."

"How often?"

He shrugged. "Whenever."

At the time of that conversation, we were grinding along a boulder-strewn track in low four-wheel drive, heading into Surprise Valley near Massacre Lake, our maximum speed: about a quarter of a mile an hour, the better to avoid high-centering his truck on a rock. We had two other government vehicles following us, because that's how they do it: if the road kills two, there is still one left. You don't want to try walking out.

"Are you maintaining this road now?" Jonas asked.

"Of course," he said with a smirk.

The truth is, the BLM, which owns a staggering 268 million acres of America (about 420,000 square miles), would prefer that there be no roads at all. They'd prefer no cows, maybe even no people.

If you want to get technical about Nowhere, the Three Corners region of Idaho, Nevada, and Oregon, generally known as the Owyhee Desert (but blending without clearly defined boundaries into the Alvord and Black Rock), amounts to seven thousand square miles with no mapped roads. But in the larger surrounding area of some seventeen thousand square miles there are no *major* roads. You may see blue lines on the maps, indicating roads, but don't let them fool you.

Most lands in that area are public. The federal government alone owns 87.6 percent of Nevada, 55.5 percent of Oregon, and 65.2 percent of Idaho. The combined holdings of the departments of the Interior and Agriculture amount to one million square miles, a third of the United States, and most of it is west of the 98th meridian. If you count land owned by state, county, and tribal governments, then only the Chinese government owns more of its nation's land.

As for population density, the four counties in the immediate Three Corners area are home to 2.0, 1.3, 1.1, and 2.6 people, respectively, *per square mile.* On the other hand, I asked the BLM archeologist what the population density was in the area we were driving, and he gave me an odd look. "Zero," he said, then had a thought: "Oh, there's that one guy who bought a place just west, so if you count him, it's one."

So the twenty-five thousand square miles that we set out to investigate, an area about the size of Lithuania, ought to satisfy even the most crazed xenophobes, some of whom we met on our hopscotch from Elko, Nevada, to Burns, Oregon, and from the Owyhee Canyon to the Black Rock Desert.

BLM literature advised us, "Access is via airstrip just north of McDermitt, Nevada (pop: 373), or in Owyhee, Nevada (pop: 908)." Unfortunately, like the myth of the maintained road, we found that to be a bit of an exaggeration.

After our night on the dry lakebed, we dragged in over the Owyhee airstrip, low on fuel, to find a crooked, badger-holed, dried-mud gash in the earth, overgrown with saltbush, hopsage, and greasewood. Not something we wanted to hit going ninety. We crept back to Elko, watching the gauges dip into the red.

Three: Wild Justice

We went back to Elko to resupply and walked into a tavern that night to find three cowboys drinking at the bar. As we came in, they turned to look at me. They were covered with dust and wore battered boots, dirty jeans, and beaver cowboy hats curled back from wind and weather. They all wore drooping moustaches, too. The big one stopped in mid-sentence to size me up with steady red eyes. He said, to my face, "Well, it ain't got no cowboy hat and it ain't got no moustache. What is it?"

While Jonas was dressed more like they were, I was wearing flip-flops, a T-shirt, and swimming trunks. I was tired and thirsty and in some dim, distant way aware that we might be about to get into our first fistfight in a real cowboy bar. We had tried before, but it had never panned out. The big guy was standing, the other two were sitting, one of them was smiling and clocking me in that way you see a lot out there, at once inviting and menacing, because you don't yet know what you're being invited to. (It turned out that he was a miner, not a cowboy.)

I walked right up to the big one, close enough to smell his breath, glared back at him, and stuck my hand out. I said my name. Then he laughed and grabbed my hand and offered me a drink.

"Aw, he's all right. He's just a Messikan." Which was half right, my mother being a Mosher with a bunch of O'Sullivans falling out of her family tree.

The third man hadn't looked up from the deep contemplation of his beer all that time. His name was Michael, and he made it plain that he didn't like to be called Mikey, which was what the big guy kept calling him. Michael was not given to idle chatter, but we managed to pry a few loose facts out of him. He was a one-legged bull rider, a cowboy by trade, who had done well on the rodeo circuit and wore the belt buckle to prove it. Then one day a bull fell on him—in Denver, I think—and the doctors took his leg off below the knee. He reached down and rapped on it. Now he was a cook, feeding cowboys from a chuck wagon on the range. He gave me his recipe for biscuits and flapjacks, which he made from the same batter. A few beers later, Michael loosened up enough to take off his hat and show us twenty new stitches in his freshly shaved pink scalp. It hurt just looking at it. Early that morning, it seemed, someone had knocked on the door of his motel room. Michael opened it, and the fellow had laid into him with a baseball bat.

"At's all right," Michael said, putting his dusty hat back on and fixing me with cold, unflinching eyes. "I'll find out who it was and fix him."

"How will you find him?" I asked.

"He'll be talkin', braggin' 'bout what he done."

Everywhere I went throughout that wild land, I encountered a strange kind of logic and justice—like that single boot on the dry lake—along with a pointed and courtly diplomacy. No one tells anyone what to do except the man who pays the wages, and he doesn't have to, because everybody understands what's expected. No two ranches out there are run by the same method, in fact, since no one tells anyone how to do anything and no one asks, either. Even seemingly insignificant things, such as the latches on the ranchland gates, are handmade, each one unique, for it is out of such details that a life is made, and nowhere had I seen lives assembled with such singular care and precision as I did out there.

So when a man came down off that vast emptiness for a few days of relaxation, as those boys at the bar had done, he wasn't bedeviled by too many rules, because he already understood all the rules that he needed to know. As for the diplomacy, the people were very polite, because they just assumed that you were either carrying a gun or could locate one on short notice. The Sav-On Drug Store in Elko sold handguns, rifles, and carloads of ammo. And if someone decided, by whatever mad logic, that he had to lay into you with a Louisville Slugger, well, fair is fair, and it was understood that no one would question it when wild justice came at last to settle the long arrears of iniquity. Late that night found me listening to Mikey's tales from when he was a sniper in Vietnam. I wouldn't have wanted to be the other guy.

Four: Where the Bones Go

The following day we would go to Hertz to get a big Ford Excursion four-by-four so that we could drive deeper into the land and challenge even the worst of the vanishing tracks and then go beyond those as far as the tires would last and see what was there. So yes, we found the place we were looking for, saw exactly how empty it was and saw the ongoing struggle to fill it, not with so many people but with the expanding dreams of the few. But we were still wrestling with a question that neither of us had spoken: Why go? What's the point?

In his classic book *Arctic Dreams,* Barry Lopez wrote, "Aspley

Cherry-Garrard, a companion of Robert Scott, said that exploration was the physical expression of an intellectual passion. . . . It points to the relationship between toil and belief, and alludes to the hope of reward that is so much a part of a decision to enter the unknown." The question is: what sort of reward? A look at history shows that those who sponsor exploration are after something different from those who actually go. "Strung out on the thinnest hopes . . . with the most sanguine expectations," Lopez observed, "men of character continued to sail to their death for men of greed." For the former were after ecstasy while the latter were after money. We must be the former, I thought, for we have little hope of the latter.

Or, speaking strictly for myself, perhaps I traveled there like my Irish ancestors, those monks who went "in search of *Terra Repromissionis Sanctorum*, the blessed landscape where one stepped over that dark abyss that separated what was profane from what was holy."

Let me first address the profane side, where we began our next day's journey:

At the Hertz counter in Elko, we stood waiting for her to get off the phone. "We had a report of you throwing rocks at it," the notunpleasant-looking woman in the Hertz shirt was saying in a notunpleasant voice. "People at the café *saw* you throwing rocks at it. And now it's got six hundred dollars in damage." Pause. "Well, how would you like to pay for that?"

Ah, Elko, Nevada, Gateway to Nowhere. It seemed that even the Hertz lady understood Mikey's brand of justice. How would you like to pay for that? (The implication being: you *are* going to pay.)

If you're not there for the justice, Elko is not much of a town, unless you want to drink, gamble, or visit an old-fashioned brothel, where you sit at a timeless wooden bar and the madam makes you a drink, then reaches underneath and presses a buzzer to alert the ladies, as they are delicately called. At Mona's, right around the corner from the Stockman's Hotel, a large one and a small one came out like prizefighters at the sound of the buzzer. We told them we were there for purely academic reasons.

The large one said, "Come on, fellas, you can't just drink, you've got to screw us, too. It's clean, it's legal, and there are no consequences.

You suck your beers, and we suck your dicks." We thanked her and left. Journalistic integrity required that we see what the dream looked like when it turned into a nightmare. So now we knew where one road went when it ended. Each of those women had a complex story and seemed eager to tell it, as if saying it out loud would make it true.

But out there, the profane was never far from the holy. We drove the Hertz Ford Excursion as far up the eastern edge of our province as it would go and then got out and walked, heading overland by sun angle and brute force. We had spotted the road from the air, and it had looked passable, given the right vehicle. It led over a hump in the mountains and down toward a little ranch, the Keddy, which Jonas had visited twenty-five years before while taking photographs for his award-winning book on Nevada. We crossed a shattered lava dome, immense fields of jagged iron-red stones, signatures of monumental forces here, but the pace deceived the human eye, made it all seem still. It was not. The landscape was in constant motion, heaving, churning, a sea of rock in turmoil. Whole mountains collapsed with the weight of years. We crossed alkali and pumice flats, climbed up through volcanic broken-glass ravines, which cut my deerskin gloves or came out in big slabs as I reached for handholds. Jonas wore no gloves, drank no water, explaining that in the eighties, that was how the rebels he'd traveled with in Afghanistan had done it. "You can't be stopping to take a leak during a Russian rocket attack," he explained.

At each high vantage we found eagle droppings, burned white by the sun. And yet nothing grew here but some burnt-over sage. So where did the eagles find their prey?

As we topped the next rise, the smell hit us. Here was the answer, the secret of that land: that wherever you pour water on stone, life explodes in a profusion and diversity that is utterly mystifying. We descended out of that dead world of dust and rock to a slow-moving brook, rich with sedges and reeds and grasses, watercress and fern, fairy rings of flowers in pink and yellow and purple. The closer we came, the stronger the perfume of life, until we saw iridescent bottle-green dragonflies, buzzing among reeds of biblical antiquity. Sign of fox, cat, rabbit. Fish swam in the waters. Fish. How did a fish cross that wasteland, where a man could die in a day, to live in a brook less than a meter across?

We retrieved the truck and inched it down across the rubble to ford the stream. We pushed on until we came to a dirt track, which we followed through low hills. Around a bend, we found a cabin, a few tents set up around it, a dog tied to one. Someone was there, but we didn't know who.

We entered the cabin and stood before a cold mud-stone fireplace, which was carved with names and initials dating back to at least the 1930s. Jonas reached up and took a crudely framed photo down from above the door frame. It showed a rough-looking man—a cowboy, I guessed—standing in the gate through which we'd passed to reach the cabin.

"Look again," he said.

I did. It was Jonas, twenty-five years younger, sporting a full beard, not a speck of gray hair.

He showed me something else, too. There on the fireplace, etched deeply with a knife, was the name "Howard Hughes" with the date, "1970." Of course, anyone could have carved it. On the other hand, back in the seventies, the owner of the Keddy, who was not a man given to lies or bragging, had told Jonas that Howard Hughes, a famously peripatetic recluse, used to stay in that cabin to get away from people. In addition, a Nevada man named Melvin Dummar had picked up an old man by the side of the road in that area at around that time. And a line from that cabin to Las Vegas, where Hughes lived, went right through Dummar's hometown of Gabbs. The old man had borrowed some money and told Dummar that he was Howard Hughes. Dummar didn't believe him, of course, but when a will, purportedly handwritten by Hughes, was found after his death, it left one-sixteenth of the estate to Dummar.

As we left the cabin, we saw a blue canopy half a mile away against the side of a cliff. We hiked over and found what we expected: archeologists. Hence the tents back at the cabin. Like all the dreamers who are seduced into that land, they had a rugged beauty about them, an air of almost giddy contentment as they worked in the hot sun, sifting the dirt that seemed hammered into every pore of their grinning faces. Kelly McGuire, head of the Far Western Anthropological Company, had brought along his nine-year-old daughter, Chloe, who was asleep with her head on a folding table in the shade of the blue canopy. Tim

EMPTY AMERICA

Carpenter, a grad student in archeology at that time, had brought his very pregnant wife, Kim, an archeologist whose natural beauty seemed about to burst the dust-covered denim overalls she wore. She showed us a perfect arrowhead, which someone had chipped out of green translucent stone more than a thousand years before. Archeologists were drawn to the area because it had been so densely populated until perhaps one thousand years ago. We chatted with them and looked at their findings, and they recommended that we visit what they referred to as "a two-mile-long art gallery" at Massacre Lake.

That's how we found ourselves, a few days later, crossing the Surprise Valley through crested wheat, where feral horses ranged free. The nearly impassable (but officially maintained) road terminated in a stand of ancient junipers. There we hiked a boulder-strewn dry wash to a crumbling reef of rock thirty feet high. Sheets of stone, which had sheared off and shattered in the declivity at its base, made for a rugged walk, but it was worth it.

Chipped into the dark brown rock, one after another, were pictures of the world those people saw or imagined. Some of the images showed the looping course of rivers in the valley below, now desert. One depicted a huge fish hanging head down, as if freshly caught. Obviously, the land they knew had plentiful game and water and vast fields of grasses to provide a wild harvest of grain.

We found one of their grinding stones wedged in a crack in the wall. It was no different from the stone I'd seen my great-grandmother use to grind corn for tortillas when I was five or six years old. We also found one of their chiseling tools, which they used to etch the petroglyphs. Those tools were cached there to await the tribe's return. But one day they didn't come back.

Another image was striking because it was so unlike all the others. It showed a quarter moon in opposition to a bright sun-like figure, hash marks beneath, as if someone had been counting. Chinese literature describes a supernova that was visible in full daylight in 1054 AD. It could have been seen from the spot where we were standing, and a quarter moon would have been out when it appeared. The hash marks ticked along at regular intervals beneath the image and then stopped abruptly. I counted twenty-three marks.

"How many days was the supernova visible?" I asked.

"Twenty-three," the archeologist told me.

We climbed the reef and found more recent signs of man. A bronze disk had been cemented into a rock near the precipice. It was inscribed "Wallace L. Griswold" and beneath: "1918–1982." Penny Carmosino, one of the archeologists, knelt down and picked up a fragment that I thought was a porous white rock. "This is part of a human skull," she said. As I held the piece of Wallace Griswold's skull in my hand, I thought: if this is all that is left when we go, then we had better come to a place like this, if only to get our bones used to the emptiness where they will come to reside anyway and for far longer than we had possession of them.

Penny was turning over pieces of what I thought was black flint. "This is cinder, see?" Cinder that had been Wallace. She looked out over the valley and said, "Someone cremated him and put his ashes here. Wallace must have loved this place." I believe that Penny understood how Wallace's soul had been captured by that place. She had lived in suburban Maryland, where she worked as a signals intelligence analyst for the super-secret National Security Agency, before wandering out here and getting lost. Or found. I asked her what she did for NSA, and she said, "I can't tell you." She was not being coy.

We hiked back over ground strewn with evidence of arrow points, chipped-off bits of obsidian called bifaces. Obsidian doesn't occur in that area. Someone had to bring it there. As the sun reached a certain low angle, the whole land lit up from reflections of the broken volcanic glass. We could see it glittering all the way to the horizon. It was eerie, because it so clearly demonstrated how teeming and busy the place had been and how deserted it was now. And that hypnotic light, which came but once a day, and mostly when not a single living soul was here to bear witness to it, now formed the last luminescent bones of the people who had lived here.

Five: How Frank Filled the Emptiness

Because we had an airplane that could go 150 miles an hour without even breathing hard, we were able to see a great deal during the two weeks that we were there. We kept our rooms at the Stockman in Elko and worked outward from there, both by land and by air. But in the plane, it was only an hour across to Cedarville, California, or up to Burns, Oregon, and so we were literally able to see the whole twenty-five thousand square miles. And while a couple of big gold mines had sunk their stair-stepped impressions into the sides of mountains, little else but for a few ranches dwelled in the bottoms. Because of how and where we traveled, we met few people. When we did, however, we could be assured that they would be worth talking to. So it was that the next day we came hurtling down a rock-strewn two-track in the Humboldt range on the far eastern edge of our claim. The overhanging juniper branches carved Nevada pinstriping into the thick coat of dust on our Ford Excursion, while the overheated brakes left a stinking cloud of blue smoke behind us. The road hairpinned back on itself, revealing a cascade of landscapes mounded shoulder-to-shoulder in the distance. Soft hills formed a high cirque around a blind valley. Jagged ranges fell away to a faint gray stone escarpment, which looked almost like a cloudbank in the distance. As we descended through aspen forests, which angled away into the sun, a stately buck kept pace beside us. It bounded off to vanish in the woods as we crossed a lava flow, a sloping expanse of rust-colored boulders, strewn and shattered in a way that suggested the catastrophic explosion that had created and transported them. In places the road narrowed to no more than an etching on the side of vertical cliffs, topped by majestic plinths and spires carved into mysterious animal shapes, as if some lesser god had auditioned here for the job of making our world.

We camped in an aromatic forest along an ice-cold river above the old mining town of Jarbidge. As the sun flared out, casting purple shadows through the pines, the air at seven thousand feet couldn't hold its heat. We huddled near a fire of fallen branches and dead saplings.

In the morning, we headed up-canyon, watching the snowmelt dash over brown stones, which were polished smooth and cut by time until they resembled the knuckle bones and socket joints of a stately beast, fallen there in the shade of a cratered red rock wall, which was topped with totems and spires. Skirts of scree and rubble descended to the water's edge, where satin grasses grew among the throngs of sapling pines along the banks. We stopped at the foot of two high minarets of stone, and as we watched, by chance, a daylight moon rose straight up between them. Only one time each year would that moon hang, full and white as a Eucharist, in the narrow notch of that natural Stonehenge. I felt a sudden, elemental connection to a spirit world, whose presence was palpable there. What had put us there on that spot at just that moment? Aztec gods or the ghosts of Irish monks?

We pressed on, up and over the ridge, where glyphs and turrets seemed like alien messages carved across the soapstone sky. Then we descended the western slopes, where the land opened into rolling hills. In the distance we saw a small motorized vehicle bouncing overland. We drove on until we caught sight of a cabin, toward which the four-wheel ATV was pitching and lurching. We parked and walked over to find two small children, wearing helmets, climbing off the ATV. Giggling, they hurried away and disappeared inside the cabin. Utter silence. High sun. Low moon. Yellow grass.

Frank Bogue came out, a thin man, perhaps seventy, wearing a sleeveless undershirt, a baseball cap, and jeans. His son, Dan, emerged behind him, along with the grandchildren, who jumped back on the ATV, stifling squeals of mischievous delight, and roared off, buck jumping through the brush.

Frank had worked his whole life in a hardware store that he didn't even own, dreaming of his own log cabin. "I read everything there was about building a log cabin," he told us. "On my sixty-fifth birthday, I told them goodbye and never went back." He found his forty acres in that river valley, which had been a migration route for Stone Age peoples, who fished and followed game and the fruiting of native grains and grasses through the seasons. Ours is a big country, but the emptiness in our bellies is bigger still. You get a sense of it if you talk to people who have chosen an emptiness that is larger than their own. You can reckon the bafflement in their words: "I came up just for the summer . . . twenty-six years ago."

It might be an archeologist burned black by the sun from sifting sand. It might be a hardware salesman who tangled with his own dream. But as pleased as they are at what they've accomplished, there is still the vague sense that they don't quite know how that hollow grew inside them or how such a sepulchral land captured their souls. And as busy as they are, they still don't quite know what to do now that they're here for good. They're not Buddhist monks. They're Americans, and they have to be about something.

At first, Frank and Dan were absorbed in realizing the dream. They hauled trees and built the cabin—and a very nice job they did, too. It's angled just right for the sun, a pumping system has turned the garden green, and the wood is all split and stacked for winter. But in due time, the work was done, the kids went home, and they looked around and took stock. There must have been an epiphany of dread and veneration as the colossal, almost willful tranquility of that place descended upon them.

As we stood talking, I noticed something shiny on the ground. It was the casing from a .50-caliber machine gun cartridge. I commented that Frank must be pretty serious about hunting, and he laughed. "No, we just shoot it at that hillside," pointing across the valley. And I thought: noise. Yes, what else could fill a space that size?

I asked what else he did to fill as much time and space as he had on his hands.

"You see that stack of bowling balls?"

Bowling balls? I hadn't noticed. But now I turned, and sure enough, thirty yards away by the outhouse was a pile of them like you might expect to see accompanying an old-fashioned Civil War sculpture. It turns out that a bowling ball has the same diameter as the inside of a large oxygen cylinder, the kind they use in hospitals. Frank and Dan cut the top off of one such tank and drilled a hole in its bottom the right size for a shotgun shell primer. They charged the bore with three ounces of mealed black powder, rigged a firing pin to set off the primer, and rolled the bowling ball in on top. There you have it: a bowling ball mortar. Just what the emptiness required.

"See that clearing over there?" Pointing again, across the valley to a circle of yellow grass with small black dots on it. "Those are bowling balls. After we shoot enough of them over there, we take the ATV down and pick 'em up and use 'em again."

He led me over to examine his cache of fort busters. They were sooty and chipped from repeated firings. When the novelty wore off, Frank came up with the idea of drilling extra holes in the balls to make them whistle in flight. "And we also stick a railroad flare in 'em so you can see 'em at night."

Frank said he couldn't wait for winter, when the snow would close the road, "so there aren't so many people coming around all the time." I asked how many people came down that way, and he said quite a few, maybe one every week or so. But in almost the same breath, he told me that in winter they get all their friends to come up on snowmobiles. "We had fifty-one snowmobiles parked right here last New Year's," he told me proudly.

Then he casually mentioned that two thousand acres (just beyond where the bowling balls landed) had recently sold for sixty-four dollars an acre, and I turned to look at Jonas. We were both thinking: *I could have had it.* Then I saw his expression change and he saw mine. We were both thinking the same thing: *But what would I do with it?*

On the ride back, Jonas idly mused, "You know, I've got enough room on my farm to build one of those mortars . . . "

And so goes the endless quest for those who chase the dream. Or for those chased by it. It's at least as old as the nation, perhaps as old as man. The area we set out to explore lies, after all, in the fork where the Oregon Trail split north from the California Trail in the Gold Rush of '49, routes now marked by the two interstate highways that divide there. But Frank's dream, and even its seemingly contradictory outcomes, was not so different from other dreams that we witnessed in that last great empty place in America.

Six: Sunday, a Day of Rest

We were invited to a barbecue up in the Ruby Mountains, where Bill and Sally were celebrating the opening of their new cabin. We followed the plume of dust from an SUV down a rutted two-track, many miles out onto the range and then down through a gate marked with a sign that said "Cabin."

Another few miles, and we came to a pond, where a house rose before us. A majestic peaked roof hung over vast picture windows above a wraparound porch, where a hefty Russian border-spotting scope sat on its tripod—for twilight viewing of the game across the valley. The kids, like Frank's, had an ATV, too, only it was amphibious and transformed itself into a boat when they drove it into the pond.

As we approached the "cabin," we were greeted by Xavier, a French chef who'd been imported for the occasion. He was flipping lamb chops over a titanic charcoal grill, attended by helpers in white aprons. Smiling bartenders poured fine wines and spirits from a capacious bar by the pond.

Having just come off the desert, unshaven and dusty, I felt like a real cowboy next to those polite revelers in their pressed jeans, starched shirts, hand-tooled boots. I had plumb neglected to wear my silver squash blossom jewelry inlaid with Navaho turquoise.

We were introduced to our hosts, Bill and Sally Searle, who (I was quietly told) got out while the getting was good—at about the time Nutri-Sweet hit big. We were seeing the other side of society in that vast tract of emptiness, but their industrious preoccupations, driven by their dreams, struck me as not so different from Frank's.

I met a few genuine ranchers there as well.

Pete Jackson (the Third, I believe) had inherited the Petan Ranch from his grandparents Pete and Anne, who had come out from Santa Barbara in the thirties and were well known, as he is, for being conservationists. Anne would not let anyone shoot a coyote on her land, which meant pretty much everywhere. Now Pete owned that land. Comprising one of the largest ranches in the United States, it spanned the borders of Oregon, Idaho, and Nevada, and he treated it with just as much respect as his grandparents had. He even seemed modestly embarrassed by his own presence in it sometimes. A few days earlier, Jonas and I happened to fly over his new house out on the range, and I mentioned to Pete that with its columns and towering trees, it reminded me of the White House.

"It is a little out of place," Pete admitted with shy good humor. "We kind of got carried away when we built it."

We sat out under the stars with china and silver on white tablecloths and ate by candlelight. Xavier made the rounds, and his helpers poured excellent wines from western vineyards, as children ran around, gleefully playing hide and seek in the advancing night. And we saw that out in that huge land, dreams could grow to any size.

Seven: The Signs of Man

Monday we were lost on a summit road somewhere, veering along in the Ford Excursion on the edge of a sheer drop to pale green valleys in an almost flesh-like overlapping of folds in the earth. We had a GPS that was not much use without the airplane, and I had lost track of where we were while listening to Hank Williams and Patsy Cline. A tumbling series of gullies, ravines, and chasms fell away as far as the eye could see to the last sawtooth peaks, which seemed to chew up into the sky in the misty gray distance. We came upon a track that fell away from the road and faded into the far sage. I got down from the truck to help Jonas navigate the dropoff without getting stuck. Then I climbed back in, and we ground overland along the time-blasted ruts that no one had traveled since beer cans were stamped out of steel.

The two-track gulched out in stony dry washes a yard deep, and we clambered up rock-strewn reaches until the last of the track petered out to grass. And then we drove some more, up and up the hill, climbing at a dizzy angle through brush and boulder, until we were stopped by heaps of stones, at a place where the land dropped straight down several hundred feet on either side. We walked the rest of the way to the promontory, from which we could see all around. Sheer red ragged walls, streaked with yellow, rose to the south. Gradual scree slopes descended to a slow-moving, late-summer river in the north. A canyon wound away to the west. We'd flown the same route a few days earlier, not twenty feet above the boulder on which I now sat to write, as the afternoon wind whistled up the back of my shirt from the arroyo. The land cried out in dissonant harmonies as each bush struck a different note.

Heading down out of that wilderness (and assuming that down was the way out), we found what appeared to be an abandoned ranch of rusted tin buildings in dry yellow hills of grass and hopsage. We gingerly climbed barbed wire and walked among weathered corrals to find a bunkhouse in back with an outdoor toilet. A claw-foot bathtub had been sunk into the ground. Clear cold water, dribbling from an iron pipe, overflowed the rim at ground level and ran off toward the creek.

We lifted the steel automobile leaf spring that was holding the bunkhouse door shut and entered to find it neatly appointed in a manner that Jonas assured me was the height of opulence for ranch hands.

Two stoves, wood and gas. Red-checked oilcloths covered the tables. Two bedrooms with spring steel beds, and a single light socket descended from the rough-troweled plaster ceiling on a twisted pair of wires, no light bulb.

"Pick up the phone," Jonas said, indicating a sixties-era aqua-green rotary dial telephone on a wooden stand in the corner.

I put the handset to my ear. I heard a dial tone.

Signs of man were plentiful. Bone. Bullet. Telephone. But few and strange were the men.

We made it back to Elko that night and met a bulky bearded fellow in a T-shirt and cut-off jeans, who said he'd ridden his bicycle down from White Horse with nothing but his backpack. He said he was just a tourist. We had seen him around Elko as we re-supplied for our forays into the wilderness. He lived here and there, surviving on food stamps and handouts, but we'd also seen him playing the slot machines in the Stockman's, and the prostitutes at Sue's House of Fantasy had told us that they'd kicked him out. He informed us that he planned to commit suicide in about three years when he was fifty-two, "because that's enough living."

"Why wait," I asked, "when you've got your momentum up?"

Bob didn't laugh. He asked us what we were doing there, and we told him that we were going where the road ends. He looked at us as if we were mad. Then he said, with a tone that suggested that even a child ought to know such a basic fact: "The road doesn't end. It just keeps going."

Eight: Flying under the Earth

Our last day but one, we took off under a pale quarter moon, skimming low over the first colorless ridge line and dipping down into a shadowed coulee. Giant owls loomed out of the darkness and went veering past the plane as we hammered on into the lifting dawn. By the time we had crossed the low mountains from Nevada into Oregon, morning had begun to break. The sun looked like a dying star, a molten blood-red dome with gilded points of light stretching halfway across the desert sky, which was streaked with coral above a landscape of flint and bistre.

Twenty minutes later, I dove the plane down into the Owyhee Canyon and leveled off about two hundred feet below the rim. I set the throttle at twenty-two inches of manifold pressure, which is to say, we were going about 175 miles an hour through that serpentine excavation, edging between jagged turrets of red volcanic rock. Cratered walls vaulted above us, opening to a river of pale blue sky, mirrored in white water, which hurtled over rocks a few scant meters below our wings. It was daylight above, but down here it was still cool and dark, as a rust-red rock face loomed ahead. It appeared from my vantage that the canyon ended there in an igneous cul-de-sac. Every instinct told me to climb, to get away, get out, but I held on and raced toward it, hoping to catch a glimpse of daylight any moment now. I was confident that the canyon would open and that I could make the turn. For one thing, I was betting on the cutting power of time and water: such a canyon can't just slam shut like a vault. Can it? For another, I was betting on the Falco I was flying, which Jonas had spent five and a half years building with his own hands out of plywood. I'd watched him craft that instrument in his barn in Massachusetts.

In his barn? You might wonder why I'd risk my life flying a plane that someone built in a barn. The answer was, Jonas wasn't just anyone. When I got my pilot's license, Jonas was the first passenger I took up, and I did not have to say, "You need to learn how to do this." After the flight, it was obvious that he would, and he did, and then no airplane was ever good enough, so he built one that was.

That was how I knew that I was flying the Stradivarius of airplanes. It was singing to me in the high woodwind whine of wind and the low tympanic strumming of its motor. If I could manage to avoid nicking one of the rock walls, which were flashing by so close to our wingtips, I knew that it would hold together, no matter how hard I flew it.

Anyway, Jonas and I had been in places more dangerous than this canyon, and I had come to know his threshold for risk, as he knew mine. Now as I watched the huge wall darken our world, I knew and he knew that we weren't going to die in any damned airplane crash. And if that darkness into which we were flying really was the shadow of death in a place where no one knew we had gone and to which no one would come if they did, well, we'd had a pretty good run. So neither of us had to say a word as we waited, my hand steady on the stick, to see what fate would bring. Was it a right turn or a left turn or no turn at all? Were we about to be pasted on that opaque windshield like a plywood bug? During all that waiting, we had passed an invisible point of no return, where we both understood that we now carried too much momentum through too short a distance to turn back or climb away. The only way out was onward, and so we waited, waited, and waited some more, as the monolith of slag seemed to take on human form, growing taller and taller, cutting into the sky, until I could see the dimples in its flesh.

Then, at last, the rock wall parted like a curtain to reveal Our Lady of the Canyon. Her mossy green thighs swooned apart, and her sparkling jewels of water trembled forth. I threw the stick hard to the left, standing on the rudder and slamming the plane into a knife-edge turn, one wing up and one wing down. We drifted through the turn and snapped out level in another section of the gorge. It was a bit like surfing a lava pipeline, the curled and weathered wave, frozen there those million years.

I smiled over at Jonas, remembering at last to breathe.

"Cheated the devil again," he said.

I pushed the nose, accelerating deeper into the shade of ragged rim-rock. The green swath made by the river's ropy course slipped beneath us in a blur. The music of that rocket violin moved through me to stir my hand, and we popped up, vertical. Big G's. Blue sky filled the bubble canopy as the canyon reappeared over my shoulder. We rolled and pivoted: straight down for a shot of the startling lush arroyo.

"I got it," Jonas said, taking the controls and diving back into the canyon. I let go and put my hands in my lap as we dropped like a hawk in the stoop, headlong through castles of rust and stone, groves of ancient juniper and white-bark aspen. Clouds skated on mirror-blue pools of water. Kindred shrikes and herons dipped and dove around us. Eagles cruised for rabbits the size of small dogs. Coves of trees released mule deer to drink at the edge of the river. Such a profusion of life, and yet just on the other side of that lava wall, one of the harshest deserts in the United States.

Jonas leveled off, face to face with another rock wall. Light winked off water and wings as he pulled hard around the next bend, where we could see the canyon begin to narrow and grow shallower. He held a trigger in his hand to trip the shutter on the Nikon mounted on the tail. I watched him, his fierce concentration, as he snapped off the frames. I looked up to see the rock face grinning. Our Lady of the Canyon was laughing, mocking us now. No more peek-a-boo turns, that was the end of the line. I vowed to shut up and die like an aviator, even as a growing tightness in my chest told me that we'd never clear the rim in time. Then I felt the pull, the heavy G's, as the wings loaded up and we took a huge gulp of blue sky. Shadows fell away like bolts of satin. In vertical flight, we emerged into sunlight. Flat yellow desert as far as the eye could see, dissolving into the smoky Steens across the Oregon flatlands. We flew west and landed on a remote strip of gravel. Our GPS said, "No Destination."

We shut down the engine and stepped down from the cockpit. Silence but for the whistling wind. Nothing but creosote bush in every direction. We saw something shiny out in the scrub brush and hiked out to find a passive radar reflector used by F-14 jet jockeys, two triangular polyhedrons, welded out of sheet steel. One reason we didn't find more people: we were in a military operations area. No one knew we were there, because we'd flown in under radar. Perhaps the airstrip was there so someone could get to the reflectors.

"I think they aim their guns at that," Jonas said.

"Oh, good . . . "

Returning to the airstrip, I knelt to examine the composition of the gravel, as Jonas and I discussed the possibility of blowing a tire or not getting out of there for some other reason.

We took out the binoculars and glassed the Steens. There on the highest ridge, a spindly antenna. A repeater. So as austere and remote and difficult to reach as that place is, people are closing in fast.

I powered up the cell phone and called home. "Guess where I am," I told my younger daughter Amelia.

"Nowhere?"

The apple doesn't fall far from the tree.

When I called my older daughter Elena to tell her where I was, she said, "Making something out of nothing again, eh, Pop?"

We departed the gravel strip without incident and made a few more passes through the canyon before heading back. It was still early morning as I tilted a wing along the Owyhee River and spied a white hat far below, drawing a long train of dust behind. The cowboy on horseback was moving steadily, leading hundreds of cattle, while other cowboys kicked zig-zag patterns in and out, scouting the stragglers on the drive north. They were so far from home and family and the lure of other lives, I was reminded of my old friend Edward Abbey, who wrote beautifully about deserts. He once found a hard-rock prospector out there and asked him why he loved the desert. Because, said the old man, "them other so-and-so's don't."

Our last day, Jonas and I took the Ford Excursion back up into the northern reaches for one last look before going home. There we found a cowboy teaching his sons calf roping as the sun went down. The calves came thundering out of a chute, kicking up clouds of dust. The men and boys came hard behind them on horseback, whooping and hollering. Ropes whirled in the air and caught the horns and back legs with an accuracy that was scarcely believable. The exercise wasn't for fun. Roping is the only way to get hold of them.

When they were done, Sam Mori, who with his brother owned thirty-five hundred deeded acres, rode over to the fence and sat his horse. He had a weathered face, branded brown by sun and hammered with dust. He was covered from head to toe in it. He wore white woolen gloves and worried a frayed rope over the saddle horn as he spoke. I asked him the same question that Ed Abbey had asked the old prospector. Sam squinted up through the dust and thought about it a moment. Then he said, "The less pretty the ground is, the easier it is to manage." By which he meant that environmentalists didn't quite see what he saw here. I could see what that land had brought into Sam Mori's countenance as he spoke to us of his forty-four years on the family ranch. His deep brown eyes fixed on mine, not shy, not challenging, not even humorous. Simply still. A half smile played upon his face, and like the land, it was both inviting and faintly menacing. His hands delicately braided the reins, absently, ceaselessly, as if he did it in his sleep. A moment before, he had been galloping in hard pursuit, raising a plume of dust. The lasso had shot out from his hand like a harpoon, and the calf's head snapped around as it hit the hardpack with a concussion that Jonas and I could feel twenty yards away through the soles of our boots. As I watched his hands gather up the rope and loop it neatly, I marveled that such violent work could take such a delicate touch, such finesse.

Sam spoke of the particular differences among types of rope. He preferred a nylon-poly blend, but straight nylon was springier. He cautioned us not to call a rope a reata, which is braided hide and not much used by real cowboys anymore, because it snaps in two. But, he reminded us, "It's about identical to golf clubs. It's whatever you like."

Then he invited us to come out for roundup in the spring. And he touched the brim of his hat and rode off, quite literally, into the setting sun.

HOUSE OF PAIN

See one, do one, teach one. That's what my friend Roberta used to say. She was chief neurosurgeon at Cook County Hospital in Chicago, and as I trailed her through the crowded hallway, through clouds of human and chemical smells and the sounds of human suffering, the wails and cries, she said, "We're going to see the train wrecks of the night." I nearly had to run to keep up with the flying gray tails of her lab coat. "Our motto is," she called over her shoulder, "See no evil, hear no evil, smell no evil." And her mad cackle echoed off the yellowed tiles.

We arrived at a room where a patient named Helen sat up in bed, her almond eyes studying me inquisitively. A girlish pout informed the expression of her full red lips, and her extravagant black eyebrows gave an intelligent cast to her broad forehead. Her Greek nose was fine and straight, and her olive skin was clear and veiled in a soft light that cast reflections on the fine hairs that glittered on her outstretched arm. It was a gorgeous day out beyond the ice crystals on the window glass, and I kept expecting Helen to smile or yawn and look out at the world, but she just stared at me. Her lips moved slightly as she breathed in and out, almost sensual in their slack expressiveness. Roberta came up and held her hand. "Helen?" she said. "Hello, Helen. Can you squeeze my fingers? Helen? Hello, Helen. Squeeze my fingers, Helen. Squeeze my fingers."

Roberta dropped her hand. She turned to me. "She may hear us, but she can't respond." I looked again at Helen, and only then did I see it: a scar in the curving shape of a horseshoe that circumscribed half of her skull in the back. In the middle of the scar was a dark and ragged hole no bigger than a nickel where the bullet had gone in. The larger scar represented the piece of bone that Roberta had removed so that she could take the bullet from Helen's brain. After the swelling had gone down, she had replaced the piece of bone.

Helen's hair was beginning to grow back. It was about like that of a marine recruit now. I could see that she had been well cared for here, clean and groomed and fed, and well cared for by her boyfriend, too, until he hired someone to shoot her in the head. He was a drug dealer, and Helen was going to inform on him, because she was pregnant and needed to change her life. Now she was going to have her baby in peace. Roberta was going to keep her alive at least that long. Helen's chart bore no name. Her whereabouts were a closely guarded secret because the boyfriend was still after her. Helen, of course, is not her real name.

I had come to regard these morning rounds as a test to see what we were made of. We left Helen staring at the empty air and went down the hall, and Roberta told me of a woman, Mrs. Green, who had a fatal form of cancer in her brain. No one would operate on her because, what the hell, she was a goner anyway. Take her home and let her die. Roberta took the case against all advice. She operated on Mrs. Green for nearly twenty hours, teasing out the nasty filaments of cancer from the healthy brain cells, and to everyone's surprise, the woman woke up. Mrs. Green went on to live another three years. And she enjoyed a remarkable and unforeseen benefit from the operation. Roberta had inadvertently removed Mr. Green from Mrs. Green's brain. In fact, the Greens had gone through a particularly nasty divorce, and Mrs. Green, said Roberta, "had absolutely no memory of him, nor of the messy divorce. It was kind of a bonus for her. She was happy. She was doing fine. But then she caught fire and burned up." Mrs. Green was making coffee in her own kitchen when her robe caught fire. "Her mother came in and watched her burn to death." I could see the pain in her face. All she could do was toss it off with a remark. Otherwise, if she became too involved with it, then all her pursuits would seem futile. The whole practice and all her skills would seem a grim joke, and she'd have to quit and go into a cushy private practice where she could be making a million dollars a year fixing slipped disks. In private practice, a neurosurgeon might open a skull ten times a year. Roberta did it a dozen times a month for a pittance at a public hospital.

Roberta was called to the ER. A construction worker had fallen off a building, and then a piece of heavy equipment had fallen on top of him. Every sort of specialist was called in because that poor man had something wrong with every part of him. His head was smashed. His left leg was crushed. His left lung had filled with blood. His heart was bruised, and at first they were concerned that he might have torn major blood vessels off of it. He was a big man with reddish-blond hair, his jeans half cut away by the paramedics. When Roberta and I entered the crowded emergency room, she took one look at his face and said, "Ooo, God, that's yucky." It was blown up and distorted until it was unrecognizable as a human face. It was purple meat. Bubbles of mucus and sputtering blood percolated out of his nose and mouth around the tape and tubes, shunts and silver clips and clamps and colored lines, red and yellow and green. There must have been a dozen people around him, and while one of Roberta's brain surgeons drilled a hole in his head, others were running metal probes into his arteries, and still others were connecting him to a variety of devices I had never seen before. Every few minutes someone would shout a warning that they were going to shoot, and we'd all scurry behind a screen to avoid being irradiated by the X-rays. ER crews tend to be young, and much gaiety attended their jokes about deformed babies. Humor to quiet the amygdala, the alarm klaxon of the brain.

A nurse came in with the man's construction boots in a plastic bag. They were filled with blood. Someone handed Roberta some X-rays of the man's head, and we went into a dark room to look at them on the light box. "Have you ever seen an emergency chest crack?" she asked me. I had not. "Oh, you've got to see them crack his chest if they decide to do that."

By the next morning we were sitting in her office, and the construction worker was still alive. Roberta had a cup of coffee that was all milk except for one teaspoon of coffee. I had wondered why she did that until I watched her operate a few times and realized that she sometimes didn't go to the bathroom between seven in the morning and seven at night. After I'd go home to dinner and to bed, sometimes Roberta would call me at eleven or midnight, and I'd hear her cackling on the other end of the line as she shouted, "I'm still in the OR, Laurence. You want to come down and watch some more?"

As we sat in her office, I noticed a photograph on the corkboard. It showed Roberta with a little girl whose head was wrapped in a turban of white bandages. I asked her about it. She said that two girls from Honduras had arrived in Chicago a few months earlier, both with terminal forms of cancer. No one would operate on them, not Children's Memorial Hospital, not Northwestern, not the University of Chicago. They didn't want the blood on their hands. The girls were too precious. Too sweet. And being the last doc who operated on them before they died would be too traumatic. Roberta brought them to Cook County and performed both operations for free. Now she looked at the photograph and smiled. In the picture the little girl was smiling. Her parents were smiling, too. Everybody was smiling.

"How did they do?" I asked.

"She lived," Roberta said, pointing to the girl with the pretty brown eyes. "The other one died."

We went to see a few more patients, and I began to get an idea of what she was thinking when she'd say something like, "Oh, this is all lightweight stuff. This is routine." At other times, I'd see her hunker down within herself and whisper: "In one day there is so much drama, there's such intensity, you have to go home and numb out. Sometimes I get home from a case, and it's two in the morning, and I've been up for days, but I'm not even tired anymore—I'm beyond being tired— and I just sit up watching *Ben Casey* or something moronic. It's what I call the Never-Ending Search for Boredom." She was describing her response to the experience of survival, only in this case it wasn't her trauma, it was someone else's, as filtered through Roberta's mirror neurons. If mirror neurons can make you wince when you see someone else cut a finger, imagine what they do when you're witnessing all that trauma and performing brain surgery all day long. Not only do you see and smell the damage, but you are the cause of some of it, too.

I was riding to the hospital with Roberta. She drove her dusty black Honda Civic because we were neighbors, and it made sense to go downtown together. She stopped at McDonald's on the way for a plain biscuit and some orange juice. "Nobody wants to touch the brain," she explained. The brain is a holy place, a dangerous place to be, and most doctors are frankly afraid of it, just as most pilots are afraid of flying upside-down. Her beeper went off, and she called the hospital. She asked someone to confirm something. Then she turned to me and said, "One of my patients is DOA in the hospital. Listen. I'm on hold." She put the phone to my ear. I could hear elevator music playing. "Isn't that great music to hear when you're waiting for someone to tell you your patient is dead?" We rode on in silence for a time. Then she heard the confirmation that her patient was dead and said, "Okay," and hung up. She drove with both hands on the wheel, looking straight ahead. Then she said, reverently, almost in a whisper, "We're going to touch the brain today."

When I turn my mind back to that first surgery—just a fast glance into the past—I see flashbulb memories: piles of bloody sponges through a curtain of blue smoke, the burn-blackened flesh of the scalp that is pinned back to the blue bunting with spider black threads and silver clamps. I see a fragment of someone's skull skittering across the cracked linoleum floor and disappearing underneath the silver-painted radiator in the corner. You may think of an operating room as the epitome of cleanliness. Think again. There are few arts that can make a grownup person faint. But when Roberta first uncovered the human brain and showed it to me, I broke out in a cold sweat and had to put my head between my knees.

My first time, a sense of panic overtook me as we went in. I mean into the skull. "Going in," that's what they say. Even before we got through the amazing fortress of the skull, I felt that I was being suffocated as I watched Roberta lift the scalp and peel it back and cut through facial muscles just over the patient's eye socket. Roberta is a vegetarian, and I think I know why. People are made of meat.

We all know about mirror neurons, even if not by name. At the time that I watched Roberta work, I had never heard of mirror neurons, in part because they hadn't yet been discovered. But here are some notes that I wrote about watching brain surgery: "The patient's flesh is my flesh. I can feel each stroke of the scalpel, I am wide awake, and they are operating on me." Even as I felt the contagion of that damage, I felt empathy for the patient. The danger was so palpable then: that this human form was coming undone before my eyes, as if we'd pulled the keystone out of the great Building of Life. I knew that we were creating a grave emergency with each new step we took, plunging deeper and deeper into the unknown, and yet on we went. Indeed, what Nature had so wonderfully stitched together, molecule by electric molecule—the beautiful, fanciful, dimpled smoothness of this lady's skin, her touchable tissues, robust and living and lovely—we were jerking apart with no hope that it would ever go back together again, not the way it was, and perhaps not at all. I was vividly aware that this woman could die right here before us.

As the knife cut, the blood vessels burst like grapes, and as they broke, the trickle of red life gleamed in the light like a molten magic metal that was sometimes red and sometimes silver. The head, the object of this elaborate and daring ritual, was at chest height, clamped in steel points, like a great living jewel on display. Beneath the head a large clear plastic bag hung down to the floor and filled with gore as Roberta proceeded with quick and rhythmic strokes. The skin is the largest organ of the body. It is an amazingly tough and resilient fabric, able to stand up to terrible torment, but under the gleaming silver blade of the scalpel it popped submissively, parting along a neat line down to the ivory surface beneath: the skull. The skin was thick and its edge was white with fat, but as it fell open, blood immediately oozed forth, and Roberta touched the vessels with electric forceps to cauterize the leaking hives of flesh. A Mozart chorus played from a speaker somewhere.

Roberta forged on into the wilderness where sane men fear to tread. With electric knives she removed the thin membrane that covered the skull. I watched clouds of smoke rise from that human skull as Roberta's head bobbed with her work, the headlight she wore dancing in the smoke and making odd reflections on the silver-red blood pouring down the drapery below the patient's head. I understood that we were about to enter the heart of darkness armed with little more than our wits and fire and a few metal implements. Here in this repository of advanced technical knowledge, I felt like a primitive at the dawn of creation.

A nurse wheeled a black tank of compressed air into view beside us, rolling it out on a black dolly with dirty rubber tires. It looked as if we were preparing to weld the muffler of an old car. On the far side of the patient, a wall of wires, tubes, and monitors hid the anesthesiologist, who was back there in that tangle, chemically manipulating the patient's metabolism. Now and then I could see the dark eyes, the Indian brown skin, the red cosmetic dot in the center of her forehead, as she peered over the blue draping and looked out at the theater of surgery from behind her mask.

"Who was the first person to operate on a meningioma?" Roberta asked the room in general as she worked. Cook County was a teaching hospital, and she was surrounded by her students, including her chief resident, who was closely assisting. Part of her job was to teach as she worked. See one, do one, teach one. No one knew the answer. "Durand in 1895," she said. And later she would tell me in frustration, "It's amazing how many neurosurgeons don't even know gross anatomy."

The resident fitted a pneumatic drill with a bit the size of a kielbasa. He attached that to a hose issuing from the black tank and handed it to Roberta. She took it up and revved the engine with a screaming whine. Then she applied the bit to the skull before us. The helical silver screw skated for a moment on the white surface of the woman's head, then caught and chewed in and began spewing out curlicues of bone, like holy candle wax. It took all of Roberta's strength to keep the drill biting. And in my own head I imagined what it must sound like in the secret vault of that woman's head.

The resident used something that looked like a bulb for basting turkey to splash water on the drill bit to keep it cool. It was a bizarre baptism of holy water and steel. The ivory bone that was being screwed up out of the growing hole mixed with water and blood and ran down the blue surgical draping into the long clear plastic bag. One of the residents changed position and his foot sent a bloody sponge skidding between my feet. The Mozart shifted gears.

When the first hole was finished we could see the dura mater covering the brain. Roberta gave the drill to her chief resident, and he began the next hole. He had to get up on his toes to bear down, an expression of fierce concentration on his face. I heard the siren scream of the device as the burning dental smell filled my nostrils, the spermy wrack of rotten seaweed and charred flesh, and I looked up and caught sight of someone reflected in the glass front of the cabinet where surgical supplies were kept. He wore clear plastic goggles (as we all did to protect our eyes from flying chips of bone and spraying blood), a blue surgical mask, a green hairnet, and swamp-green scrubs. His eyes were wide with amazement at what he was seeing, the skin of his face was pale and blotchy with shock. It took me a moment to realize that I was looking at my own face.

At last six holes were drilled, and a French safe cracker's tool known as a gili saw was inserted between two of the holes, a wire with an abrasive coating. By running it back and forth with an upward pull, the bone between the holes could be cut. Roberta and her resident took turns cutting from one hole to the next. Then at last she lifted out a tea saucer of bone from the woman's head and placed it in a stainless-steel bowl of saline solution. With the vestments, the incense, the ritualistic nature of surgery, even the music, it was difficult not to think of the Catholic sacraments with which I grew up, the priests in their vestments whom I used to serve at Mass. "Surgery is all ritual," Roberta once remarked.

The final barrier was the dura mater, the membrane that encloses the brain, and as Roberta plucked at it with a stainless-steel pick as fine as a sewing needle, then cut it with a scalpel, she said again what she'd told me many times: "No one wants to touch the brain. The general surgeon will do almost anything, but no one wants to touch the brain. It's too mysterious." She meant that it was too risky. There is no wiring diagram for the human brain. Even with all that we know today from magnetic resonance imaging and positron emission tomography, every individual brain is different, like individual faces. Sometimes, Roberta said, they could take great slabs out of a person's brain, and she might suffer no ill effects. Other times, they might nick a tiny blood vessel and render a patient unable to speak. In fact, you can actually remove half the brain in a child under the age of eight, and he'll grow up normally. The damage might produce a completely unexpected effect. "In one study," wrote the cognitive neuroscientist Elkhonon Goldberg, "a patient who was unable to name a peach or an orange had no difficulty naming an abacus and a sphinx."

The functioning of the human brain is so powerful, so nearly magical, that like a nuclear power plant, it takes tremendous and risky resources to make it work at all. It takes so much blood to keep it func-

tioning that a tidal surge of it collects at the top of the head in the sag-
gital sinus, which is not so much a blood vessel as a canyon from which
an estuary of blood flows back out of the brain toward the far shores
of the body. One of Roberta's main concerns was staying out of there.
If that dam burst, there would be no way to stop it. I once saw it nicked
ever so slightly, and we were awash in blood in seconds. One morning
I saw a chief resident coming out of the OR as we were going in. He
looked pale and shaken. He said, "I'd begun to think I should do neurosurgery wearing rubber boots."

When the woman's brain was exposed at last, Roberta quickly
unveiled the laser. Before she began, she picked up a wooden tongue
depressor, pointed the laser at it, and pulled the trigger. A soft pop. A
black hole appeared in the wood. A wisp of smoke arose. "I guess it's
turned on," she said. Then she addressed the woman's brain. The
tumor was fatty, convoluted, a red and angry blob, and as the laser light
penetrated, it began to glow from within like the special effects in a
bad horror movie. Only it was real, and it was inside a woman's brain.
A real woman with real children waiting to hear what we'd done with
Mommy. The thing in her brain was the size of a baseball. Roberta
attacked it with the shimmering blade of light and gradually reduced
it, inch by smoking inch, to a glowing coal flowing with bright hot
lava. The anesthesiologist started a unit of blood. The crisis was over,
the big drama done. We were about to finish and pull out. Mozart
switched to rock and roll (to speed things up, Roberta told me).

I don't remember a lot about the rest of that night. Roberta's residents closed for her. She was done, spent. Somehow we got home.
Roberta drove. I probably shouldn't have let her. But here's the whacky
thing, the thing that kept Roberta from being a full-blown mental case.
The next morning we were doing rounds, and we went to the room of
the woman she'd operated on the day before. This was a woman who
had been in a coma, mind you. On death's door, as it were. With a
growth the size of a baseball inside of her brain. We arrived to find her
sitting up in bed, a youthful, beautiful woman with an open smile, dis-
playing no sign that she had undergone a traumatic experience except
for the bandages surrounding her head.

Roberta held her hand and smiled. "How do you feel?" she asked.

"Fine," the woman said. She wasn't even in much pain.

As we walked away, I asked how the woman would do.

"She'll be completely cured," Roberta said.

Making rounds, we passed through the pediatric ward and saw a baby that weighed five hundred grams, seventeen and a half ounces.

"I've never seen a baby that small," Roberta said. She told me how she had recently become very sensitive about anything that happens to children. "I can't stand it with children," she said. "It kills me."

We walked up the stairs and down the hall to stop by and see Helen, the pregnant woman whose boyfriend had her shot in the head. She was sitting up, too, or someone had propped her up. Her vacant eyes stared out the dirty window through the ice at the little park across the street. Her mouth was working, and bubbles of saliva swelled and popped and grew again.

"Look at that." Roberta said that sometimes people who are in a coma will move their mouths that way before they come out of it. "She might wake up." She took the pretty woman's hand. "Good morning, Helen. Good morning."

NIGHT IN THE CITY OF SUN

The Night Was Just Beginning

When the full moon comes, the Haitian drummers congregate on the beach and play out under a canopy of stars. Somewhere out on the Atlantic, waves are gathering in long rafts of gleaming swells, pulling moonlight down in oily shafts. Then as they heave toward land, the waves lift and flicker, curling white as if they were paper catching fire, until finally they smoke and tumble, dissolving once again to the held-back, squid-black sea. When they withdraw, they leave only white sand, like a luminescent fog, and footsteps and drumbeats.

The night was just beginning.

"It's Not America Here."

We drove out Highway 1, Janie and Brian and I, in Brian's Saab convertible, which he'd just bought with the advance for his first novel, *Paradise Overdose*. The top was down, and the wet night was heaving all around us in a wicked roar. From the back seat I could hardly hear what Janie was saying. Her blond hair stood up in undulating waves, like a model in underwater photography. She was pointing at the Vagabond Hotel's sculpture of three nude women, white as soap carvings, with dolphins for companions, in a giant clamshell.

The Gourmet Diner was an original stainless-steel 1950s diner, which the owners had towed to a spot beside the highway and set down and anchored there like a gleaming, sculpted nugget of silver with festive lights burning inside and people rushing to and fro among the pastel tables and behind the counter. The food was French provincial. Janie and Brian and I ate hearty and shared a chocolate mousse.

Suburbs slipped away beneath the wheels as we crossed the causeway to A1A and drove down the narrow strip of land along the Intracoastal Waterway. The last ancient world of Miami seashore motels lies up around 180th Street. The Saraha with its caravan of camels in front. The Suez featuring pyramids, a faux desert. The Colonial with a huge observation tower, which seemed to excite Brian greatly. "That is quintessential Morris Lapidus fifties staircase-to-nowhere architecture." Lapidus was the neo-Baroque architect who designed the Fontainebleau Hotel and gave Miami the so-called MiMo (Miami modern) look it is best known for. The full moon followed us as we spun along past Tiki huts, Sun City, Olympia, Beach Cove, and the Dunes with a Roman chariot on top. Roofs tilted in isosceles triangles of broken-down concrete and glass.

Janie and I decided to run up and down the highway, going from lobby to lobby, collecting postcards. This might be our last chance to have such postcards, because developers were going to knock all this down to put up high-rise condominiums. As we entered the first motel, we could see that we were almost too late: hideous shag carpeting, bullet-proof glass, and uniformed guards with dime-store badges and real Glock nines. The clerk offered us an ocean-front suite at eighty-five dollars. Just the two of us. We looked at each other. We could have done it. We eventually did. But Brian was out in the car.

"Have you got any postcards?" Janie asked.

Brian walked in while we were paying and bent to pick at the shag carpeting, saying, "Oh, God, there has to be terrazzo under there. I just know it's under there. Why did they destroy this lobby with all this shit? We used to go to lobbies and sit there when we first came to South Beach," he recalled. "There was nothing else to do. I miss it. Now we have to go to openings of Prince's new club and Planet Hollywood and all that." Brian, a creature of the Caribbean, is right at home in Miami. He grew up, in his words, at the Freeport Holiday Inn in the Bahamas, where his father, a physician, founded Robert's Black and White Clinic. He decorated it in black and white. "He had a black nurse dressed in white and a white nurse dressed in black. It was really sick. Everything was black and white. Even the coffee cups were black and white," Brian said. It became somewhat celebrated, and people from all over the world showed up wearing black and white. They say Robert removed a wart from Mick Jagger's penis. Now Miami is the only place that Brian can live. Raised on a tiny Caribbean island, he can never become a New Yorker. "Miami is the new capital of the Americas," he said. "It is the focal point of culture, business, civilization, all the way south to Chile, a place where you can be in touch and out of touch at the same time. Ian Schrager, who was Steve Rubell's partner in Studio 54, the premier New York nightclub of the 1970s, is renovating the Delano Hotel. Drag queens are the cultural heroes of the nightlife scene.

Janie, on the other hand, is from New York. She is one of the country's most successful makeup artists in fashion, film, and advertising. She was Andy Warhol's stylist on all those DayGlo portraits. "Miami is a third world city in first world clothes," she said, a place where New Yorkers and Caribbean islanders can feel instantly at home, a place where both a Nobel laureate such as Isaac Bashevis Singer and conceptual fetishists such as Madonna can relax—and make a living. When I complained to Janie about the fact that the Raleigh Hotel, an otherwise interesting place to stay, could not take a telephone message and actually deliver it to me, she said, "It's the Caribbean. It's the heat and the siesta mentality. You get used to it after a while."

I thought I was getting to like Janie a lot. She was tall and thin and provocative. I guess she had to be to work with Warhol. She had a great smile.

After a while, we saw that we were attracting too much interest from bizarre-looking people with beepers, who all seemed to be talking on pay phones outside these motels. So with our collection of tacky postcards, we decided to push on south.

We passed through the fashionable Bal Harbor shopping district and cruised the vintage architecture of Surfside. A sky like a Jackson Pollock canvas of stars unrolled overhead. We whipped along the seashore into North Beach, past the North Shore Community Center band shell, where the big band scene was filmed for the movie the *Body Heat*. A scowling muscle man with a yellow Walkman gave us the evil eye as we slowed. The beach at Seventy-third Street: the Day's Inn has an ocean view for thirty-five dollars a night.

"I'd stay here," Janie said, and she craned her neck around to look at me in the back seat. I smiled.

Next door the Seagate serves great fried fish and Cubano food. "It's not America here," Brian said as he pushed the gas pedal to the floor and took us away. Down, down we drove along the peninsula. Brian looked at the encroaching high-rise apartments and shook his head, black hair flying in the breeze, his black baseball cap with a light bulb on the front cocked down against the moon. "They're ruining the whole strip. I'd like to buy the whole thing and rehab it myself. They just knocked down my favorite building, and they're putting up Paco Rabanne Maison." I thought: It's Miami. What can we ask of Miami? To be more tasteful?

"We'll Probably Be Killed Here."

One morning Brian picked me up, and we crossed MacArthur Causeway to see the dramatic skyline of Architectonica buildings. One was built like a staircase down to the sea. Another had an immense square cut out of its center. A giant palm grew inside the square. We passed Star Island, the most expensive real estate in Florida, where Vanilla Ice and Thomas Kramer and Gloria Estefan live. Their homes have marble driveways. As I said, we can't ask Miami to be more taste-ful. It is about taste that is so bad that it transcends judgment and becomes a completely new category: Miami.

We dropped down I-95 to Southwest Eighth Street in Little Havana, Calle Ocho. The spring festival there rivals carnival in Rio. We drank sweet espresso *cafecitos*. People milled around in colorful *guayaberas*. A tremulous saxophone played somewhere. We crossed to La Gloria Cubana to see old people roll handmade cigars in wooden tobacco presses. Each person makes two hundred a day, cutting tobacco leaf with razor knives, wetting the edges, and pressing them expertly together into perfectly sculpted cylinders. Bundles of aromatic cigars lay tied in white cotton ribbon. It almost makes you think that smoking ought to be good for you.

Calle Ocho becomes highways 41 and 90. We raced along, top down, and Brian told me stories of his family. His brother, Robert Antoni, is the author of *Divina Trace*, a novel that earned him a reputation as the new James Joyce. Brian said that his sister, Janine, came home from school when she was eighteen and spent her vacation pounding a huge boulder into sand with a hammer as an art project. "We thought she was in big trouble," said Brian. "We thought she'd never make it." Followers of the art world will recognize the famous Janine Antoni, conceptual artist, whose work includes *Gnaw*, in which she gnawed at six-hundred-pound blocks of chocolate and lard, spitting out the nibbles to make chocolate hearts and lipsticks. In a piece called *Lick and Lather*, Janine cast herself in soap, which she washed, and then in chocolate, which she licked. Janine washed a gallery floor with her hair (*Loving Care*). Janine transformed her mother and father into each other. Janine's movements are tracked more closely than the space shuttle's. She receives immense checks for doing these strange things.

We stopped at Uncle Tom's Barbecue for a pork sandwich. I asked Brian how safe it was in Miami these days. That gave rise to a discussion about the inverse relationship between safety and freedom and the tyranny of safety that is now imposed upon us by all of the repressed Nazis in the guise of lawyers. Brian said something periphrastic that amounted to, "Give me liberty or give me death." Putting his money where his mouth was, he shopped the thrift stores of Overtown. True, tourists had been murdered in Miami, specifically German tourists in the Overtown area (where the freeway passes over a poor part of town). But the days when drug planes were zinging overhead and bales of cocaine were bouncing down suburban streets, the days of *Miami Vice* and of machine gun fire in shopping malls—that's all over with now.

Mostly.

The local Wild West answer to all this rumble is the venerable Florida state "carry law," allowing concealed weapons. Since that law was passed, there has been a proliferation of ranges where an ordinary citizen may enroll in a course in combat arms and exit onto the street with a police permit that grants the legal right to strut around town with a .357 magnum in a jackass rig. Trail Glades Range at Florida

Highway 997 and US 41 is a public park dedicated to a shooting range. Anyone can bring a gun and bang away for a nominal fee. It's a family thing. It's a civic thing.

We passed the Miccosuki Bingo gambling site, an immense sea of concrete in which floated a steel and rock building of unspeakable proportions that looked like a nerve-gas plant in Nebraska. Then everything before Brian's Saab convertible spread out flat and lay in green and yellow fabric all around, as if we rode an ever-unrolling bolt of soft scented cloth.

A sign crudely painted on a board in ocher brush strokes said "Frog City," and Brian hit the antilock brakes hard, and we swerved into the thickly overgrown driveway, scattering shells and pebbles.

"We'll probably be killed here," he muttered, hunching over the wheel now and creeping forward slowly among the exploded corpses of RVs and the rusted remains of airboats, their old propellers snapped off like twigs. We crawled along an oyster shell path near the sea and found ourselves in a shady jungle clearing of some sort, and all around us rusted trucks, corrugated steel lean-to shelters, a tool shop of some sort, open to the weather, an old school bus infested with wasps and birds' nests. Iridescent green and blue dragonflies hovered. Junked Cadillacs, mobile homes with smashed windows, rusted acetylene tanks, garbage cans, and palms with great bunches of reddish coconuts ripening high in their branches. We got down from our shiny auto and walked in a bit on the lane. I poked my head into the open-sided tool shop, its roof yawning at the sky. It looked as if a mortar round had hit it. Vines had crept in to claim everything, an abandoned refrigerator; a motorcycle, its seat torn to shreds; a couch, its stuffing blossoming in gray tufts of cotton. A peacock stood proudly on a rusted table saw and displayed its magnificent blue fan.

We encountered Eveleen Yates and Wayne Fountain sitting in plastic lawn chairs under a canvas canopy with a beer cooler between them. They looked up placidly as we approached with caution. They grinned at us happily. A Doberman pincer nuzzled my leg. I stepped closer, close enough to see that the cooler at their feet was filled with blood and frogs. Eveleen smiled, picked up a live frog in her left hand, gripped it firmly, and with a pair of pliers in her right hand, deftly, without even looking at what she was doing, ripped its skin clean off. She dropped the peeled pink frog into the cooler. Wayne reached down and churned the dozens of frogs back and forth with his hand. "What're you doing?" Brian asked.

Eveleen picked up another and with a flick of her wrist stripped it of its skin. Wayne was doing the same now, each of them with a pair of pliers, zip, zip, zip, one by one, in a rhythm that never stopped, and dropping each freshly skinned frog into the bloody water, and every now and then Wayne would reach down and agitate them absently with his left hand, just give them a little whirl. The frogs lived quite a while in there, struggling in the albuminous fluid, before they expired.

Eveleen and Wayne told us that they were gigging frogs, or *frogging*, as Wayne put it, and would sell the frogs to Miami restaurants. "My daddy frogged," Eveleen said. "His daddy frogged, too. I been frogging since I was little." Wayne and Eveleen weren't little anymore.

A rooster crowed. Chickens pecked around the compound. The Doberman circled and approached again, and I scratched its nose. Frog City was the remains of an old tourist business, airboat rides and an unlicensed zoo, which had been shut down. What the authorities didn't get was taken by Hurricane Andrew in 1992, and now the chickens and roosters and feral peacocks were all that remained. Here and there the land simply weakened and seemed to fall in and give way to lily ponds. Beyond that the whole of the Everglades stretched endlessly away in all directions. Nowhere before on that faintly scribbled road had it been so evident that we were in the middle of such a confounding and measureless patchwork wilderness.

We talked with Eveleen and Wayne for a time and then walked around their compound just to see what was what. The path we walked grew fainter the farther we ventured, past castor bean and night-blooming jasmine and sausage tree. Buzzards, fat and black as Labrador retrievers, sat in treetops waiting for calamity. The ceaseless death of the swamp was a never-ending meal for them. We walked until the road gave out and let go into the Everglades, and when we returned, Wayne and Eveleen were just getting a fire going in a barbecue kettle.

Eveleen stopped skinning frogs and stood and walked around. She was huge on top, tapering gradually to an odd shape like a broad exclamation point in flip-flops. She said her folks were farmers, and her daddy worked the central Florida sugar-cane fields some, but he also gigged frogs now and then. "Wayne's folks hunted alligators. Sold 'em. They moonshined a little bit, too," she added with a high, sweet laugh. She and Wayne exchanged a look of genuine joy and affection.

"What are you going to cook?" I asked, having just seen all the fish in the world hiding under lily pads.

"Steaks," Wayne said, as it if were obvious.

"Where's the Fry Bread?"

On the Miccosuki Indian reservation Brian and I saw the thirteen-hundred-pound alligator Tiny, the fourteen-foot, 110-year-old beast with a brain the size of a US quarter—Tiny, whom the Miccosuki Indians have possessed all these years in a moat fenced by chain link, his beautiful pink mouth so pale like the sun seen through fog at evening time, pale and pink as Bahamian coral sand, his rows of teeth like a startling tableau of minute scrimshaw carvings, his whole tremendous black and green body scabbed over with the rude shock of this terrible existence here in a six-foot space and the whole four thousand square miles of the Everglades rippling away on every side of it.

Our guide, Angela, had big blue eyes and a big gap between her teeth and long brown hair splashed with red. She wore a thin mini-dress and sandals and handled baby alligators, talking to them and cooing at them as if they were her children. "Maybe I'll take you home and feed you," she said to a small one. "You look like you're not getting enough to eat." She went into the pit with the Miccosuki alligator wrestler, a big bored-looking Indian with a ponytail. Angela says she might consider learning to wrestle alligators one day. "It's a career path," she told me.

It rained briefly, and then we took an airboat into the swamp. The Everglades can look like the midwestern prairie, endless blowing sedges punctuated by stands of trees. The boat, with its deafening motor, moved so smoothly over that landscape, without a bump or hesitation, no matter what it flattened in its path, that I couldn't overcome the feeling that at any moment we'd hit something solid and be pitched out, our faces smashed on the Plexiglas windshield.

NIGHT IN THE CITY OF SUN

We skipped out over the pale green and yellow plains under the building slate-and-white clouds and visited an Indian village, where real Miccosuki Indian women made little baskets to sell. Brian rushed around the tiny island in the swamp, saying, "Where's the fry bread? They always take you out to a faux Indian village where they sell you fry bread." Hawks kept watch, turning in great slow circles, silhouetted against the hazy sun.

The word of the moment in Miami was the French word *faux*, which means false, as in *faux pas*, false step. Only in this case it meant ersatz, intentionally faked for the effect, like the faux cowboy bar, Davey's, between Lauderdale and Miami, with five-star rodeo riders and a hitching post out back. Or La Cavacha, another *taverna*, where on Saturday nights patrons arrived on horseback to hear great Latin music and eat Cuban barbecue. Little Haiti is not Haiti. Little Havana is not Havana. Everyone looks like Robinson Crusoe in sandals and long hair, washed up on the beach by some catastrophe. But even the dispossessed are faux dispossessed, for they have money and jobs, or better yet, like Brian, they have money and no job. The beach is faux beach, the sand pumped in from ocean depths. The only thing real is what was here in the first place, the immense undulating fabric of the two-and-a-half-million-acre swamp. And on its edge, this city with its air of a 1950s nuclear test site taken over by Dominicans, Jamaicans, Peruvians, Bahamians, Bolivians, Salvadorans, Puerto Ricans, Cubans, steaming in the provisional Caribbean air of decay and permissiveness and a lack of clear rules. What happens in Miami is not precedent, it's just what happens.

On the way home, stopping at a red light, Brian told me that an ordinance had been passed to allow tourists to run red lights "if they feel threatened." Everyone drives seventy-five, eighty miles an hour. "People are allowed to drive in the manner to which they were accustomed in their native land," he said.

"People Are Having Sex Down There. I Guarantee It."

First of evening: full moon in a pewter sky and delta kites with spinners for tails over white sands and hurtling stallion waves. I was getting ready at the Raleigh Hotel, getting ready to pick up Tom Austin, King of the

Night in South Beach. We were going to do the nightclub scene. Or should I say the *Nightclub Scene*. Many things in Miami need italics.

I worked out at the Raleigh's free-weight room, an open-sided tent facing the pool and the beach. One of the many fashion models who stayed at the Raleigh was working out beside me. She was tall and thin and had a haunting mask-like beauty, as if she'd already died but was too beautiful to lie down. She wore tights so tight that no anatomical detail, not a hair, remained a mystery to me.

I finished my workout and swam in the legendary pool, which had been featured on the cover of *Life* magazine in the 1950s. The deck and pool at the Raleigh are comparable to the Playa Mimosa in Cuernavaca. Guys in combat boots, khaki shorts, white T's, silver earrings, sucking Tootsie Roll pops. Terrazzo, concrete, and hibiscus. Women in skin-tight Speedos or in no suits at all.

God had sent angels to tell me to go out. So I showered and dressed and went out.

Now the sky was beaten copper, guttering liquid light. The traffic stirred up and down Collins Avenue. I picked up Tom, and we went to Pacific Time. In Miami the best restaurants and nightclubs change so rapidly that writing about them is like mapping the clouds. But my transit of Venus occurred when Pacific Time was *Bon Apetit*'s choice for Miami's best new restaurant. The restaurant had a long black marble bar in back where customers could sit and eat while watching the chefs, the Blodgett ovens and Garland stoves all blackened from constant use.

Tom Austin looks like a beaten intellectual, an Under-the-Volcano outcast, who skipped like a stone on the waves of some sadder, deeper sea and landed here. He has long sandy hair. Miami is a casual town, but Tom wears clothes that look as if he found them at the bottom of the laundry bin, and sometimes his pockets are inadvertently turned out, too. Sometimes he wears shoes. And yet no matter where we went, we were greeted with open arms, because everyone in Miami knows that he is the Nightlife Guru. Everyone reads his column "Swelter" in Miami's hip free weekly, *New Times*. People in Miami rush to the newsstand just to see if they've been savaged in Tom's cultural bondage and discipline column. He wrote his philosophy thusly: "The fountain of filth that is the modern world has come to embrace the universe, past and present, and the tide can no longer be turned back. . . . From desperate teenagers in Cuba selling themselves for a bar of soap to deluded models preying on the powerful in hope of major pay dirt, it's all the same filthy business." Consequently, the waiters at Pacific Time were falling all over themselves to suck up to Tom and bring him whatever he wanted. Such as numerous fortifying margaritas for the rough trip ahead of us. Spicy duck pancakes with tamari.

Tom once wrote for the *Herald*, covering what passed for society in Miami. "In 1988, 1989, the money was supercharged," he told me over tuna tartare. "They were throwing it away. They had bowling alleys in their houses. It was all coke, Arabs, S&L's, laundering—all crooks, and I covered it as 'society.' This place," he said, indicating the new construction chic decor of Pacific Time, "was formerly Italian, an arson job called Johnny's," Tom added, as if that was the usual way restaurants changed hands here. We finished our meal, which had clearly been put through the fabulizer for Tom, and lurched out into the night in search of someone who was having sex. After all, when you get right down to it, Miami is about nothing if it's not about sex. Even if you're ancient in Miami, you used to have sex.

Out on the street it was full dark now. The last copper light had set somewhere over the swamp, and neon lights came up aqua-pink, flickering hard against the steamy blackness of the star-hot night. We stopped at a club called Amnesia. Faux secret police standing outside guarded the doors. They dressed in black and wore secret service earphones, radios, and lapel pins. The building was an immense white mosque, towering against the green jungle foliage, the black night sky.

Inside, the center of the building was open to the night, a scrap of tent material flying several stories above. An intensely loud Latin band played under a Great White Goddess sculpture. Everything was on a Cecil B. DeMille scale. A fountain with a sculpture in it. Smoke and spotlights heightened the Harlem, 1958, effect. Bars on several levels communicated by staircases, and around each bar people sat in comfortable booths and couches to form little circles of exclusion. It was not about friends, it was about who we didn't want to have as our friends. Everybody except us. We climbed to the heights and looked down. Tiny people, each wearing many thousands of dollars' worth of clothes, danced to the Latin beat on the shiny wooden floor below.

Boring.

We drove up the peninsula to Stephen Talkhouse on Collins Avenue. Nil Lara, the Cuban singing sensation, was on stage when we walked in. He wasn't scheduled. He just happened to drop in to play with an Afro-Caribbean jazz ensemble that had been pulled together for the night. In one hop we had gone from total fantasy to total realism. (Or was it actually faux realism?) Stephen Talkhouse was old, dark, knocked together, under-designed, with a raised wooden stage. It looked like a folk nightclub in Chicago circa 1973. Giant canvases of primitive art. A chandelier of beads. Behind the bar: the glass doors of a refrigerator, a virtual room of beer bottles lit in red neon. A stainless-steel tap protruding from a red wall served nothing.

On stage a dozen bongo and conga players sat on folding chairs, as motley a crew as I've ever seen. One man looked like Timothy Leary with dark sunglasses. A thin black man in dreadlocks played a Roland D-50 vintage synthesizer keyboard. A huge African woman with a golden bow in her locks played bass. A woman who looked like a middle-class housewife from Miami played conga. Two women in long print skirts danced by their tables beneath the stage, one of them an exhibitionist so limber and thin and white, who twisted herself into tree-limb knots and threw her skirt out as if she could barely restrain herself from tearing it off.

Miami seemed to run on a meterless source of sex and violence. Everywhere the music was Latin, a constant drumming, like insects mating. We walked up Washington to a club called Bash, where darkness itself was a structural element. Smoke. Strobes simulate heli-arc welding. A bad catastrophe had happened here, the décor seemed to say, with much loss of life. We were merely the witnesses to the aftermath of something. Burned walls of buffed and tarnished steel reminiscent of the movie *Metropolis*. Tinfoil streamers hung as bunting over the narrow dance floor. Spotlights pierced the gloom. Concrete abutments and sound so huge that the bass notes made my new unconstructed linen pants flutter. When we couldn't stand it any longer, we shoved our way past the pumped-up security guards in black T-shirts and into the back, where we found a faux jungle bar with animal eyes painted in among the painted leaves. Scenes change in Miami with the restless logic of a dream.

"Woah," Tom said, "there's my competition," meaning Tara Solomon, the night-life columnist for the *Herald* ("the press—" Tom wrote in his column, "a lowly but integral element in the pimp ecosystem"). She wore her hair in a topknot like Cleopatra. Red high heels and a dark gray miniskirt. Big hoop earrings. As she passed us, Tom said, "I hate it when I go someplace and I'm the most fabulous person there."

At a gay bar called Twist two transvestites in bad makeup and good clothes sat next to a blinking cash machine. We stayed only long enough for several people to recognize Tom, and that was enough for him. We left.

From club to club we went throughout the night, and everywhere we went, Tom was welcome. People on the street at two a.m. stopped him and grinned and told him tidbits of gossip for the broad-reaching skein of his acid wit. Murmured at night, printed next morning. Everywhere we went the music was either a relentless Latin conga or sounded like a car with a broken starter. The South Beach nightclub scene is pure Roman spectacle on the farthest edge of America. Latin is as Latin does.

The culmination of the evening was Warsaw, tremendous in scale, equally disastrous. Not since seeing Dr. John's midnight show at Tipitina's in New Orleans had I seen such a jammed-in, pumped-up crowd, smoke so thick that Tom dissolved as he walked ahead of me.

I remembered Brian telling me that I might witness "the most beautiful people you've ever seen in ecstasy. It's body worship. They'll be fucking on the floor. Only during carnival in Rio can you see such purely physical, open, and uninhibited religious ecstasy and strangeness. I saw a midget dancing with a ten-foot penis. Miami has the hottest fifteen blocks of night life in the world right now." In fact, South Beach has today what Havana had in 1958. Soon, they say, it'll even have casinos.

The great high vaulted warehouse spaces of Warsaw were filled with smoke transpierced by red and blue and green spotlights—the room turned on spokes of light—and a sea of seething bodies rose in tiers, level upon level, from the great sweating blackness of the main dance floor, where men, half of them shirtless, jammed shoulder to shoulder, swaying in sandals and shorts.

"People are having sex down there," Tom said. "I guarantee it."

A man appeared on stage now (or was he standing on the bar?) in full Indian headdress, feathers cascading from his head down his naked back. He wore nothing but thin cotton thigh-length stretch workout pants, and he had (is this real?) a twelve-inch erection, which he was stroking with every other beat of the song, dancing rhythmically, hips gyrating, a convivial grin on his handsome face. The crowd was howling with delight as strobes took evil snapshots of this onanistic phantasmagoria.

As we left, Tom admonished me, "The amateur strip contest starts in fifteen minutes. You sure you don't want to hang out?"

We were already on the street. We could hear the bass notes from the speaker system inside. I touched the wall. Tom saw my expression and put his hand on the wall, too. We looked at each other. The rock wall was hot and pulsing, like flesh. "Jesus," he said, and we walked on down the street.

At three in the morning we ended at a quiet and elegant little club filled with the former-dealer disinherited drag queen outcast wealthy. Reginald, for example, a man-boy, a heroin dabbler with a high school education, making three hundred thousand dollars a year putting together parties for people at nightclubs such as we'd already seen tonight. Theme parties. Big nightclubs would give him a cut of the door for bringing people in. He had a network. He put out the word. People flocked to his parties. He was the king of an industry that didn't exist yesterday, wouldn't exist tomorrow, but he was in it now, so what difference did it make?

Reginald was thin and only very discreetly tattooed and had a slight nervous palsy. He had "Six Degrees of Separation" written all over him, a kind of sociopathic sincerity, behind which loomed enormous lies. When Tom introduced us, Reginald's handshake was a code of some kind, a conspicuously circumspect signal, like passing money beneath the table, and he looked me right in the eye and said, "Come to Amnesia tomorrow night around eleven. We're doing Tito Puente Night. I'll put your name at the door. We'll have a space at our table. You won't have any trouble getting in." And he drifted out into the world. I had been moved up the food chain in the South Beach ecosystem.

"It's Gonna Come Down and Good. It's Gonna Be Fun."

Top down. Rain and sunshine. Wipers tapping rhythm to a Latin score coming from the streets, as if we were in a movie about ourselves. Brian wore black shorts, purple socks, and an Ashley Bickerton T-shirt, "Good Stuff" on the front and "Bad Stuff" (such as a swastika) on the back. Backward baseball cap. We passed the new Bacardi headquarters, a ten-story blue tile mosaic depicting leaves and fruit.

Going north, the neighborhood turned Caribbean, with colorful saints painted on the stucco facades. We stopped in at the market at Fifty-ninth Street, a great open building with Haitian voodoo music playing and tables of goods for sale inside. Counterfeit copies of works by famous Haitian folk artists.

The rain, which had been off and on before, now began in earnest, the way it does in the islands: shocking in its sudden and brutal power. And yet sunlight persisted through it. Sunshine and rain.

A black man named Charlie tried to trade Brian a red plastic shopping cart for his Saab convertible.

When the rain stopped, we drove out to Coconut Grove. We saw a small airplane towing a rainbow banner announcing Gay Tuesday nights at a fashionable restaurant called Starfish.

Coconut Grove, the edge of a great shopping mall, CocoWalk, on Main Highway, towering shops and forbidding middle-class hordes in shorts and sunglasses, grim troops stalking the main streets.

"When South Beach is over," Brian said, "it'll turn into this. This is all about the future of South Beach." An anthropologist who wanted me to get the full life span of this creature.

Yet when we entered the neighborhoods of Coconut Grove, we found ourselves in a completely different place. Because Coconut Grove lies in a hummock of the land, it is the northernmost growing range of many tropical plants. Coconut Grove, in other words, is the closest thing to a tropical rain forest that can be found in the United States. The street markers were made of old coral stone. Domes of yellow hibiscus and bougainvillea rose from the dark green surroundings. Bushes of fuchsia. Giant trees with red-orange blossoms cascading down toward the roadway. "Those are called woman's tongue in the islands," Brian said, "because the pods make so much noise." The jungle exploded in sprays of yellow alder. Spanish moss hung in silver-gray tresses from cypress and evergreen. We passed homes set back in quiet streets, where mangoes, ripe and glazed in reddish purple, hung in clusters from backyard trees. At the end of one street, overlooking Biscayne Bay, we saw buttressing root systems so mammoth that they seemed to make cathedrals of the trees.

Leaving Coconut Grove, we crossed the bay to Key Biscayne and drove down to Cape Florida. The devastation that Hurricane Andrew had wrought was nuclear, a marvelous and haunting beauty. The endless beach by the Cape Florida lighthouse, once visited by a million people annually, was now deserted.

As we headed back to the hotel, the sky grew black, and the bright sunlit pastel buildings of South Beach stood out in unreal, joyful, terrifying relief, like a Magritte. "It's gonna come down and good," Brian mused. "It's gonna be fun." Suddenly he sounded like the island boy he was, a Jamaican twang in his voice. Brian loved Miami, because it was crazy like the islands. He loved it because it was crazy like New York City, too.

Big Fish

The water taxi leaves from Bayside, a mall in the heart of downtown Miami. It's difficult to miss: the Hard Rock cafe with a towering Fender Telecaster on top is right across the water from it. Bayside has the greatest food court of any mall in the United States, featuring Cajun, Japanese, Cuban, Argentine, Chilean, Peruvian, French, Italian, and on and on. More exotic birds on bicycles. Live reggae bands at water's edge.

The most important stop on the water taxi route is Big Fish, and it's easier to find this way than by trying to drive there through the confounding concrete rain forest of highway underpasses. Big Fish is one of the few truly important Miami eating experiences, sitting on the riverside on a stolen park bench, eating freshly caught dolphin sandwiches and conch fritters. Although it looks as if the building is just there for the afternoon, Eric Santos, the Panamanian chef, has operated this outdoor restaurant since 1982. Which in Miami time is centuries.

Brian and I watched a one-hundred-foot metal boat across the river loading and a swamped Haitian skiff sinking slowly downstream, as we drank iced tea and poured on the Matouk's Pepper Sauce. He said, "My grandfather made my grandmother carry Matouk's in her purse. He had to have it with everything he ate. You can't make conch salad without Matouk's." He took a conch fritter and dipped it in the hot sauce. He tasted it, grimaced. "These bear no resemblance to any conch fritter in the world," he announced. I'd had conch fritters in the Bahamas, and I had to agree, but the dolphin sandwiches were good. Matouk's is very, very hot.

Sonny

Brian and I sailed from Bayside, past the Port of Miami (largest port for cruise ships in the world), beneath MacArthur Causeway, around Star Island, and out west across Biscayne Bay. Coming back in we chanced to pass Watson Island and could see from the water that along a spit of land shrouded in Australian pines, a shantytown had grown up, a knocked-together village on the water's edge made up of lean-tos and plywood and campers for the homeless, the squatters, the outcasts.

After we docked, we drove the Saab through construction barriers and down long sandy access roads, until we found ourselves at the water's edge, tracing the route we'd sailed an hour before. We were just a few hundred yards across the water from Howard Hughes's old pink stucco house and Julio Iglesias's Moorish-style red-tile-and-white-stucco mansion and the place where the venture capitalist Thomas Kramer was spending forty million dollars to build himself a new home next to the home of Vanilla Ice. Jet-skiers were posting like equestrians out on the blue swells in the bay as we approached this island-like shantytown, where our Heart-of-Darkness tale ended, far up the river where we found our Kurtz.

As a journalist now these twenty-odd years, I've discovered that you can walk in almost anywhere, walk in quickly, look around, chin up, purposeful expression, and there is a grace period before people get the sense that they want to take something from you or hurt you. There is an animal shyness that keeps them at bay for five minutes, ten minutes. But like a blush, it wears off, so timing is important.

We parked the Saab in plain view and walked right into the shanty-town. Chickens and ducks scattered at our approach. The houses were mostly plywood, some with indoor-outdoor carpeting flowing from an interior darkness onto the beach sand under the diaphanous shade of the towering pines. We walked all the way back in, and the space between the two rows of houses narrowed with the land. People looked up sleepily and nodded or even said hello to us. They didn't yet know what to make of us. They were dark and thin and wary. Here and there, shirtless children in shorts played up and down the beach. If we'd come upon this on the far side of a Bahamian Island instead of in downtown Miami, we might have mistaken it, naively, for a gritty little Eden.

Cast-off RVs and campers and busted trucks dissolved in rust, as if exotic orange termites had attacked the steel. A vague scent of excrement, rotting vegetation, and seawater, and the slow suspicious glances we received made me think that everyone had fallen under a spell of some sort. Look up *zombie* in the dictionary. There's a picture of these people there.

As we walked back out, a man caught my eye and said, "You're journalists, right?" I don't know how he knew. He said he'd come here by way of a bank robbery in 1979. He was a powerfully built man, almost black from the sun, with pale gray-green eyes and shoulder-length dark brown hair. He might have been in his forties. "Welcome," he said, standing to greet us and to show us around, as if he'd been expecting us all along. Call him Sonny. He looked like Sonny Crockett from the old *Miami Vice* television series, only after years of hard drinking and living as a fugitive from justice, he had changed. He was heavier. He wore no shoes. Dirt was hammered into his skin so deeply that it had become like a full-body tattoo, a fine reticulation of filaments that enclosed him in its carbon darkness, and now only those gleaming eyes peered out at us, that white-toothed grin. Sonny drank from a long-neck bottle of beer.

"These are all your subculture radicals, drug dependent dropouts, this is a mental graveyard," he announced, as if giving us the tour we'd come for. A man swept the ground with a broom outside his plywood-and-tarpaper house. "That's Poppy," Sonny said. "He's a Marielito," referring to the Cuban refugees who came on the Mariel boatlift in 1980. "He has a step-down living room. His place is one of the nicest. He hustles food stamps and helps people out."

Sonny pointed at a trailer behind us. "There's an alcoholic lives in there. He does day labor pool. Henry has the chickens and that duck. Steve and his wife have been on Watson Island ten years. They're crack addicts. Five huts down on the right are the Cubans who have the kids. And Bea across from them, she has a house full of books like Jackie O. All she does is read and do crack." Sonny pointed at a boat half sunk in the shallows. "Lobster Eddie lives in that sailboat with four dogs. He hunts lobsters. He dives sixty feet to get them, holding his breath."

I asked if his community had any activities, ceremonies, projects. "There's no sense of spiritual unity here," he said sadly. "There's no gatherings. What you've got here is a major drug happening. When the bridge comes around the corner," he said, pointing to the construction through which we'd driven to get here, "they'll flatten this." He pointed toward Hibiscus Island and Palm Island across the water. "If I lived over there, I'd call an airstrike on this shit."

I was beginning to understand that people don't arrive here by luck, they travel to this place by logic, twisted to match their twisted path, and now Sonny's monologue was unraveling his logic before us. He spent the sixties hitchhiking around the country looking for himself. He got his girl pregnant. They married. He was about to go to Vietnam, but he contracted hepatitis and became 4-F. "Divorce followed," he said, as if it had stalked him. He became a roofer in the 1970s, and he fell off a roof and shattered his foot. I had noticed a slight limp, and now he pointed out the swollen ankle, which had healed badly. In 1979, he pulled a bank job. "I did it with a note instead of a gun. It was the stupidest thing I ever did."

Then Sonny was on the run. He believed that the police knew who he was, that he had been caught on the security camera, but he had not. He wasn't even hunted. But somehow in the act of passing that note, threatening someone, taking someone's money, of fleeing on foot and continuing to flee, Sonny had crossed over to a place—a spiritual place—from which he could not cross back. Now, he told us, he had a scrap business, which he ran out of his truck. He was forty-four years old and lived in his green and rusting pickup truck with the springs coming through the seats.

And then just as suddenly as he had recognized us, he turned, saying, "Gotta go, fellas." And he walked away. That grace period had elapsed. Some instinctive animal protection had taken over inside of him—that we were getting too close, that he had revealed too much—and the curtain came down.

Sonny walked away and sat in the nylon webbing of a has-been lawn chair in front of a tarpaper shack beside a black woman, who seemed to be talking to herself. Sonny kicked back grimly, sucked on his beer, and looked straight ahead as if we'd never been there in the first place. And we left rather quickly.

"What Do You Want to Do Now?"

We drove out past half of a crumbling coral stone house with a green tile roof, the last such house on the waterway, out through hibiscus and jungle palm, purple pui, lace, croton, corkscrew pandarus, and bottleneck palm and red bananas and alamanda, white birds, angel's trumpet and ginger and heliconia.

We were driving across the water now. The South Beach skyline was dissolving in the mist. "Take a good look at that," Brian said. "A year from now, you'll come back and it won't be there. It'll all be high-rise condos." South Beach was being overrun by the reinforced concrete blight of developers. A few weeks later we returned to see Sonny and his people, and the whole Watson Island shantytown had been bulldozed under, nothing left but a spit of sand. Not a trace of that community, not even a child's toy, remained.

"What do you want to do now?" I asked Brian.

"We could go to the Woolworth's on Washington Street," he said. "The lunch line is great. That ought to be part of everyone's tour of South Beach."

RITES OF SPRING

In the late 1980s, my wife Carolyn and I were getting ready for a trip. I can't remember where we were going. It was spring, and the lilacs were in bloom. The air was filled with flowers, and Carolyn especially loved lilacs. The windows were open in our bedroom, and morning light was streaming into the sitting room as she stood by her chest of drawers getting dressed. I was watching her because she was beautiful, and she turned with a strange look on her face and touched her right breast. "I can feel a lump," she whispered.

"But you just had a mammogram," I said.

A sudden stillness held the room, as if the air itself had stopped moving. The light changed. Then everything changed.

We were at Highland Park Hospital north of Chicago. Our two daughters had been born there, and we had always felt a sense of well-being in that place. The rooms looked out onto trees and lawns. But when we went there for her biopsy that feeling was gone. I was holding her hand as I watched the silver needle glide into the side of her breast. I felt the pain, saw her wince, and felt her fingernails dig into my skin. I couldn't watch the scalpel. In a few moments, the doctor had removed a lump the size of a pea, and it was whisked away to be studied under a microscope.

We sat in the sunny lobby waiting. Carolyn gently held her wound and looked around as if she might burst into tears. Carolyn's name was called much too quickly. If you are an ordinary patient, they make you wait and wait. It must be taught that way in medical school: the worse the news, the better the service. We were led to a room no larger than a closet with two chairs and a stainless-steel table. The doctor came in and closed the door with his palms flat against it as if to keep out something that was pursuing him. This was not the posture of someone bearing good tidings. I felt a strong jolt of panic, surging adrenaline, and I thought: *If I feel this way, how must she feel?* Then he said, "This is not a death sentence." I felt a hard bubble form inside my heart. I turned and saw how determined Carolyn looked. She planted both her feet and squared off as I'd seen her do on her brother's sailboat when the sea was pitching things about.

I don't remember what else was said in that tiny room. We walked out into the spring sunshine and saw a different world. The colors had dimmed. My mind was spinning, rationalizing and bargaining, trying to list all the evidence against this. My father was a scientist. My mother had raised seven sons, and they were all alive and healthy. One of my brothers was a doctor. Another played saxophone. That must count for something. Carolyn and I owned a house, a Volvo, two dogs. We had kids who needed their mother. This wasn't supposed to happen to us. We were the most beautiful couple in the world. We were only forty-one years old. We led a charmed life.

Didn't we?

We entered a whirlwind of dizzying appointments. "Get the best surgeon," people told us, but they missed the point. Surgeons are tradespeople, like plumbers. Surgeons are also not necessarily the best people to talk to when you're in a vulnerable state of mind. After all, they get paid to cut. One surgeon, trying to convince Carolyn to have a radical mastectomy, said, "What do you need breasts for? You've had children." Both Carolyn and I recognized that we needed a team. A surgeon would be on that team, but the team needed a leader.

Her name was Melody Cobleigh. She was an oncologist, perhaps the ideal doctor, a combination of scientist and artist, healer and scholar. She read everything, did original research, wrote books and papers, and saw patients nearly every day. Most importantly, she had golden hands. She undoubtedly saved Carolyn's life, and she did it all on the first visit for about sixty-five dollars.

Carolyn wore a sleeveless blue paper gown, and when Melody directed her to lift her arms, I could see her right breast through the armhole. I did not know that it would be one of the last times I'd ever see it. I merely noticed how different Melody's examination was from those of the surgeons, all men. Melody closed her eyes, the better to read what she could not see. Then unexpectedly, she called another doctor in, a Dickensian figure, young, fine-pointed, aloof, who called himself DeMay and whose expertise was a new technique known as fine needle biopsy.

"She has breast cancer on the right," Melody told DeMay, "and I'm feeling something on the left." Then she turned to me and asked in a level tone, "You aren't the type who faints at the sight of needles, are you?"

I said I was not.

"Because you can stay or you can leave, but I don't want you to faint."

I promised that I would not. I tried to look inside myself to see what was there. This was several days and a dozen doctors past the initial biopsy, and I felt as if something had crawled inside of me and died there. I looked up and winced again as the needle went in. No anesthesia this time. Carolyn cried out and dug her fingernails into my hand once more. It was the first cry she'd uttered since this all began, the first evidence that cancer was physical, not at all like what you see on television with smiling people fighting the good fight and pink ribbons and fun runs for the cure, whatever that is. This was deeply personal. Our lives, so recently filled with myriad thoughts and plans and purposes, had narrowed to a single ugly thing.

When the needle came out, Melody and DeMay left the room, and we were alone. "What does this mean?" Carolyn asked. I could hear the fear in her voice. This was completely unfair. No one had said anything about the left breast. The lump had been in her right breast. The left breast had never been on the bargaining table. The game was rigged. The house was crooked. But all I could do was look at her.

Melody returned, again too soon, and said, "You've got cancer in that other breast." I saw Carolyn recoil toward the open window. The world was wreathed in gloom. Clouds hung like gray jellyfish sending tentacles of wet mist down to invade the spring earth. I felt that we existed in a bathyscaph at the bottom of the sea. All of a sudden the room seemed terribly hot and close. I thought: Maybe she's right. Maybe I am going to faint after all.

As my consciousness passed back through the window and

returned to the room, Melody was asking if we did anything carcinogenic. Did we, for example, work with chemicals? Maybe we were scientists or crop duster pilots. But we weren't. Was it leaded gasoline? Living in the city? Was it that we'd eaten too many fish from the Great Lakes? Was it VDTs or PCBs or DDT? We'd put chlordane in the basement to kill termites in 1977, and it was banned soon afterward as a carcinogen. Surely this was someone's fault.

As my mind raced through the possibilities, Melody had Carolyn up on the table and was systematically going through her body as if through a crowded closet, looking everywhere now for signs of cancer. I understood: if both breasts had cancer, then maybe the Big Tumor lay somewhere else. Melody was thinking: Maybe you don't have breast cancer. Maybe you have, say, liver cancer, and it's already spread to both breasts. On the other hand, if she had two primary tumors, one in each breast, then it may already have spread to other places in her body. I could practically feel the fire racing through the structure that was my wife.

I slumped into a chair beside the examining table, staring at the wall, waiting to hear what other horrible surprises Melody had in store for us.

"Your cervix looks entirely normal," she said after a few minutes of rummaging in her bones. Then, sotto voce: "I'm going to do a rectal now." When illness comes, the self is stolen by strangers. Part of getting well is finding ways to steal it back.

When word traveled out along the trembling web of filaments that connects everyone to everyone else, the phone calls began coming, cards and letters arrived, packages and casseroles and flowers were dropped at the door, and an outpouring of care and help and attention came cascading down on us. A friend from Santa Fe sent a Native American medicine pouch full of crystals by FedEx. One of my brothers gave me an Apache tear, a shiny black rock that was meant to absorb my grief. It was as if we had won some obscure contest, and in our newly elevated status we had become the royal couple of pathology.

Elena, our oldest daughter, who was eight at the time, came home

RITES OF SPRING

from school and said, "Mom, Annie said they were going to put plastic bags in your breasts. That's not true, is it?"

It was true.

We did things in response to cancer that superficially seemed to make no sense but that deep down in the emotional brain were really important. I began to stockpile food in the basement as if nuclear war might be the next step in this galloping progression. Carolyn decided to have the house remodeled, and workmen began stomping around, closing off sections of the house with plastic sheeting and hammering through walls in clouds of dust. It seemed to match our emotional state

We continued to visit surgeons to interview them for the job we needed done. I went along and took notes, because that's what I'm good at. It helped. Doctors who were made too nervous by my notebook were off the list; they were thinking about malpractice. My father was a professor in a medical school, and I grew up working in his labs. I knew from him what doctors were. One evening he was sitting in his easy chair grading exams when he called me over. He said, "Doctors are not gods," and showed me where a student had spelled the word for that muscular thing in your mouth *tung*. A few are artists like Melody. The rest are plumbers.

On our first visit to Dr. Witt, Carolyn wore a new navy jacket with three big rows of blue buttons. "How do you like my triple-breasted jacket?" she asked after we'd been introduced.

"It's very nice," said the surgeon, clearly unsure of what she was driving at.

"I need all the breasts I can get," Carolyn said. Dr. Witt laughed. He was a tall, thin, boyish fellow with blond hair. His hobby was making fine furniture in his basement with electric power tools. When I suggested that it seemed odd to be a surgeon and to play with instruments that could so easily cut off all his fingers, he just smiled. He got the job. After we had talked for a while, he recommended that Carolyn read *Love, Medicine, and Miracles* by Bernie Segal. At first I was surprised at how many of the physicians we saw embraced the spiritual side of healing. That was before I learned how little they knew about breast cancer. It was their subtle way of saying, "I hope you like to pray, because we don't know what we're doing here."

This was around the time people had begun to use the word *ugly* to describe what they saw under the microscope. A friend of mine, a pathologist, took a look at the slides and pulled a face. Out of the Universal Substance, Nature had gone wild in proliferating strange, prodigious, and freakish forms. There are as many kinds of cancer as there are weeds in the fields of Our Lord. Sadly, neither of the ones that Carolyn had, neither the left nor the right, would fit into any of the categories they had for garden-variety cancers. So the doctors could not say with any degree of certainty what the outcome might be. Even if they could have said it about one of the cancers, they could not hazard a guess about a case in which a woman contracted both kinds. Neither could they tell us that a certain number of people with Carolyn's condition responded to this or that treatment, while another number did not. What we did with regard to surgery, what we did afterward—it was anybody's guess. It just so happened that most of the research had been done on infiltrating ductile carcinoma, the most common variety of breast cancer. If you had another variety, they couldn't tell you much at that time. You missed out on the NIH grants. You got the wrong disease.

Outside the waiting room windows, window washers hung in their harnesses, swinging in the wind. Hanging by a thread, I thought. A familiar feeling now. Looking back, seeing myself and Carolyn dressed up, going to the ballet just before she found the lump, I realized that we're all hanging by a thread. The difference is that window washers know it. And now we did, too. I looked down the El tracks coming up the Congress Expressway and running out to O'Hare Airport. It was a remarkably clear day. As I stared out the window, I realized what the central issue was. At the same time, I understood how scared I was. At any moment someone might walk through that door and tell me that Carolyn was dead. How would I tell the girls? How would I raise them without her? I felt physically ill thinking about it. I almost felt guilty for having to deal with my own fear. After all, no one was cutting me. It would take me years to understand how trauma moves out in circles from the focus of the injury to damage all the people in its path, me and the girls and Carolyn's parents and her brother, and on and on in echoing rings.

Dr. Witt had agreed to try to perform a lumpectomy on both sides, but we didn't hold out much hope. When he called at last, it scared me so badly that I could hardly catch my breath. I let him talk. He said the left breast would have to go. The cancer had spread throughout the tissue. He wasn't sure about the right until the lab work was done. But he had made a pact with Carolyn. She didn't want to go to sleep thinking she was getting a lumpectomy and wake up with no breasts. He had agreed to wake her up and let her adjust to the idea. This was a first step in Carolyn's strategy for surviving cancer and then surviving her own survival afterward: predictability and control. Viktor Frankl wrote, "Even the helpless victim of a hopeless situation, facing a fate he cannot change, may rise above himself, may grow beyond himself." Carolyn was supplying her brain, so besieged by emotional turmoil, with the ingredients of rational, orderly thought: a predictable plan embodying those things that she could control in a situation that was mostly out of control.

Shortly after Witt called, I spoke to Melody. She had been to the lab to look at the tissue that Witt had cut out of Carolyn. "This thing is huge," she said, meaning what Witt had taken from Carolyn's left breast. The breast that a number of surgeons had not even examined. Those who had examined it had missed a five-centimeter area "entirely involved by cancer," Melody said. I put the phone down. For a long time all I did was count seconds, watching the clock on the wall. I realized that I was waiting for something to explode, like in the movies.

When Carolyn walked into the house, ladders and dust were everywhere, the radio was trumpeting rock and roll, and workmen were smashing out walls and putting up new sheetrock and wallpaper. The plastic sheeting made a prism of pastel sunlight through the rooms as Carolyn went around inspecting the flowers that had been sent in her absence. She ordered them removed. They were all dying, and she was superstitious. She toured the house, wrapped in her coat, looking at everything as if it belonged to someone else, and then she sat on the sofa in the living room looking forlorn. Sitting beside her, I suppose I must have looked the same.

Everyone had expected Carolyn to stay in the hospital for a week, and she was home in a day and a half. Everyone assumed that meant the worst, although it took me a few days to realize what I was seeing.

Some of our friends were afraid to ask what it meant that Carolyn was home so soon. Finally someone asked if the cancer was "inoperable," and I got it. I was shocked at how ready everyone was to believe that Carolyn had come home to die. It wasn't that they were uncaring or callous. They loved Carolyn, and they were scared, too, as the waves of trauma spread out from the center and engulfed them.

After many hours in the waiting room someone was called to tell me that I could go to Carolyn's room and wait there if I wanted. The aids and nurses were all so nice. "The room's not ready yet, but that's okay, you can go in. Do you want another chair? Can I get you something to drink?" And I saw again what I had seen in our neighborhood, how nice people could be when they were really scared for you. I sat stiffly in a chair by the window, and each time a car or person passed in the hall, I jumped, thinking that it might be Carolyn. What would the living corpse of my wife look like? Would there be blood all over like in neurosurgery? Would she be as pale as death? The bodies of those we love live within us. Harm to them does harm to us. The self is deranged.

They brought her on a steel cart. She had an IV needle as thick as a pencil stuck into her neck. Tubes ran everywhere around her as if she slept in a bed of translucent snakes. Her body looked so small, so flat, so thin beneath the sheets and bandages, and her beautiful once-gleaming brown hair was matted and moist and tangled as if she'd been shipwrecked here. Her face was pale, her eyes were swollen, her limbs slack. Then I saw her lips move. She smiled. She was trying to say something. I leaned down and put my ear to her lips.

"They have great drugs," she said. And I saw another element of her strategy unfold in that stroke of humor. She was creating some order, a predictability in her control over decisions about her own health. And she was laughing, because to laugh was to triumph over unruly and frightening emotions. I had not thought about strategy yet, because I didn't yet know I needed one.

RITES OF SPRING

For the longest time I couldn't look. When the resident came in and peeked under the bandages the next morning, I turned my head and looked out the window at Chicago. Far in the distance I saw smoke and the scintillating strobe lights of the fire trucks. I felt a mirror of pain reflecting back at me. But when the doctors left us alone, she began telling me what she remembered of a wild dream in which the surgeon said he'd been up drinking all night and the residents were urging him to take another drink, shouting, "Hair of the dog!" We had to be careful how much we laughed lest the snakes in her bed get excited and begin biting.

I was astonished at her good humor, her resilience and laughter in the face of this. Soon we were walking the halls together, looking for people to make us feel lucky. There's always someone who's worse off than you are, and one of the keys to surviving your own survival is to find them: see one, do one, teach one. Carolyn had lost her breasts, but that guy lost his tongue and vocal chords. Yuck! We became ghouls, out in search of whatever was gruesome. I brought Elena and Amelia, eight and four, to visit. I brought a cooler with Dove bars in it, fearing that I might not be able to drag them away once they saw their mother. Fearing hysterics. Fearing, fearing, fearing. But they were champs. Amelia, who was crazy about horses, gave Carolyn her favorite toy pony.

After five days, I brought Carolyn home. Ten days after surgery, she was up and dressed in her finery, and we went to the church for Elena's first communion. Life, as they say, goes on. And much too quickly. For at last I had to look. I had to change the bandages. The doctors refused to come home with us. They had given me salve to put on the stitches. I could not avoid it. We were like two pilots trapped in a plane that was going down, saying, "No, you take the controls."

"No, you do it."

"No, you."

"Did you take a bath?" I asked.

"Yes, but I didn't look," she admitted.

"How did you avoid it?"

"I closed my eyes."

We stood in the bathroom. The girls were at school. She stood by the sink before the mirror. She could not yet lift her arms, so I helped her take off her gown. They had wrapped her like a mummy in Kerlix gauze, and I unwrapped her the same way. It was awkward, and I kept thinking: This is a big mistake. I should not be doing this. Things will never be the same. I shouldn't be the one.

First she turned around while I held still, but the turning made her dizzy. Above all we did not want her to fall. I walked the bandage around and around her as if she were a Maypole. Even before the bandage was off I could see how different her shape was. I knew her shape. Her shape had mapped out a vast landscape in my brain, and the discord I felt now at the mismatch between the map in my brain and what I was seeing made me feel physically ill. The birdcage of her ribs seemed so frail now. She was like a child again, her long neck, her small head, her faint smile. I could see how afraid she was of what we were doing, so far out on this precipice, and so I tried to pretend that it was no big deal. I'd been to gross anatomy class at my father's medical school. I'd been to the morgue there. In fact, I accidentally locked myself in a freezer full of dead bodies once. I saw the site of a plane crash with 273 dead people scattered in a field, four of them my friends. I'd seen it all. So how could a few stitches bother me? Still, deep down I knew that it was a mistake.

She held her head high, her chin elevated, proud, as I unreeled the last of her wrappings and saw for the first time the terrible thing that had been done to her. The doves had flown. I felt a bubble burst inside my heart.

She was looking at the ceiling, tears flowing down her cheeks. This job was all mine now. I dropped the Kerlix into the wastebasket and picked up the tube of salve, marveling at the horror of it, the profundity of what they'd done. If I hadn't been so heartbroken, I would have been fascinated. But as it was, I had to look closely enough at the black infestation of the wounds that traversed her chest from side to side and up and down, as if she'd been in a knife fight. And here the curling edges of her flesh met and meshed in the crisscross macramé of black thread, some dried blood. I felt like a coward, that in some essential way I had failed as a husband, as a friend, as a man. But I still pretended it was all right.

"What do you see?" she asked.

"It looks excellent," I said. "No sign of infection." Imitating as well as I could that medical school demeanor I had learned from my father, the professor. But I knew that was not what she was asking. She was asking, *Am I still here? Is it the same me that you used to know? Am I whole?*

"You're fine," I said. "You're just fine."

Carolyn asked Melody how her hair would come out. One strand at a time? Bit by bit? How did one lose it anyway?

"All at once," Melody said. "One morning you'll wake up, and it'll be on your pillow."

"Just like that," Carolyn said, and I saw something in her eye that I'd seen before. A narrowing, penetrating look. She was hatching another plan, another strategy. Carolyn, a woman of great style who made her own clothing, even her own hats, had said that she feared losing her hair more than losing her breasts. She's not the only woman who's told me that over the years.

"Just like that," Melody said. I loved her for her honesty, but she didn't know what she was dealing with.

The day before the first treatment a truck pulled up to our house, and a guy in a uniform gave me a box. I had to sign for it. It was labeled, "Caution! Chemotherapy! Handle with gloves. Dispose of properly." My immediate impulse was to dispose of it promptly. Of course, I opened it to look. Inside were all sorts of fiendish devices and toxic potions in Ziploc bags. Miniature injection bottles, "precision guide" needles, butterfly infusion sets with mini-bore luer lock extension tubes. A box of fifty pairs of rubber gloves. (*Mercy*, I thought. *Fifty? This is going to go on and on, isn't it?*) A case of alcohol wipes. Then the chemicals themselves, each in its own syringe, wrapped in plastic, sealed in a transparent bag and labeled with warnings. One had this command: "Keep Refrigerated!" The label had a penguin on it. The other read: "Do Not Freeze!" It featured the same drawing of a penguin with a red slash mark drawn through him. Over the six months that Carolyn went through chemotherapy, she came to refer to her drugs as "Penguin" and "Do-Not-Penguin."

When Kathy the chemotherapy nurse was about to put the first needle in, Carolyn held up her hand to mark a pause in the unstoppable galloping of events. We were in the second-floor sitting room off the master bedroom in our home. Tall windows on all sides opened onto the green crowns of the trees. "When we're finished with this," Carolyn told us, "we're going to be looking out these windows, and the leaves are going to be turning fall colors. It'll be beautiful." Then Carolyn took my hand in hers, and as Kathy pierced a slim vein on the back of her hand, Carolyn's fingernails dug into the back of my hand. It had become something of a ritual of shared suffering for us.

As Kathy worked, she began asking a barrage of what seemed to me rather strange questions. "How often do you move your bowels?" she asked. And: "Is it normal? Brown?"

"Well, I'll tell you," Carolyn began. "I was shitting up a storm when I was first diagnosed."

The doors were open, and people drifted in out of the green world. A neighbor came by, the pathologist we knew, who had first called the cells under the microscope "ugly." He brought a bouquet of lilies of the valley and a purple flower in a vase shaped like a uterus. He kissed Carolyn, and the coiled snake wriggled on her arm. It was a windy sunny day, and he wore shorts and a T-shirt. He wished Carolyn good luck and left. A little while later, while we were waiting for her shot of Do-Not-Penguin, we saw him and his wife, a neuroscientist, as they wheeled their new baby past our window. The world was going on out there, and we were in here waiting for Carolyn to get sick. After her first round of chemotherapy we went straight to a theater to see a comedy movie and sat in the dark laughing and laughing. Then we went home and waited for her hair to fall out. The second round of chemotherapy came and went. Then the third. Still nothing happened. Carolyn was ravenous after chemotherapy. We began going out to restaurants and then to more comedy movies. We began to wonder if Melody had given us the wrong drugs.

When Kathy came, Carolyn would taunt her, saying, "What kind of wimpy drugs are you giving me? Don't you have anything stronger?" The doctors had given her loads of narcotics and sedative hypnotics, but they sat in the medicine cabinet untouched. I warned her that she'd never amount to much as a drug addict.

It wasn't all fun and games. The back of the hand is extremely sensitive (which I guess is why they put needles in there), and sometimes when the IV wouldn't go in right, Carolyn would sit there with tears streaming down her face. Then she'd smile just to let us know what she was made of. But her hair never fell out, and she never threw up. People began to look at her the way the bad guys look at Superman when they empty their guns at him and he just stands there smiling. She wasn't all steel, though, and I couldn't do what I did and remain unchanged either. I always stood and held her other hand while Kathy did the injections. Another part of me died during that process. I could feel myself slowly being pulled free and drifting away.

The Methotrexate went in first, and then Kathy taped the butterfly set down, and she and Carolyn talked for an hour before the fluorouracil injection. That was the procedure.

Always, right after chemotherapy, she would want two things: to go somewhere and eat and to be entertained in some spectacular way, a movie, a play, the demolition of a large building . . . More than once we sat in the dark with great tubs of buttered popcorn and watched *Bill and Ted's Excellent Adventure,* which had just been released.

My friend Jeanne Giles was diagnosed with breast cancer some years later when she was only thirty-seven. She photographed the families and friends of people who'd had breast cancer in order to demonstrate how the disease "touches the circle of all the people a woman loves." The show is called *The Circle Project* and tours the country. It vividly illustrates the long shadow cast by cancer. I fell into its shadow in those years, though I didn't fully understand it until Jeanne showed me.

A strange thing had happened to me right after Carolyn's surgery when we were still in the hospital. Because, as Jeanne would attest, it isn't just the patient who goes to the hospital, nor even under the knife. Many lives are cut by every stroke of the blade. I was looking out the window during one of those days, then, sitting with Carolyn, surrounded by the flowers and balloons that people had sent and all the photographs of family that we'd pasted to the walls to remind her of all the support she had. To remind her of the reason she was returning to us. I don't think she needed reminding. I think the truth of her ability to survive was her innate resilience. Hardiness, they call it.

For a long time psychologists and psychiatrists didn't believe in resilience. Most people will have a traumatic experience at some point. And most will then do something remarkable: they'll snap out of it. Or they'll work their way out. Or they'll crawl out on hands and knees. But they will move on. Most people find ways of coping, strategies for adapting, and their negative thoughts and feelings pass. They get busy getting on with their lives.

I think Carolyn's decision to redecorate the house right after she was diagnosed was such a strategy. It made perfect sense. The house was an extension of her self. And in the shock and fear and loss of control that surrounded her diagnosis, redecorating the house was a way of making that part of herself whole again. By the time she was undergoing chemotherapy, the remodeling was finished, and she could live in it and draw from it a feeling of new wholeness, not to mention aesthetic pleasure. In her brain, she could make new maps of the house as she made new maps of her body. Finding joy is part of being well. She took ballet classes with the girls, went ice skating, took tap dancing lessons, and on the first anniversary of her surgery we went to Paris together on the theory that you can't feel too sorry for yourself if you're in Paris. Which brings me to the strange thing that happened to me in the hospital.

I'm not the tap dancing kind. I don't do much ballet either. Although I ice skated a lot with Amelia when she was little, I found it interesting only because it gave me an opportunity to spend time with Amelia. I don't get much out of redecorating either. But as I sat in the hospital room in the days immediately after Carolyn's surgery, staring out the window, out of the blue, so to speak, I had this thought: this seems like a good time to start flying upside-down. I guess everybody is wired differently. Suddenly, looking out the window, I thought that would be the most therapeutic thing I could do at that juncture in my life.

I had started flying small airplanes about fifteen years earlier, but I hadn't flown in a couple of years. Carolyn was perhaps a day or two from going home at that point. I turned to her and asked, "Do you mind if I go back to flying?" I didn't mention the upside-down part.

She said, "No, I don't mind. Go. You should go." She was lying propped up in bed, flat as a paper doll, looking out the window at the majestic view of the industrial works and the rail lines, smoke and steam rising in white flags. "I'll think of you up there."

Cancer doesn't end like other diseases. It just goes on and on. It's a major change in life, and it stays changed, and it gets stranger as time goes on. We were part of the system then, as if we'd joined a cult: the money was flowing at an alarming rate, and we had zoomed past important questions into the world of "winners" who had "beaten" cancer. We even wound up on TV somehow, and in the hot lights when the hostess asked me how breast cancer had changed my life, I was suddenly seized by the nearly irresistible impulse to leap across the stage and strangle her on live television. But I muttered something about not wanting to be the Man of Steel anymore, and everyone laughed, and the show went on. At that point, we still hadn't completed all the reconstructive surgery and the surgery to correct that surgery.

It was spring again, the time to go through the annual hall of fire at the hospital, the iodine injections, bone scans, X-rays, and all the concentration camp tests that could be dreamed up in the thrall of greater profits—barium enemas, the tomography scan, the blood tests and needles and the basket of plastic snakes. Since no one has discovered a test for cancer, the strategy was to assault the walls of the citadel of the flesh from all sides at once until a bright light would shine through it.

Breast cancer is a family disease. Suddenly life is slit open, and you find everyone peering in, asking questions they'd never think to ask otherwise. For two years, I was afraid to walk along the street in my own hometown, because no matter who I ran into, the question was the same: "How's Carolyn? So, any signs of . . . you know . . . "

———————

Her breast cancer of 1988 never came back. But in 2007, she was diagnosed with peritoneal cancer, which is the same disease as ovarian cancer. Carolyn and I are not married any longer, but we are family. We get together and have family dinners. We celebrate holidays together and the birthdays of our daughters, Elena and Amelia, and my son,

Jonas. Many times my wife Debbie and I took Carolyn to chemotherapy, sometimes with Elena and Amelia, and everyone brought along snacks and music and movies to watch. We became a notorious crew at the hospital, because when Carolyn had chemotherapy, a party would erupt and sometimes spill over into the halls. We all sat in on appointments with her doctors and took notes to keep the medical establishment honest.

She went through rounds of chemotherapy and long periods of reprieve. Near the end in the spring of 2012, the first time she met the palliative care doctor, who calls himself Dr. Mike, he asked when she had been diagnosed. When she told him, he said, "You've lived a long time."

A long time! She was sixty-five years old, and her first grandchild had just turned one. How about seeing him graduate high school? College? How about him just remembering who she was? It was outrageous. The whole thing was vile.

But the cancer had become resistant to treatment. Carolyn gradually became weaker and less able to eat. We were in Dr. Mike's office, and he was encouraging her to get in a hospice program. As weak as she was, as foul as she felt, she was sitting up, saying, "What are you talking about?" In the days to come she grew rapidly weaker. Her condition deteriorated so fast that it was shocking.

As I write this, only weeks after that first conversation with Dr. Mike, we have installed a bed in the first floor of her two-story house, and all of us—friends and family alike—are taking turns being with her. As weak as she is, Carolyn is reveling in her new role as a grandmother to little Emmett. I have sat with her many a day, as I sat with her in the past in many a hospital recovery room and through many rounds of chemotherapy. Even in this dire circumstance, she is one of the resilient people, the hardy people, as her parents were in their time. Her Polish mother and father both survived cancers that doctors had expected to kill them. Her father survived malignant melanoma. When her mother had lymphoma, the doctors wanted to amputate her leg, and she said, "Are you crazy? I have to dance on that leg." And her parents kept on dancing well into their eighties and lived into their nineties.

As we go through this struggle, I see my daughters rise to towering stature as women of great strength and fortitude and even wisdom. I knew them as children, and although I assumed the depth of their compassion and abilities, I had never seen it so powerfully demonstrated before now, as we travel together into uncharted territory. This is April. Amelia has scheduled her marriage to Terry in November. Clearly, the date is not tenable. Carolyn can barely speak. A voluble thinker, a literary force, she has been reduced to a whisper. Amelia moved the date up to April 21, and today she and Terry were married in a brief but beautiful ceremony in their church. The priest, Father Chris, was respectful, even eloquent, and when the surprise operatic singer broke into "Ave Maria" at the end, Carolyn smiled and nodded, as if to say: *That's the wedding I was looking for.* We are gathered around her now, a tribe around a low fire in the middle of these wild nights. We don't know what will come, only that we face it together. Carolyn is choosing the music for a party that she will not attend. And if Carolyn and the girls were ever good at anything, it was throwing a party.

Carolyn's life has been completely dedicated to art. Amazing art. She made her own clothes. She turned ordinary objects into beautiful experiences that arrested you as you walked into a room. She dedicated her life to making life beautiful for others as well as for herself. And she was dedicated to spending life, not saving it. She had a deep philosophy of living for the moment, because she knew that it was fleeting.

On one particular day I remember from recent times, I was driving Carolyn home from an appointment with one of her doctors. I'd shuttled her there because her arm was broken, and she couldn't drive. She'd been ice-skating, celebrating life, when a small boy torpedoed her. I asked if she had developed a conscious strategy of adaptation through all that she'd been through.

She smiled and said, "Keep on dancing."

BUSH PILOTS

Kotzebue, Alaska, is a village of rusted ductwork and plywood sheds for homes and house trailers up on cinderblock footings and mudhole gravel streets (and two old, old log cabins), where Eskimos live mostly with no running water, among agonized blossoms of twisted pipe that bloom in fields of low and leathery grass. Little scoured backpaths cut through shoulder-high scrub and sedge, where great oxidized brambles of furred steel fittings and scaly aluminum conduit spring up, the squalid littoral, purlieu of scavenger birds and of tundra rats and four-wheeled ATVs on the salty permafrost tableland. Wash hangs in the icy breeze. Every other house is bedecked with weathered hides and horns set on galvanized steel roofs or nailed to the outer walls. Forsaken sled dogs whimper in their chains. The only pavement other than the airport ramps lies on the parking apron of the National Bank, where lithe and limber Eskimo girls in sheaths of spandex flow back and forth on rollerblades at sundown before this pearl of cast concrete and glass set among the shacks.

One Sunday morning, waiting for a bush pilot to take me out, I had wandered to the eastern end of the airstrip and watched the sun rise. Here, thirty miles above the arctic circle, it wouldn't rise until after eight-thirty, and Kotzebue was losing more than ten minutes of light every day. Within the week, the sun would rise at nine-thirty. Within a month it wouldn't come up until noon. Even now the first cerise rays tunneled through the last dark fungus of clouds, revealing a daylight luminescence, the sapphire sky far above. The sun did not so much rise as it stalled. Small and tarnished and solidifying like a bead of molten glass from which the flame has been withdrawn, it scraped along the level hills beyond the quicksilver surface of the sound.

Still no sign of Jim Rood. I wandered around a hangar that bore a sign proclaiming, "Alaska International Air." The rear door, wide as a wall, was raised a few inches off the concrete footing. I knelt in the parking lot among weeds and oilcans, and peered into the darkness beneath the doorseal. A bear claw? Yes, a great black bear claw reached out of darkness toward me. Reek of carrion.

I walked around the side, climbing a fence to get past airport security, and found a severed caribou skull, still festooned with green dissolving clots of meat. The cervical vertebra of a Greenland right whale, famed of *Moby Dick*, lay among truck parts and thistles. Around on the ramp side of the building, where Rood would park his plane when he arrived, I found a small man-sized door. I pulled it open, and the stench of rotting flesh hit me. As my eyes adjusted to the darkness, I could see that five moose and countless caribou lay slaughtered and decomposing on wooden pallets in cheesecloth game bags or shiny black garbage bags or just in scattered heaps of blackening meat left out in the open in that great empty cavern of silver insulation, large enough to hold four or five old-fashioned DC-3s.

The darkness deepened as I moved farther from the framed patch of white sunlight through which I'd stepped. Blue and brown plastic tarps hung from rafters. I pushed past a dozen tan dog cages, a shattered bubble helicopter, and meat boxes labeled "TOFU WO CHONG SF, CA." I stumbled in darkness upon the flensed hide of the bear I had seen. It had been salted and now lay supine as if submitting in its leisure to the tedious tanning of time itself. Far in back, a large shop and a small office with heater and telephone and scheduled trips on a grease-pencil board.

I stepped back through the burning white threshold and blindly waited for Jim. My shadow fell far across the ramp like a thin and strangely jointed puppet. Presently, Jim Rood came taxiing up in his red Piper Super Cub. It wore a set of Racemasters, the so-called wrinklewalls, drag racing tires so deflated that the sides caved and cracked. He was in his late fifties and wore a perpetual expression of quiet, studied pessimism beneath his institutional-looking clear plastic spectacles and the black baseball cap with his company's logo: Northwestern Aviation. He had a dim, abstracted, and diffident air, a face cool and bland on the surface but betraying here and there the hints of a fitful inner counsel he kept with himself. His navy blue jumpsuit was clean. He put tarps under the meat he carried so that his plane would stay clean. His largest item of luggage was his survival bag.

He'd just brought a hunter in from several days in the bush. I overheard Jim say, "I'm sorry you saw so many people." Then he motioned for me to get in, muttered something about the fire extinguisher being under his seat, and taxied out. He turned sideways on the big runway, and for a moment I thought he was running up the engine. Bush pilots always take off and land as directly into the wind as possible, but some, I suppose, take it to an extreme that I wasn't prepared for. He took off *across* the 150-foot width of the asphalt runway rather than use its 5,900-foot length. No takeoff run. We rose as in an elevator.

Cruising out over the sound into a bank of low thin clouds and haze, Jim held the stick between his knees and poured himself coffee from a thermos. As tundra sneaked beneath our wings, he told me about his life. In 1969 Jim came to Anchorage from a machinist's job in upstate New York. He met a girl. So often a bush pilot's tale turns on the meeting of a girl. They lived in the bush for three years. Her father, a guide, had two Super Cubs. "I arrived with five hundred dollars, and I didn't know anybody." Jim spoke easily through the headsets we wore. "Then I met him. He was a good-hearted con artist, and the girl was a wild child. I worked the season and used the Super Cub to get my license. It was an outlaw operation. I flew side-by-side with him, flying formation." Jim and the girl lived in a bush cabin until 1972. Then in 1973 he went to Kotzebue for a two-week job ferrying oil exploration crews for Buck Maxin, an old-time bush pilot who was legendary in the area. Jim Rood never left.

He worked for Buck until 1978, when Buck retired. Jim bought the business and Maxin's coveted Part 135 certificate, the federal license essential to being in the charter business. But Buck apparently couldn't stay away. When I was there, he was at the other end of the field flying float planes. He and Jim weren't on speaking terms.

Along the way, the loneliness deepened, became chronic. He had two sons in Kotzebue from different women he called Eskimo girls. "I'm living with a girl now. I still maintain contact with the boys, but

I don't get along with their mothers too well." So often a bush pilot's tale turns on the girl estranged, the sons not seen nearly enough.

We fell through whistling snow to a river bottom called Hugo Creek and followed the fork upstream to a narrow crevasse it had cut in the tundra, as if acid, not water, flowed among the stones. Gold lived in the land, and blooms of blazing quartz exploded here and there from the pastel earth. Wild grottoes of time-eaten sediment beckoned from cornice and plinth. A brown stain down the mountainside, the slack ejaculation of mud, a recent avalanche. Herds of caribou shuttled across the boreal plain and through the forest like brown bubbles shifting and rising in a jade sea. On the high entablature of one white mountain someone had painstakingly spelled out, in stones, "Jesus Loves You."

We flew up the Agashashok River in a small valley of rolling brown tundra with hundreds, maybe thousands, of caribou fleeing our footprint of sound. Chalk-white gravel bars appeared in ice-clad waters that riffled along in shallow serpentine channels. Moth-like movements of the Cub within a wingspan of the gravel and the gin-clear water, a splendid moment of singularities: gravity and wind tugging on us as we pivoted slowly there, almost stopped on air, yet revolving somehow, as Jim looked over the gravel bar for changes since his last visit. "Aw, the wind's shifted," he complained, then banked the other way. It was all so smooth, like a dream of flying, as if we were a picture painted on Chinese silk, unraveling over the river in a silent, ceaseless ribbon. Then we were earthbound, still. Jim was so proficient and his touch so effortless that I scarcely understood what he had done. One moment we rotated on a wingtip. The next we walked a gravel bar in a landscape that no one on earth could imagine, the hazy rock of the distant Brooks Range like a great machine that had seized in the midst of its terrible motion. Jim stuffed his hands in his pockets and inspected the gravel bar with a proprietary air. "I spent four hours cleaning up this strip the other day," he said. The bush pilots find their own places to land and claim them by cleaning them of logs and large rocks, perhaps filling in low places with smaller stones or putting up a bit of cloth on a stick for a wind sock.

The talky stream was clotted with frail reefs of translucent ice. We walked away from each other, and I turned to watch him in his blue jumpsuit, like some mislaid attendant, small and lost in this bewildering landscape: the hacked and pallid peaks around us and the trembling earthen sky shot with capes of cobalt blue. A far copse, the spikes of scrawny stilted trees, then hordes of them more distant. Jim unzipped his fly and urinated on the stones. Then he blew his nose loudly into a white handkerchief he took from a concealed pocket. He looked up at ravens passing overhead, squawking in their powerful contraltos. Then it was so quiet that their huge black wings cut the cold air with a sound like tearing silk. Jim knelt at the stream and put his face in the water and drank like a wolf. Then he crossed to me and said, "I'd like to leave you here for a few hours just to enjoy the landscape, but I'm afraid I might not get back." I thought: Yes. Leave me here and don't come back. For what was this landscape if not the very isomer of our loneliness? I asked Jim about his own loneliness, and he said, "I like to go where nobody knows me and forget everything."

But I couldn't stay, not at least without tent and sleeping bag. Not without a gun. So I climbed back into the Cub with Jim, and we took off. Jim squeezed out that last inch of flaps with the handle as we lifted off the river bottom. We flew low up the river, searching for new places to land. Surviving the landings was not the biggest challenge. It was getting out again if the airplane was damaged in landing. The pilots refer to the places they land as airports. "This'd be a good airport," Jim said of one gravel bar, "except for a few big rocks."

We retraced Hugo Creek to the south, and something caught my eye. "I think there's a hunter down there," I said.

"No, I don't think so," he said, circling.

"Well, there's a dead caribou," I said.

He dipped a wing. "Look," he pointed. Then the picture resolved itself, and I saw: two wolves had killed a caribou and were sharing it with a dozen carrion birds. At our approach they scattered, twisting and snarling up at us. One was an enormous black male, bigger than any dog. Its companion was a beautiful silver-gray female. The Brooks Range hung faintly all around them in dream curtains of bluish ether and around us as we wheeled on the scene of the kill. Now, running for their lives, the wolf couple flowed over the land, she like mercury, he like a supernatural oil. I could see the big black one abandon himself to the urge of flight, allowing all that is brutal, willful, and delicious about the savage necessity of survival to pour through him and turning now and then to display his countenance, his body twisted in its passage up the hillside, tongue flashing pink and atavistic, and his huge shoulders rolling smooth and loose in his marvelous hide as he scrambled up the scree to evade us, vanishing now in withered clefts of stone with the warm heart of a caribou fresh in his gut.

We veered away, leaving the couple to its mountain keeps. The slag-like molten serpent's flow of the Agashashok drainage poured through slits of tundra grass, as sunlight candled distant clouds and spilled in silken swarms of rays and pooled in bright lagoons.

Across the field from Jim Rood's operation was Alaska Island Air, a bush pilot service that delivered mail and flew charter and ferried hunters and fishermen into the wild. Before the company changed its name, it was called Ram Air, and the business cards advertised such hyperbole as counterinsurgency, small land wars, and revolution. Its owner, Mike Spisak, said, "Our motto was we fly anyone anywhere, anytime." Blond, clean-shaven, and youthful, Mike was a contrast to most bush pilots I met, who gave the outward appearance of men who had come to Alaska to wrestle grizzly bears. In jeans and a Columbia nylon jacket, Mike, although usually covered with grease and dust, gave off the impression of being a kid from the suburbs. He had a chance to play college baseball ("Pitcher, of course," he said modestly), but he came up here instead. When I first arrived, he pointed at me and ordered one of his pilots, "Take this guy out and get some grease on those pants."

The Alaska Island Air offices were nothing but a simple shed with white walls, fluorescent lights, a desk with a computer, apparatus for brewing coffee, and the state-record arctic char on the wall above the contour map of Alaska. In Mike's small office, a .22 rifle leaned against a bookshelf, "my dog killer," he called it. Outside on the gravel ramp where the airplanes parked lay skids of caribou and moose, cut up and packed in boxes or in bloody game bags in the open. Mongrel dogs were forever stealing bits of rotted gristle.

One morning Mike's copilot, Kerry Cope, drove out across the ramp in a shattered truck to load the DC-3 for a mail run to the villages. A restless wind gathered snow around our feet. Although an FAA flight service station operated on the field, along with the National Weather Service office located just behind it, and although the Federal Aviation Administration sent up weather balloons twice a day to formulate its detailed predictions, I saw no pilot obtain a weather briefing at any time before a flight.

If you'd like to roll back the clock to the days of Antoine de Saint-Exupéry and the airmail flights over the Andes, the days of his famous novel *Night Flight*, it's just a matter of going to the Arctic and flying the mail in a DC-3. Ours was a 1944 model that still bore the stretcher hooks and ashtrays from its days as a hospital ship for soldiers wounded in World War Two.

Using cables and come-alongs, Kerry and I winched skids of Coke tight behind the pilot's seat, and then we strapped them down with nylon belts. We loaded crates of valve fittings. We carried Lexan panels that caught the wind like kites. We hoisted radio antennas and strapped them in. This stevedore activity, as much as anything, was bush pilot work.

When we had filled the plane with cargo, we topped off the tanks from a rusted old fuel truck, which ran out of fuel halfway through the operation. It had to be filled itself from a newer fuel truck that moved about the field on a continuous circuit, servicing aircraft. Mike came out of the office, calling "Clear!" as he shrugged past the pallets, and he was cranking the right engine even before Kerry and I came scrambling up the ladder to strap ourselves in. "I hope you don't have any other plans for today," he shouted at me over the noise of the battering propeller blades, dropping a spare headset on the floor for me to pick up. Or not. His insouciance went beyond ordinary rudeness into a realm of hard-ass pilot style not even seen among fighter pilots.

"Why?" I asked.

"Because we're going to Barrow," he said, cranking the left engine. A huge greasy eruption of smoke filled the air behind us and billowed away in the prop wash, rolling across the ramp like a giant tumbleweed.

The DC-3 was a wonderful contraption of pleated aluminum

painted gray and green and lathered with a deep meringue of adhesive soot and crystallized grease, which grew everywhere around us like a fungus and migrated in the crevices beneath our feet. Knobs of the garden faucet variety hung from pipes and plumbing such as you'd expect to see in a basement.

"Forty-seven on take off," Mike told Kerry, and a moment later we were rolling down one of the few paved runways above the arctic circle. Kerry set the throttles, tuning them with the precision and care of a symphony player. One characteristic bush pilots share by necessity is a light and delicate touch, a smoothness on the controls that makes ordinary pilots seem clumsy.

Mike steered the big plane with soft dream-like motions of his feet and let it lift gently from the runway, as Kerry tilted his head to the side as if listening and moved the throttles by millimeters with thumb and forefinger, setting forty-seven inches of manifold pressure as requested. The airplane clattered and shook as if an angry old bird had been caught in a flimsy cage.

We departed flat out over the water, topping a small hill. Mike said, "Gear up." Then: "Climb power." Kerry powered up the hydraulic system, then lifted the squat yellow gear lever on the floor, and the wheels struggled into the belly with a groan and a thump. He reduced manifold pressure for the long slow climb and set the red mixture knobs to auto-lean. With thumb and forefinger, he delicately rocked them back and forth to check that they were locked in place. I saw a strange beauty in every part of the plane. The pool-ball-white prop controls were crazed with a black reticulation of age and of the human tradesman's oily hand.

I sat in the jump seat between them, with the old radio bay all but empty beside me. A few items of ancient vacuum tube equipment lay dead inside it. The old crank-style ADF radios were still in use. We flew at two hundred feet over a roadless tundra infiltrated with lakes, rivers, pools, swamps, and invaginations of the ever-leaching sea. The snow-covered mountains in the distance were shot with sunlight through a hole in the iron overcast. The tundra was spongy, yellow-brown, pocked and whorled like the brains of slain giants laid out flat to dry. Occasional twisting lines of trees marked the river's course. A dozen caribou spilled forth as we dialed in the 070 heading directed by the GPS and climbed to six hundred feet. Bush pilots fly low. One reason they don't often check the weather is that they are usually beneath it. Besides, it is an academic question: they have to go anyway. One bush pilot told me, "If you're training a new pilot, you take him out and make him fly the route at fifty feet, because one day he'll have to do it anyway. He might as well know what it looks like."

As we hammered on toward the northeast, Mike reminisced about the old Ram Air days. "When we started, we were the biggest bandits up here. The FAA had a picture of me on the wall they used as a dartboard." They all take pride in their banditry. They're all, of course, reformed. A bandit, in bush pilot terminology, is someone who operates extralegally, running charter flights without a Part 135 certificate. "We used to fly seven a.m. until two a.m. then get three hours of sleep, get back up, and do it all over again." It's illegal for a commercial pilot to fly more than eight hours each day, but no one I met adhered to that. "We'd log three hundred hours a month, fly external loads, you name it. Kerry and I were a lot more exciting. You've got to remember that up here everything you do is to make money."

Every bush pilot I met seemed to subscribe to this fiction: the Get-Rich-in-Alaska Myth. The truth was that they lived in squalor, in wretched shacks and house trailers, in conditions befitting a wartime outpost. The cost of living was devastating. The pay was spotty. Mike was an exception. By spending himself at a prodigious rate, by aggression and lunacy that went far beyond that of the ordinary bush pilot, he had succeeded in putting together a large operation. When I asked him, "What's your dream?" he said, "This is my dream. I've achieved my dream."

Look. A settlement in the distance. White gleam of rooftin and the black rhomboids of primitive architecture. Frail bars of tea-smoked sunlight passed through luminous clouds of steam. A smooth landing on a gravel strip. The sign on the shed said "Selawik, Home of the Wolves." And it was.

Men in hooded, grease-dimmed coveralls descended upon us in growling four-wheel Honda ATVs. The wind seemed worse up there. We unloaded three skids of Coke and Dr. Pepper and 7Up, the stuff of civilization in a town that had no roads. A wooden walkway led from the gravel airport out among the crude and solitary shanties thatched with steel, each issuing a flag of smoke into the clay banks of cloud. Afar, a yellow diesel backhoe reared up, the frozen and improbable guardian of these forsaken ramparts thrown up in haste against the nothingness.

When we had finished loading, my head and hands ached from the cold, and my back hurt. Before I snapped my seatbelt on, Mike was cranking the right engine again, shrouding the men in smoke as they ripped apart the pallets. He hogged the DC-3 out of there, shortfield, calling "Gear up!" as we cleared the gravel. Around the corner at 130 knots to heading of 352 degrees for Barrow, the farthest point north in the United States.

We clamored through clouds, then drifted between ethereal pennants of vapor on our way to ninety-five hundred, sandwiched between layers of gray—then grayer—darkness as we drove on toward an area of light, shining like the end of a tunnel. Somewhere shy of infinity we were swallowed again in the murky abstraction of the mist.

Now a fractal vegetation of ice began to grow on the windshield. Through cracks in the emergency exit I could see the flickering light of the cloud mass through which we were passing like a cold fire burning in a dark hearth. The door was rattling, and I finally noticed that my whole left side was cold from the wind coming through the cracks. I stuck my hand through the open doorway behind me and felt a wall of icy air in the cargo bay. This plane was a maze of dark green-painted recesses and insulation, padding, exposed wires, and fuel lines.

I looked up: now we were driving through snow. I jabbed Kerry's shoulder. "Are we on an IFR flight plan?" I asked. He shook his head, "No." I asked him how we were supposed to avoid hitting someone else. "There's nobody else up here," he said.

"Is it legal?" I asked.

He shrugged.

The snow accreted on the windscreen flake by flake. Mike called for alcohol, and I turned the valve, but nothing happened. "Maybe it's empty," Mike said, and I wondered what else was empty that we didn't know about on this airplane of my father's youth. Kerry steadied the

BUSH PILOTS

throttles and prop, adjusting as we went. The steady throb of the engines shifted, settled, and synchronized once more. He set in a small amount of carburetor heat. The old plane required constant attention. Kerry pulled the gear lever up over and over as we flew, and each time it would sag again in flight. Before the flight, we had poured about twenty-five gallons of oil from a steel drum into gas cans to carry for the two great rotary engines. The cowlings were black with oil.

The snow stopped as we proceeded out over the Brooks Range at ninety-five hundred. I poured coffee into Styrofoam cups from a battered stainless-steel Stanley bottle and studied the CC-8 WAC chart, on which I found no settlement until Barrow. One tractor trail left its spider track, and a pinpoint along it bore the name Brady, and then other than an abandoned cabin here and there, nothing for the next 280 miles. The maximum elevation figures showed that fifty-three hundred would clear the highest peaks, but despite their relatively low elevation, the mountains were forbidding. When once the mists parted for a moment, we could see through the gray and hazy clouds, plunging down and down in stained and dreary chasms, that were we to ditch, we'd have no prospect of rescue. We'd be on our own. The clouds closed up once again, and I was relieved. I'd rather not see that truth.

Mike got up and tapped me on the shoulder, jerking his thumb at the cockpit. I was to fly to Barrow. I settled into the ancient seat and strapped in, taking the controls, turning left and right to feel the feel of things. A big airplane. Slow and heavy. The yoke was large and felt like the old black steering wheel of my father's 1950 Ford, cast from a fractured Bakelite analog.

The snow began again. We entered an area of turbulence. Mike and Kerry joked and drank coffee, and when a hole opened up again we could see the Noatak River. "That's that gravel bar that gave me such a hard time last year," Mike told Kerry. We looked down on the tortuous course of the river flanked by intermittent gravel bars, all ivory cut with curving pearly tributaries. The ADF was picking up staccato Russian civilian radio broadcasts.

I backed off on the throttles to begin the long slow descent. I checked the chart. North of Barrow, it read, simply, *pack ice*. We were heading for the Arctic Ocean. There is something keen and hard and vivid about flying into a cloudbank at four thousand feet, talking to no one, on no flight plan, with no weather report. Such a ritual as this, as much as anything I've seen up here, is the wilderness of it all, the wildness, the gear of insanity that makes us mesh with this alien land. Pilots and other people up here give themselves over to being lost in ways that we can't or won't tolerate back home.

Mike had told a story about the days when he ferried fuel to the gold mines in a converted crop duster called an AgTruck. He was hauling 270 gallons on each trip, five trips a day, to "a one-way, dogshit, dogleg strip with a bluff at one end and no way out when the wind was blowing wrong." Once he had been unable to get in for several days, when the miners called to let him know he could come on out, the wind was just right. Mike was naive back then and had no way of knowing that they were lying just to get fuel for their mining operations.

The normal weight of the plane was twenty-three hundred pounds, and he was grossly overweight at forty-five hundred. He came staggering in behind the power curve, a condition of extremely slow flight, in which the drag of the airplane pushing through the air becomes greater than the lift the wings can produce. Behind the power curve it takes *more* power to go slower. Under those conditions, he had one try.

A creek just before the strip meant that he could not land short without tearing off his landing gear. He knew that if he didn't hit the first thirty feet of runway, he'd hit the cliff at the other end. That was the moment bush pilots train for.

By the time he saw that the wind was blowing in the *wrong direction*, by the time he understood that they had *lied to him*, it was too late. "I touched, bounced, then railed it and pulled the lever to dump the load of fuel." Fortunately, crop dusters, such as the AgTruck, have a mechanism for unloading, at an instant, the fluids they carry. "Those two guys were standing there waiting for me, and I douched them with 270 gallons of diesel. Of course, without the weight my trim went to shit, and with full power I shot straight up like a rocket. Since the ceiling was only a thousand feet overcast, I immediately found myself in the clouds at about sixty-five hundred feet. All I had was a turn-and-bank indicator and a compass, no instruments, no approach plates, nothing. Well, I knew it was thirty-five minutes back to Kotzebue, so I turned to my heading and timed it. I descended where I thought Kotzebue ought to be and broke out at four hundred feet over the open ocean. There was no land anywhere in *any direction*." With more tailwind than he'd anticipated, he had accidentally passed Kotzebue and flown forty miles out over the ocean toward Russia. He had no way of knowing precisely where he was, but he picked a compass direction out of a hat and headed back. As luck would have it, he struggled back to Kotzebue with the ocean licking at his wheels.

I gave the controls to Mike for the landing. The windshield went all Christmasy, as coronets of ice spun about the windowlights like a celestial vespine clockwork. We broke out at sixteen hundred feet over frozen tundra. A flat earth. Legion the dragons of snow and fog leaching down through optic gloom to touch sienna soil and filter through the lakes of pale ice. I turned to fiddle with the alcohol again, perhaps to clear the windshield before landing. Then I noticed the small placard that said, "Remove tank before going into Combat." We slid onto the runway so smoothly that I hardly felt the commotion of the wheels on gravel.

It was fifteen below zero when Mike leaped out of the cargo door at Barrow, Alaska, and dashed across the ramp to relieve himself. It was September 17, and in a phone call to my daughters, Elena and Amelia, I'd heard earlier that it was going to be ninety degrees down in Illinois that morning. Kerry and I fetched the ladder out of the cargo hold and put covers over the engines to keep the oil warm.

I stood on the edge of the Arctic Ocean and looked all around me, turning in a complete circle. When we learn to fly, our old world drops away, and we learn the new and subtle cues of another world. So when we come to the Arctic, that familiar world of the pilot drops away, and this is what we find. The sunlight was bright but sourceless, unreal, as if we stood for an overlit studio portrait in a luminous rice paper world. The land was not entirely featureless, but low and flat, stretching out to the seamless wonder of infinity.

We left the Barrow ground crew to load the DC-3 with more cargo and walked across the gravel expanse to eat at the Japanese restaurant that had recently opened there. Mike seemed to have two moods, one grim and brooding and introspective, the other explosive, deranged, and beset with a diabolical glee. When it came to food, he grew expansive. He came to Alaska in 1979. By 1982, he was "hooked for good." He originally worked for his father-in-law (another tale that turned on the favors of a girl) who was the operations agent for Wein Airlines, the only airline in Kotzebue at the time. Mike was flying commercially by 1984. Money, of course, was his motivation. But he also wanted something almost everyone who came up here wanted. The pilots all have different names for it. Some call it independence. Others say, "I wanted to be my own boss." But I thought again of what Jim Rood had told me: "I like to go where nobody knows me and forget everything." I thought of him now, wistfully regretting that he could not leave me in the wilderness. The decision to live in the Arctic, to fly under such extreme conditions, is a reckless measure that could be propelled only by affairs of the heart and spirit that cannot be fully told.

Mike learned to fly in a Taylorcraft and used to fly people in it as an assistant guide. He graduated to a Cessna 170-B and flew that as a guide for a while, too. He went to Fairbanks with a commercial pilot's license and an instrument rating on December 23, and on December 24, he was on his way back with a Part 135 certificate, the official document that allows one to operate charter and scheduled services. He moved up to a Cessna 206, a good economical six-seater capable of carrying a big load and landing short. Along the way he had Super Cubs, AgTrucks, Cessna light twins, a Turbo 207, three 402s (bigger twins), and now the DC-3. Along the way, he beat out everyone for the mail and cargo business.

As we waited in the vast plywood restaurant for our lunch, Mike and Kerry fell to telling stories, and they laughed until their eyes watered. Mike told of the good old days, when they'd break the spar on a Super Cub's wing and have to ferry it out.

"Ferry it out?" I asked. "How can you ferry a plane with a broken spar?" This being the structural beam that runs transversely through a wing and makes it a wing in the first place.

"Easy," he said. "You cut off the fabric and shove a log through the wings. You tape the log to the spar with one-hundred-mile-an-hour tape," by which he meant duct tape. "Then you take one of those blue plastic tarps, wrap the wing in it, tape the tarp to the wing, and fly it the hell out." Peals of laughter. Amazing platters of seafood began to arrive. Silence fell.

When we headed out of Barrow for Peard Bay, the wind was blowing aloft, and chaplets of foam fanned out from treacherous towering whitecaps below. Great wheeling blades of sunlight pierced dark voluptuous clouds. We flew at one thousand feet over the ocean with radio chatter in the background. Two pilots were shooting the breeze. It was like eavesdropping on the spirit world. Point Franklin passed below, just a thin spit of beach carved by the waves and separated from the land by water just north of Wainwright. As far from civilization as it was, the sand was littered with fifty-five-gallon drums from sea traffic, and as Mike let down to wavetop level, I stood between him and Kerry, roaring along at 160 knots, surfing the turbulence, and I could feel our speed, our tremendous momentum, our marvelous audacity in being there, ripping along on the edge of the world with bleached white deadwood trees that had drifted in from Asia, flickering past beneath our wings. You have to know what you're doing to fly this low. An ancient wrecked whaler, a defiled carcass of ribs, was gone in a flash. An abandoned fishing shack. The smoky mystery of the landscape spinning by in dancing motes of yellow light.

We dropped cargo at Wainwright, lifting one thousand pounds of pipe fittings and handing them down to ground crew, growing colder and colder as the day wore on and exhaustion set in. Mike was the boss and didn't have to, but he worked as hard as anyone, hogging pallets around for the forklift to carry from the bay and hefting boxes and boxes of steel valves. The villages we visited were gravel strips set beside boardwalk communities that looked as if they could be dismantled in an afternoon, warrens of beaverboard and galvanized steel, littered with the trash of constant construction, sheet metal, Tyvek, and nail-gun ammunition.

At Point Lay the DEW line looked like a space ship that had just landed, bright and new and geodesic, pale green house trailers coupled into rows of offices behind razor wire. People would come out to the plane on four-wheel Hondas through the incessant whistling of the wind to holler their requests. "Anything for CTS Construction?" Mike shook his head, and the man in the yellow construction worker's parka flipped the motorcycle throttle and spun away in a cloud of dust. This is the last frontier, then, just like the Alaska license plates say, but they're building it so fast that it won't be for long. The license plates ought to say, "Alaska: Hardhat Area."

———————

We were done unloading cargo for the day. Mike took off, and I crawled into the empty bay for the ride home. Tops at twenty-eight hundred, we burst into bright sunshine. I sat on a cardboard scrap on the cold floor, looking out, feeling the rumbling vibrations of old, old times. The ashtray beside my arm was painted white. Asbestos padding, old fittings for stretchers, and grease and gravel embedded in chewed plywood, heel-gnawed and stricken with the disease of time. The doors barely fit anymore. I could see the whistling white world out there and feel the bitter cold. Wind whipped the bungees and cargo straps, hanging empty now. I put up the hood of my parka against the cold. Around me: chain and ladders and oil and a roll of paper towels bolted to the wall, a lonely pennant that gradually unwound in the fitful draft that rummaged in my bones. My father had a photo he took from the window of a B-17 he was piloting in the year this airplane was built, and it looked just like my view now of that rounded aluminum wing over those sun-shot clouds in this strange northern place.

Heading back at eighty-five hundred I could see the jagged black and white brilliance of the Brooks Range gutting the cloudbank fifty miles ahead. Bright cumulus at sunset, illuminated from above, made secret dusky grottoes of the world. The moon rose full against shirred clouds, freaking the mountains in a frenzied cross-hatching.

We encountered a large and perfectly formed lenticular cloud as we came up over the range, signal of the wrecking-ball winds there. In a few minutes we were kicked all around the sky with wild slamming gyrations. I took my seat and locked my seatbelt.

The clouds broke up below, revealing open bowls choked with snow and sandy cones and river bottoms. Dark began to claim the surrounding hills in bulky increments, these opaque palisades, sea reefs thrust up here by the accrual of eons, scarlet earth and razorous rock etched and gullied with the failing sun and low-order yellow growth in purple shadow on the scree slopes. Sooty, coal-colored, slatted mountains and the wild melee of stick-figure pines rushing down like the disruption of a puppet colony, frozen forever in this Pompeii of salmon-colored mist.

A huge valley opened up. Then more hills. Then tundra once again. We crossed the Brooks Range twice today.

Landing at Kotzebue, Mike called for flaps on the flare, even though we had plenty of runway. Just before we hit the ground, Kerry dumped the flaps, our residual lift, and the plane settled heavily as if a machine could be tired. The last rind of the sun, peeled and leaking, lay upon the unfractured pewter platter of the bay.

———————

At last, I found someone who could leave me in the wilderness, as Jim Rood had wanted to do. His name was Matt Owen, and he wore red long johns and ripped woolen pants and a grease-blackened baseball cap. A single black pigtail braided down his back past his waist. With his never-shaved full beard and a little gray creeping in, Matt looked like a real mountain man, as most men did after only a short time in this country. A few days earlier, Matt had inserted a friend of Mike's, a bush pilot named Glen Earls, into the Brooks Range to hunt caribou, and now Matt wanted to go check on Glen to see if he was ready to come out. Matt would drop me, and I'd stay with Glen and help him clean up his campsite.

At thirty-eight, Matt was a registered guide as well as a bush pilot. He had come to aviation by way of the family business. His father was Morris Owen, famed bush pilot, the only man to acquire an Airline Transport Pilot rating while blind in one eye, whose name appears in *Who's Who in Aviation* and who was taught to fly by Matt's uncle Jess, proprietor of Owen's Flying Service in Missoula, Montana. Morris Owen still ran Trans Mountain Flying Service when I flew with Matt.

Matt was supposedly one of Mike's pilots at Alaska Island Air, but Matt owned his own Super Cub, and Matt didn't exactly work for Mike. Matt worked out of Mike's offices. He was there every morning drinking Mike's coffee. I asked more than once about how this arrangement worked, but no one could quite describe the contract between Mike and his various pilots. No bush pilot wants to admit that he works for another man. Everyone has to be his own boss, an independent. They all just help one another out because that's the way it's done. Everything is voluntary, or it just doesn't happen.

As Matt and I were fueling the Cub out on the ramp early one morning, Mike came out and tossed me a blue sleeping bag, saying, "Take this." And with his best demonic grin: "Just in case I don't make it." It was Mike's job to retrieve me from the bush before night fell.

Matt and I took off into a sky that looked like wet concrete troweled in cold swirls. We crossed the Hotham Inlet at two hundred feet as flocks of trumpeter swans lifted at the sound of our clatter and drifted away over the mud flats. As we followed the scalloped jade course of the Noatak River, Canada geese flew south in elongated Vs, huge flocks rising and meshing with impossible precision. Half-moon gravel bars slipped beneath our wings. We spanned a forest of gaunt and bony pines. Soon we began to see herds of caribou, first in dozens, then in scores, and eventually by the thousands, flowing over the land with a smooth, unswerving, and purposeful concentration that seemed as unstoppable as the course of the river itself. A big bull moose concealed in pines swung its antlers, catching the light: this dark and ragged monolith of muscle carried an immense rack of bone like an unsheathed sawblade. Matt circled the Cub lower still, turning a wingtip on the tundra, then dove and climbed away.

A blond sow with black legs escorted three cubs through a clearing. Her rolling motion and the great hump on her back made her unmistakable as an arctic grizzly. A pulsing halo seemed to pursue and compass her as her honey hair was hived in the sun's rays. Even though we passed over at fifty feet, she reared up and undertook to strike us out of the air with her tremendous paw. Matt dipped a wing, and I found myself looking down her throat. Pink tongue, white teeth, the gliding scythe of claws that would have snatched us down to make mincemeat for her cubs. Stories passed among the pilots of grizzlies taking small airplanes out of the air that had flown too low. Certainly they were capable of it. Matt's plane was always bloody from caribou and moose meat, and bears had attacked it in the wild.

Another herd of caribou. Another great bull moose. Then a cow with calf, lying in a hollow of the land. We pressed on into the mountains upriver, crossing the Nana region, where six thousand Inupiaq Eskimos live in an area the size of Kansas. We found ourselves in an area of numerous white stone hills with flat tops of broken rock. With no intercom, Matt had to yell above the engine noise to speak to me. "You can land on any of those!" he shouted. "Problem is getting off again!"

From above we came upon a scene of fallen statuary, two great toppled caribou, one pointing east, one pointing west, with huge and complex antlers for antennae, harkening to the last dim message from the ether. And in between, fifty yards from each, an upright hominid, running and gesticulating and waving at us, grinning, an empty green packframe jerking up and down on his back. Matt had dipped the Cub so close that we could see the tan coveralls smeared with gore. The running man looked like a mad killer exiled here in this wilderness on his naked heap of chert. Matt circled, then let down to a place where cliff met the flat ridge at an oblique angle and palisades of stone fell away to the faintly forested river bottom. Flying slower than I would have believed possible, Matt was approaching the sheer wall of rock when a downward burst of wind shoved us below the cliffside. We would hit the wall.

He yanked the flap handle for all the lift he could get (there's an extra inch or two there if you need it), added full power, and climbed smoothly away. As we went around for a second try, he called back at me, "You only make one bad landing up here."

We could see Glen waving as we came in for the next pass, a stout and jolly man with a round head, his short arms pumping as he jogged toward us. Matt approached with the heel brakes already partially depressed for immediate traction. He dumped the flaps a second before touchdown, then applied hard braking once the wheels were firmly on. No rollout to speak of. We scraped in on a dust cloud of our own making, and the little airplane jerked to a halt. Matt had already cut the engine and stepped out before I knew what was happening, and little bits of shale grit were falling and ticking on the fabric of the plane in the unexpected silence that followed.

I grabbed a structural tube above me and hauled myself out of the back seat to take a look. We had landed sideways on the long ridge, owing to the wind pouring over the top. The temperature was in the forties. A pale sun was out. I looked over the sheer sides and wondered how he'd ever get off.

Matt hitched up his pants, his shirt open to reveal his red long johns, and he admired one of the caribou that Glen had already dressed and beheaded. Matt tilted back his baseball cap, examining the antlers. "That'll go 410, I'll bet you anything," he assured Glen. "You'll want that mounted."

"You think?" Glen asked, scratching his head with a gory hand. He was covered with blood from his once-white jogging shoes to his baseball cap, with a smear across the bridge of his nose for war paint.

I studied the severed bloody head, the magnificent set of antlers. Glen had simply hacked the head off with no thoughts of the taxidermist's art. Yet I could see that even in death the old bull's long and prehistoric equine face, its bladed antlers, were of proud and noble lineage. Its eye was turning white in the wind. The inert oculus, fogging over with a slow accrual of wax, stared austere and indifferent at the valley floor he yearly compassed with his kin. He had been migrating to the south when he was detained on this forsaken capital. He'd had an amazing life in these arctic regions, and now Glen considered memorializing it in his urban basement.

We loaded the Cub with bloody cheesecloth bags of meat. Glen had crudely quartered three other caribou and put them in game bags, gauze bandages on these ghastly wounds. Blood tarnishes like fine silver. It turns black in this dry wind and soaks the bags and grows a tough black pellicle. Hefting the weight of flesh into the plane, I felt something in it, a force that made it feel different from hefting a rock, a log, a dumbbell. It was a living thing, now dead, and its death was a special state of matter, just as its life had been.

Glen and I stood on the lonely crag and watched Matt take off in a smoking clatter of pebbles. The little airplane with the big tires sank out of sight: it seemed to shoot off the cliff in a suicidal cloud of dust, then collapse like a hawk and succumb to gravity, only to catch itself at the last moment and struggle upward once more, clawing the air as it gained speed. The noise had died away to a faint mechanical racket. The tremendous silence of the Arctic descended on us once again. Glen and I hiked down the ridge and set to on the cervine carcass farthest from the camp.

Glen laid his stainless-steel shotgun beside us on the ground. The ground looked like the molars of a mastodon, and in the crevices and on the cusps, there beneath the gray meniscus of the sun, grew the scant green-silver blooms, the dried and bone-white skeletal plants that told a story about this remote precinct of nature: how harsh it would get, how wild it was. Flying in, I had seen below wide expanses of tundra colored in the same shades we'd find on autumn leaves down south. I learned later that they were, indeed, forests. Stunted, aged birch and willow, some more than two hundred years old, so dwarfed by growing over permafrost, where liquid water is available only a few months a year, that they had formed a carpeting beneath the feet of caribou. We were on a far edge of the envelope of life. Beyond, conditions would become Martian. And yet we found life in such profusion.

The ridge on which we worked, a heap of shattered shale three thousand feet long, fell away abruptly to an immense valley of forest and yellow tundra cut by tangled rivers that looped and spliced in coils of white and pewter as they dipped and curved, flat metal ribbons mending dark and ragged wounds, darning in and out of fissures cut through multitudes of pine. This ocher tableland fanned out from our hilltop and spanned more than one hundred miles. We were in the foothills of the Brooks Range, and we could lift our heads from our work to see how its ascending crescent surrounded this valley.

Glen and I set about field dressing the caribou, which lay not quite on top of the ridge, its right eye exploded outward from the hydrostatic shock of a 180-grain 300-magnum round that Glen had put in its neck a short while earlier. The buck had throw up a huge swath of green and stinking vomit, and its last reflex breath was still blowing gouts of blood from its nostrils as Glen slit it up the furred middle with his skinning knife and let the greenish heap of steaming viscera fall gently down the sloping terrain into his waiting arms. "Come here, buddy," he muttered underneath his breath, which came in snorts from the effort. With the huge snot-blue and silver-green guts slick and stinking in his arms, Glen reached up inside the dark interior of the animal and began working his blade blindly to detach the mess from the cavity. He withdrew his arm covered in gore and excrement, slinging great gobs of it off in annoyance. "Damn," he said. "I meant not to do that." He smeared the brown fecal matter on the tundra beside him, turning his hand this way and that, then plunged in again up to his armpit, this time freeing the last of the viscera.

I caught hold of the antlers and pulled the animal to a cleaner spot a few feet up the hill. I tipped out several quarts of blood from the gaping cavity and then rolled it by its hooves onto its back. Glen removed a well-worn bone saw from a leather sheath on his belt and sawed through the pubic bone and stood athwart the animal and pried it apart spanwise to free its laden rectum. With his hunting knife he cut out the anus and then he flung it away and we started on the hide. He stripped back skin with one knife while I worked with another, the fat like clabbered milk against the bright red meat, the grand and shining socketbones like giant pearls lashed in the still-warm muscle with white and hollow twines of tendon. Soon we had the animal apart. I held the body, embracing it, while Glen sawed through the spine across the abdomen. I cut off forejoints and feet, working the blade carefully into the enigmatic structure of the joints, and tossed the hooves away. The workings of these attachments and the means by which they transferred the tremendous power required to move this mass were incomprehensible to me. It made all the machines of civilization seem the crude conceits of our primitive tribe. I saw that nothing I did would ever be this smooth nor have this effortless artistry.

I removed the hindquarters with easy strokes, dressing the knife now and then on a small campstone. All this while and with every cut we made, blood leaked in prodigious thickening accretions from the sweet and tepid hives, until we both were slathered in the adhesive reek of carnage and our own sweat and the deranged joy of butchery.

I had never cut an animal up before. But my squeamishness

quickly turned to fascination with how marvelously the thing was put together, this intoxicating device. This was a work of nature, as was everything I could see for one hundred miles around me, and everything beyond that, too. I was suddenly awed by our audacity, to inject ourselves into this genius and savagery with such a fragile thing as an airplane. The scale was completely bizarre, the scale of size, but also the scale of sophistication. Look at the frictionless design of this leg joint in my hand, the way it defied the laws of physics. The enemy we were up against was so far advanced beyond us, it might as well be from another star. We were not in this league. It seemed that this kingly being had conquered entropy itself. And we were a piece of gristle in a box kite. The madness of our pursuit was intoxicating. I tinkered with what was not rightfully mine. I was overwhelmed with wonder at the strength and sentience built into this hooved being, for survival in these arctic reaches, for navigation across this grievous continent with nothing but eyes and nose to lead him, the magnificence of his respiration and his once-thunderous locomotion. And I, this squatting ape, had wrecked it all in half an hour with a four-inch knife blade.

Glen and I cut up two caribou that afternoon and packed the meat to the top of the hill, carrying guns against the grizzlies that would sooner or later find this charnel heap. Then we sat in the lee of the tent to get out of the hectic wind and ate ham sandwiches, spreading mayonnaise on Roman Meal bread with a bloody hunting knife, keeping rifle and shotgun near at hand. Glen talked about his days as a coal miner back in North Carolina, working thirty-inch shafts seven miles deep in the earth in the 1980s. Glen said that learning to fly and becoming a bush pilot was "the dumbest thing I ever did." He was making one hundred thousand dollars a year as a coal miner, which was how he found the wherewithal to take flying lessons. "There's no money in being a bush pilot," he said sadly. "Very few people can make it." Retired from bush piloting, Glen now works for the Aircraft Owners and Pilots Association in Anchorage.

We watched the valley fill with mist. Out on the Brooks Range, the tilted, chamfered cones of blue and white were slowly inlaid with the beaten pastel colors of the sun. Streams and bars of sunlight fell in saffron curtains from a long and gloomy ridge, and we slapped our hands together as the cold began to settle in, where nothing more than the small green tent stood between us and the long centrifugal fetch of the wind across the tundra. A towering double sun flared up, an artifact of ice fog, trademark illusion of the arctic sundown. Glen laughed at our predicament. "Either Mike's going to leave us here all night just for fun," he said, "or he'll wait until the last possible moment before dark."

And it did seem like the last possible moment before dark when we heard the far-off buzzing of Mike's engine and saw the Cessna 185 beating a course toward us. He circled several times, passing low over the landing area to inspect it thoroughly before finally settling and skidding to a stop. When he stepped out, I asked, "How do you like the new landing strip?"

"I'm here," he said. While Glen and I loaded meat into the plane, Mike walked the runway, inspecting with grim intensity its ruts and bumps and widowmakers, pointed pieces of rock that could slash a tire. When we thought we'd put enough cargo in the back, we waited for Mike's return. He glanced at the remaining meat and said, "What about all this?"

Glen said he didn't want the plane to be too heavy.

Mike hefted a leg of caribou and started throwing it in. "Heavy's not the problem," he said, and we loaded all the rest. I recalled him telling me that his rule of thumb was a pound to a pound and a half per foot of runway. "Six hundred foot runway means you can take eight hundred pounds. Roughly. With wind, you can take more." I also recalled Matt telling me that approximately six of their fellow bush pilots had died in the past year in crashes. Before Mike cranked the engine, we had five caribou, three men, and camping gear in the four-seater Cessna, and I was forced to wonder if I might be in more danger leaving than staying. I'd been a pilot for much of my life and had never heard of that sort of weight-and-balance calculation. The truth was that what we were doing was insanely risky, not to mention illegal.

Mike put in full power, and the engine bawled and clamored, scattering gravel behind us, and we set off down the desolate mountain ridge with clone suns hanging pale and woeful on the ridge, as if we now departed a hostile satellite hung on the catenary of this remote double star. I was in the back seat with the bloody bags of meat, which fell heavily against me like a drunk. We were fast approaching a wall of rock that rose, sheer and white before us, when Mike yanked the handle to give us full flaps and eased back on the yoke. We lifted, bounced once, and with the stall horn blaring, he made a sharp right turn, and we ran off the cliff, still throwing gravel. We fell toward the black spikes of pine forest while Mike cranked the trim wheel like mad. We crawled across the treetops at fifty feet. As soon as it became clear that we were not going to be impaled on the pines—one pilot in an identical plane had recently died that way—Mike's grim features disjointed into a smirk, and then he and Glen burst into uncontrollable laughter. It was this moment, to experience fear, delight, and wonder in one's own continued existence and to have had a hand in making it so, that circumscribed and defined the bush pilot's world. To go in, to breathe in the ferocious Arctic, and to get out again, still carrying it in our lungs. This was the laugh of someone who'd been holding his breath.

This then is how it happens. I sat in back with the sacks of flesh, watching late light reflect white banks of riverstone, the watercourses plaited like silver hawsers through the pastel grass, as the darkening landscape veered away to a shapeless infinity. And I fell in love with that moment. I saw my life back home as pain and chaos and futility and this as the perfect clarity, the peace I'd always been seeking. I knew the lure of this place and our bizarre conduct in it. It is not bravery or derring-do that takes us overloaded into a three-hundred-foot dogleg gravel bar on a riverbank. It is not sport. Only a cornered animal fights this hard. Perhaps it is a final despair that we cannot whip with all our might. Or perhaps it's the only way to find the delicious abandon that a wolf can feel when he's on the run.

We crossed gleaming ash-gray mud flats cut with capillary intricacy. Flocks of birds in lingering transport, undulating congregations, made oblique angles to our course. Abandoned in a channel, a ruptured skiff drifted past.

Here the sunset lasts forever. I kept expecting it to finish, and it just kept on coming and coming, distended and red and creaming all over the sky in freak striations as if the body of time itself had stopped athwart the rim of the earth and vented all its gas across the stars.

At last the squirming lights of Kotzebue wheeled into view and turned as we turned, like a carnival ride stranded on this shabby spit of land.

Late that night, Matt and his girlfriend Linda, a researcher from the Department of Fish and Wildlife, and Dave Leonard, Matt's alter-ego pilot, sat in the office drinking beer. Dave, thirty-seven, like Matt, was an independent arctic guide and owned his own Cub but flew with Alaska Island Air and somehow exchanged services with Mike. Twenty years earlier, in high school, Dave and his best friend Danny Cowan had read Jack London and Robert Service together and then dreamed of arctic adventures. Dave worked as a taxidermist's assistant after school and on weekends, and he'd seen the big game hunters come in and spin tall tales of strange things done 'neath the midnight sun. In 1974, between their junior and senior years in high school, Danny and Dave visited Alaska for the first time. The next year they made the trip again and stayed. They hired on as packers, camp jacks, for an old master guide who still used horses. The boys were seventeen years old.

From packer to assistant guide to registered guide, they worked their way up, and as soon as they could, they learned to fly. Dave acquired his guide certificate in 1981 and was finally able to buy his own Super Cub in 1986 from a pilot who was in trouble with the IRS and was forced to sell. Shortly afterward Danny Cowan was killed in a crash. Dave admitted that it was difficult for him to go back to flying after that. "I thought Danny was invincible," he said.

Dave and Matt got together in 1989, odd isomers, the hobo ministers of such marginal pursuits as can exist only in those storybooks they'd read and in this raw, disordered province, so recently shaped by some ghastly intelligence, a land so new, so savage. Matt and Dave have been laboring side by side ever since, sharing the miscellaneous warrens of the borough, crafty and vigilant of the providential. Ad hoc, unstructured, abstracted as monks, they live by reading the wind, sentinels against happenstance, and by walking the ridges and gravel bars looking for that singular stone, that rift in the land, the white driftwood spar camouflaged on white stone that would end once and for all the realized adventure of their youthful dreams.

In first light, with hands cupped round a smoking mug of coffee, they stepped out onto the ramp amid pallets piled high with meat boxes and moose antlers, to inspect their Cubs, side by side like two wary old wolves. They laughed (they always laughed), but then their stolen looks before first flight told a story, too. Surreptitious glances as they checked each other, perhaps for the last time. And each night when the deed was done that look was gone, and in what might have been waves of relief, as they drank their beer, they laughed and laughed, shooting down their watches with the airplanes they made of their hands. "There we were, coming in overloaded, *way* behind the power curve, full flaps . . ." Or: "We was coming onto that one old stretch of the Kuguruwok and man, it was blowing, I mean it was just *howling* . . ."

Why did they keep going out? I knew now, I knew. And I longed to stay in that landscape, because here the feeling of being lost and the fact of being lost were one, while at home the feeling was merely a confounding contradiction, a character flaw, a personality disorder. I understood how a bush pilot came to be, came to take an ordinary life and set himself out here and make himself poor and doomed to work so hard every day: For these are passionate and ultimately lonely men. These are men who—back in the world—knew that a grizzly bear was eating them alive. They just couldn't see it. Now they've come to a place where a grizzly bear really might eat them alive. But it's all right, because they can see it. Each morning they rise to greet a vast landscape that stretches away like the restless dream of a poet. And in a life where nothing ever felt authentic, this finally feels right. This place was in his heart, and so he brought his heart to this place. He came in order to sit here on these riverbanks and look at those mountains, to watch what animals happened by, and simply to listen to the sense this stream of life made when it spoke.

BIG BEND

The calcite cliffs behind me were pink at sunset. I drove the old Maverick Road north. The entablature of those cliffs ran for miles and miles like that, fifteen-hundred-foot walls of sheer rock ruled flat against a paper sky. The daylight was so intense that we seemed to be caught in an invisible flame, tequila on fire. Now crashing through dry washes of chert and shale, leaping over their far banks, Maria and I could see the sun dip behind the low hills of ash, peppered with stunted trees like an arctic tundra. All life here was dwarfed by the silent thunder of the sun. We spun out a wagon train of dust behind us. It would soon be night, and we would have no light to speak of at the camp along Terlingua Creek. I stole glimpses in the rear-view mirror. The cliffrock ran to deep purple, streaked with bister. The truck danced through flinty draws on spider legs, throwing its awkward shadow all the way down the desert floor. Bats on leather wings veered and jerked around us like spirits freed from destiny.

Down on Terlingua Creek at last, Maria and I huddled on our haunches in the sand and felt night come on like a power failure. It was 108 degrees when we pitched camp. Terlingua Abaja was known to be the hottest place in the park. Maria was a naturalist, small and vulpine, beautiful. She knew these things: The creek ran mostly underground at that time of the year. The desert did not come alive at night as in a nature film. Few things yet moved. A pair of doves made listless dives and skimmed along the desert floor in trail. No, the desert simply sat there with its hot tongue all over us. That was its secret: it would sit there until it had sucked everything out of us, and we were left like the dried molting of a cicada. It was a place of contradictions. For there in the deathly crepuscular light as we squatted on a rock, small fish were swimming in stagnant pools, and the green fingers of some unnamable saltweed reached up like dead and moldering hands to grasp the air.

We found our sleep at last light around nine-thirty. The temperature was 103 by the Jeep's thermometer.

———

Stark naked in the mountains, Maria and I sat before our scullery fire. She knew enough not to interrupt the silence of this place. An early wind bent the stoveflame like a pennant and tilted it to the earth. It felt as if we wore clothes, though we did not. The air and our skin were exactly the same temperature. It felt as if a few swimmer's strokes could take us to the surface where that full moon, chased by Mars and Venus, floated like a luminous ball of cosmic gas on the surface of that lake of air. But we were stranded at the bottom, drowned Argonauts, yet still conscious.

During the night big winds shook the tent and threatened to pick it up. But in the morning that front had passed, clearing the world of the smoke from forest fires in Texas and Mexico. Unlike the night, dawn was a long time coming. Saturn was so bright in the east that it looked artificial. My citysense told me it was an airplane, but it wouldn't come to me. Anyway, I saw no airplanes there, no tic-tac-toe of contrails to spoil the sky in its first daylight quaking. Big Bend was on the path to nowhere.

We were going to see the canyon that in the 1700s confused the Spanish so badly that they turned back in humiliation from their imperial advance north.

———

Vast reliquary valleys always there at my elbow, offering up the bones of the dead to those who would walk there. Huge purgatorial voids of white volcanic ash and endless fields of ejecta, as if a tremendous explosion vomited all these rust-colored rocks out here, which is more or less what happened, said Maria. She gave me these tidbits when she bothered to speak at all. We both preferred the silence. The land and the mountains were built by volcanic action followed by erosion. Hot bile rose out of the earth, which was stove through to its spinning iron armature. And the ash was still ash, and the lava was still lava, and if you looked closely, if you stood in it for days and days, as we did, it began to form a picture. You could see the volcano. We were inside of it.

Glen Springs Road to Juniper Canyon was politely referred to as unimproved, although someone with a machine may have graded it at some forgotten time long past. Like grading the wind. The jolting, bucking, swerving chaos of our vehicle threatened to toss us off into the cactus. Though every rock, no matter how small, threw a long magenta shadow, our shadow was the only one moving across those huge flats, faintly green plains, through the bulging mountains, in the lee of the jagged castellated Chisos Mountains.

No one was on the road. No one would be.

Sometimes we'd stop and turn off the engine and simply listen to the nothing of which we were the sole occupants. Maria and I stepped down from the truck and held hands and just looked, saying nothing for a long time. The world seemed entirely empty, but after a while, she told me that we were in the company of about ten thousand coyotes, a few bears and mountain lions, scores of collared peccaries, eight million jackrabbits with ears as big as donkeys' ears, deer, fowl, rats, snakes, and wasps the size of hummingbirds, hummingbirds the size of bats. All of them invisible in the daylight.

The Dead Horse Mountains to the east caught the light. Boquillas Canyon and Sierra del Carmen, all layers of light and shadow, as if they were just poured there out of the beaker of the sky. Yucca blooms twelve feet high stood like sentinels all around. Prickly pear as purple as a bruise and green ones blushing with yellow flowers that felt like wax. Armies of harvester ants dragged things, unlikely large, into their cold caverns in the earth.

We remounted the truck. I started the engine. Aluminum air conditioning fooled us for a time. We were not really there. That was just a movie, a video game: "Drive through Hell."

Climbing and dipping through rock and bedrock and more rock, we found ourselves in a place of tremendous heaps of flint and shale that climbed to naked lava and crevasses that swallowed us from sunlight and then spit us out the other side. The shocks bottomed out.

The truck groaned and complained but kept going. Our gear in back leaped, floated, and crashed back down again as I drove more and more recklessly. A wayward meteorite hit the undercarriage with a stony gonglike sound, and I wondered about that gas tank. How would this cartoon vehicle, conceived in the mind of an advertising executive, fare in the real world of rocks?

We emerged into an area of low trees that grabbed at the side mirrors. Sometimes whole cactus plants leaped in through the side window to join us on our way, and out of the corner of my eye I saw Maria recoil from thorns as big as surgical needles, yellow and lethal looking. As she clutched my shoulder, a huge spray of fragrant purple flowers intruded through her window. The desert offered up such contradictions. For a few days, our minds recoiled, then we gradually began to accept anything, anything at all. A whole dead deer, gutted out by turkey vultures and coyotes before being left to mummify, as black and leathery as an old saddle in the sun. Bones. Skulls. And in the distance something green. That land held water if we could find it.

The road presented spike rocks here and there that would tear a tire in half. They stuck up like sabers and were buried deep like dragon's teeth for maximum effect. As an experienced American driver, all my instincts told me that the road just had to get better. It did not. It got worse.

Like many vessels I've piloted—airplane, boat—that vehicle was a paradox. It was our friend and our enemy both. For it could carry us beyond help farther and faster than our feet ever would. And then it could leave us there without recourse just as quickly. The hiking trails of Big Bend go up the mountains, where conditions are cool and safe. Those trails are populated by happy packers. Not so the roads. Some are little more than cart tracks made two hundred years ago, now fading into these chartless wastes. Others are the original network of crisscrossing trails made by Comanche and Apache. The road down from Marathon to Persimmon Gap, Route 385, is the Great Comanche Trail. No one, not even the US Army, ever owned this place like the Comanche. No one ever will. For to own a place, we've all learned, one must live there. And even then, it's just on loan.

"Be prepared to walk out," we were told by a guide. "There's nobody out there. You see lots of tourists here at the Basin or the Visitor Center, but out where you're going, you're pretty much on your own." He did river rafting and Jeep tours, and he'd been in the park a while. Maria and I met him at the Terlingua Store just outside the boundary of the park, where people gather on the porch at the end of the day, where the beer is cheap and the advice is free. "One hose, one fan belt, and you're basically going to walk out. Might carry extra of those. A shovel can go a long way, too. Sometimes you move a few rocks, toss a couple shovels full of dirt, and it means the difference between getting through and not getting through. People go missing here all the time. Takes a while to find them."

Takes a while to walk out, too. Distances in the park are not far by ordinary standards. Twenty minutes here, half an hour there by car if you want to rush from historic marker to historic marker on the paved roads with the kids in back. But on the back roads, when that radiator blows up or that tire deflates perched on a spire of stone, when you get out with a ten- or twelve-mile hike before you, then suddenly you feel as if you're on the mountains of the moon. So we had a tarp and tent stakes and parachute cord to make a lean-to. Wait out the midday heat. We had packs, our tent, sleeping bags, loads of water, gallons of it, in MSR Cordura nylon Dromedary bags, along with bottles and jugs, and then some food, as if we might have had an appetite in that heat. "Down a quart and put three in your pack," one ranger told me. "That way you're carrying a gallon." A gallon is one day's supply of water for one person. The best time to hike out would be between one and five a.m., if you don't mind the wild pigs.

———————

Santa Elena Canyon. Not a sound but for birds and insects. The high-water mark from the October 1990 flood of the Rio Grande was higher than the cab of our vehicle. Maria and I got out and walked across sand flats, the low dry wash of Terlingua Creek, to the mouth of the canyon. The rock was still cool from the night as the sun lifted a hand's width above the horizon. I guessed that it was eight in the morning or so in the lee of those tremendous cliffs. So confounding is the area, and especially its canyons, that it resisted even the rudimentary efforts of cartographers until 1902, when the US Geological Survey sent Arthur A. Styles to make the first accurate maps.

The Rio before us was brown and still but for a few ripples where it braided over stones as it turned from east to south. The so-called Big Bend, sharp as an elbow. We stood at the base of the cliffs and looked up. Once a seabed. The walls rose in layer upon layer of nameless shades, heavy with skirts of scree, which in turn were dotted by prickly pear, rooted in rock seams, bright green in the immense field of gray. And on the east side, rolling hills led to the dark Chisos, the upper peaks of which seemed to spread black wings against the morning sun the way the turkey vultures do to dissipate the chill of the night. We could see them at the base, those tremendous and angular copings that descend to boulders, which looked like building blocks tossed away, the tumble-down ruins of a lost civilization, purlieu of giants. Above mud banks lined with common reeds and grasses that resembled bamboo, the cliffs were falling. At that rate, they would be gone in the blink of an eye, speaking in geologic terms. Say fifty thousand years. A thousand generations of people, like the ones who left the scattered palings of their bones in the pumice flats out there.

We set out among the cliffs. A path had been cut, so it wasn't difficult. Like climbing the choir-loft stairs of a church, though a misplaced step would put you in the river, and it would be a long ride down. A couple of hundred vertical feet, half an hour later, and the narrow trail descended and then petered out along the banks to pig tracks though reeds. We followed, deep in Santa Elena Canyon, until we couldn't follow anymore and found ourselves face to face with a sheer wall of rock that rose to a slit of sky. No sunlight down there that early. It was a dead end without a canoe. We could hear the mocking laughter.

"It's a canyon wren," Maria said. "Santa Elena Canyon is one of the few places in the US that the canyon wren lives." This was a great deal of talk from her in our gentle pact of silence. "We're just barely in the US now," she went on. "Or maybe we've already walked into Mexico. Nobody cares," she added. "There's nobody here."

"There's us," I said.

She took my hand in her handsome hand, and her broad mobile mouth smiled.

The walls towered, arched, and shelved over us. It was a good place. A huge fish rose and turned in the river, blistering the surface for a moment, then vanished. Maria found a beaver dam wedged into the cleft of a great rock and then another that was exploded by flood. The pattern of its destruction was clear, a swath of dried ocotillo sticks and thick reeds chewed at the ends. After a while, the sun flared and found its way back there, and it was time to get out.

We were both wondering where the boulders were. The cliffs must be crumbling, we thought, as all cliffs do. We had been looking across to the other side of the river and had seen slides and scree. So where were the bits and pieces that were falling off on this side of the cliffs? As we made our way back along overgrown trails, Maria came to a sudden realization and pointed out that the boulders were all around us. They were so large that we couldn't see their limits. We had to crawl through the spaces between them to touch the flank of the actual cliff itself. The boulders were larger than houses.

As we emerged from the canyon through banks overgrown with juniper and grass, the river gleamed silver in the sun. The light was blinding. We could feel the first great pressure of the sun on us like divers descending. Here comes the desert day.

———————

At high noon the crickets made a sound like a diamond drill cutting through steel. Our shadows sat directly beneath us, black stacks of stone. Nothing moved, not even the dust cloud we kicked up getting there. It sat like a brown river over the road and just hung there. We filled our water bottles from one of the big bags, put on our day packs, and headed down into the river bottom that led to the Burro Mesa Pouroff.

It was once a huge whitewater river, as grand and tumbling as the Colorado. Anyone with canoe sense could see by those rocks how it would have ridden. The bottom where we walked in midday heat was a bed of gravel, white as gypsum, with polished limestone boulders like a tremendous string of pearls. Rising on either side to a height of a hundred feet or more were crooked walls of lava embedded with stones picked up along the way during the eruption, so that now the whole structure had the look of a mad aggregate put there against a terrible purpose and cut through by the blade of time, right down to the quick where we walked in each other's footsteps. If the sun hadn't been straight overhead, there would have been shade, for the vault of that river was a great jagged groove. The riverbed ended abruptly in a sheer wall, a bad surprise for someone on the run.

We sat in the meager spot of shade created by that chute. It came off of Burro Mesa above, a flat tableland whose drainage ended here. The chute was a three-quarter cylinder of black rock polished smooth as chrome. It was about twenty feet across and a hundred feet tall, a cave for bats where the obsidian-looking rock met the porous reach of aggregate beneath it. It was the vertical flume where the river went from up there to down here, and if it ever rained again, the water would explode in a tremendous waterfall pool right where we sat.

It hadn't rained for more than sixty days when Maria and I visited Big Bend. Not real rain, not appreciable. In Terlingua the people told us it hadn't rained since Christmas. And I wondered how that desolation came to be. Big Bend had once been a grassland used for grazing cattle.

Ten thousand years ago people lived here. They called themselves the Human Beings, as do most indigenous peoples in whatever their own language happens to be. Deer and bison were plentiful. This was some of the finest grassland in all the Southwest, and the lions hunted with the Human Beings, and the little wolves followed them for scraps, and the mourning doves filled the morning with their sad weeping. Other people lived along the river, too. They irrigated the flood plain and grew crops. Now and then the river flooded and washed the soil clean and made it good again. By that means, it never went to waste through too much farming. As dry as much of the land was even then, freshwater springs ran all year. Dense thickets of forest had grown up along those streams, so they always had firewood. Fire, water, food: it was a good land, if harsh.

Then the Spaniards came marching up from across the river in armor, and they saw this place and saw the Human Beings (whom they called Jumanos) who squatted by their *jacals* and ate by their fires. The Spanish had come from cities and so could imagine only cities. They came from imperial Spain and were after more empire. That and the missionary zeal to spread Christianity drove them ever northward from the place where in 1521 Hernán Cortés murdered Montezuma, who believed that Spaniard to be a god. Cortés stole every art object made of gold or silver that he could get his hands on and melted it all down to ingot and sent it back on ships for tribute to the king of Spain.

Those were the people who claimed this land.

Álvar Núñez Cabeza de Vaca was shipwrecked while attempting to reach this rich new world. In 1528, he washed ashore near what would later be called Galveston, Texas. He spent seven years there, living among the Indians, so called, and escaped, eventually passing in his mad peregrinations through what is now Big Bend National Park. Thought to be the first non-Human Being to cross this land.

Cabeza de Vaca forded the Pecos River near Reagan Canyon and descended into Chihuahua, Mexico, near Presidio, Texas. In his trackless wanderings, he had inadvertently discovered an overland route for the Spanish into the Rio Grande valley. Upon their return, Cabeza de Vaca and his party regaled their countrymen with tales of cities of gold. Remarkable though their lies were, considering what they'd been through, they inspired official exploration of the region. Convinced that he would discover something akin to the Aztec empire so recently sacked and looted, Francisco Vásquez de Coronado y Luján set out on a two-year trek but discovered nothing worth plundering.

A silver lode, turned up at Zacatecas in Mexico in 1546, touched off a new migration, with the inevitable war between Indians and Spanish being one result. All this while, the Human Beings continued to live and farm along the Rio Grande. The Spanish military viewed them primarily as soulless beasts, subhuman creatures that could provide a steady source of slave labor for the silver mines. Paradoxically, the Spanish missionaries viewed them, at the same time, as souls ripe for conversion to Christianity and ready to be sent to heaven, preferably with as little delay as possible. Eager Franciscans went to work this out in 1581, which was only the second penetration of the Big Bend area by the Spanish. They followed the Rio Conchos north, crossed at

La Junta into present-day Texas, and proceeded all the way to New Mexico, where the Pueblo Indians killed them for their trouble.

A rescue party retraced their steps the following year, establishing two facts that would be important for Big Bend country: first, that thousands of Indians lived up there, waiting to be converted and enslaved and worked to death; second, that the Rio Conchos was a direct route to that territory.

For the next century, however, few Spanish ventured that far north. But Robert Sieur de La Salle's trip down the Mississippi for France in 1682 set off a panicky response in Spain. Discovering a land was one thing. Claiming it was another. But to really own it, one had to occupy it, and that meant having people who were willing to live there. As it happened, not too many people wanted to live there. To begin with, it was harsh and unlike Europe. Second, Apache and Comanche warriors of astonishing ferocity had begun to drift down from the northern plains in search of new buffalo herds to hunt and had become the most notorious raiders in the history of the Americas. People were terrified of them. And with good reason. The Indians tortured, mutilated, and scalped their victims, set fire to houses, and took all the horses. The Comanche had no regard for human life, not even their own. If they found infants or toddlers in the place they raided, the Indians mutilated and killed them. They chopped into the skulls of babies with their primitive hand axes and pulled out their brains. The Comanche would take the older children for slaves. Occasionally, a child would be accepted as a member of the tribe and would forget all his former habits and customs and even the Spanish language itself.

When I was a small child, my great-grandmother sang a song to me as I went to sleep.

> Allá vienen los indios
> Por la chaparral
> Allá vienen los indios
> Por la chaparral
> Ai, NMaria, ai, Tatita
> Me quieren matár.

Her mother had sung the same song to her, because when my great-grandmother went outside to play as a child, *indios* still raided and killed people. (When my great-grandmother married one of those Comanche Indians, her mother was horrified and refused to speak to their firstborn for the rest of her life.) So no one wanted to live in Texas. In 1731 the king of Spain had his emissaries canvass the dirt farmers living in the Canary Islands and offer land and a title of nobility to anyone who would come and face the Comanche. Some of my relatives were among the ragged group of families that accepted that pitch.

Less than a mile from the beginning of Black Gap Road, the bedrock opened to reveal a huge valley, a panorama of rolling hills, and the angular shapes of mountains beyond like the buckled wreck of some blue-gray vessel come adrift from another world to run aground right before our eyes. Volcanic debris and ash, cliffs and buttes, and dotted here and there, green flags of vegetation, signature of the subterranean aquifer. And yet all this world seemed made out of dust, as if the hills had been loaves freshly handled by their bakers. To the east, tumbling successions of ranges in ranks vanished to mist and smoke at midday. Maria and I climbed back into the truck and descended into that land-scape. The tires made a sound as if I drove across a field of broken crockery. The road was already bad. And then it became terrible. The road turned southeast, and Talley Mountain consumed us. It was a trick of peripheral vision, but the immensity of the mountain caused it to close in from both sides like a trap. Its great shadowy flanks were faintly green from the cactus plants that dotted its rocky surface. At 3.6 miles I pulled up before a crevasse through which the road appeared to run. I had been warned that at times Black Gap Road, which was not maintained by the Park Service, would barely exist at all, would fade out to wagon tracks, and could vanish altogether. Here it seemed to cross an impossible obstacle. It simply disappeared into an incision in a solid block of black and copper-colored rock about thirty feet tall.

"Shoot," said Maria.

I got out and walked into the breach. I found a space through which one might attempt to drive. Someone had even come up with a kind of crude cobble of boulders to make a surface. The rocks were as big as the tires on the truck, though, and none of them flat. Then a mixture that looked like concrete, decked with stones like skulls, had been poured in to mend the lurch from stone to stone.

"What do you see?" Maria called.

"Nothing good."

I climbed back in. I crept forward, the cab bucking and lurching, tipping drunkenly toward the close black walls and never quite finding its footing. In a couple of places it seemed to dig in hard, and then all the power of the engine lifted it back and rolled it into the next hole, over the next sharp thing.

"You want me to get out and help?" Maria asked.

"I'm afraid the truck might tip over and crush you."

Our pace was by inches. Then with a slamming of the undercarriage and the labored scream of steel on stone, the machine hauled itself into the light like a monster being born out of a naked slit in that mother rock. We reared up the hill leaving a gnarled umbilicus of dust behind us.

Perched on a rise, we took stock of this place we'd worked so hard to come into. In all directions we viewed a compassless waste of pumice, lava, gypsum, sand, all baked to more than one hundred degrees now and fiercely lit by the white disc of the sun.

Nights I'd wake to the blue meridian of the moon, washed in smoke like a dissolving lozenge, though yet so bright that I could sit up and scribble notes by its light. At dawn the moon would be trailing Mars and Venus like bright barges aflame to the waterline. And yet, the stars at night were not big and bright deep in the heart of Texas, not anymore. Here's how that came to be.

Big Bend National Park was the center of an area known to the Spanish and the Americans alike as the Gran Apacheria, the home of the Apaches. To the south: Comanches, the worst of the lot for pure, wanton savagery. The Apaches attacked and killed the Human Beings, but they attacked with equal fury the Europeans or anyone else in their path. In 1683 Juan Sabeata, chief of the Human Beings, led his mortally whipped people to the Spanish fort in El Paso. (It was the same place where my grandfather, a descendant of the Human Beings and wearied of the Mexican Revolution, crossed the river in 1914 with nothing but a rifle to his name, there to work in a clothing store until he could move farther east to San Antonio, where he would meet and marry my grandmother, Rosa Hernández, descendant of the Canary Islanders.) Sabaeta's retreat to El Paso and his conversion to Catholicism (not to mention his helpful claim of having had a vision) set in motion a series of Spanish intrusions into Big Bend that would spell the end of Apacheria and lead to the ultimate ruin of the fragile ecosystem that had rendered the land habitable. Those expeditions discovered a French presence in Texas, making it an urgent matter to have Spanish people actually living there, if Spain wished to sustain its claim that Big Bend was part of the Spanish Empire. From the latter part of the seventeenth century through the first quarter of the eighteenth, Spain continued to send its expeditions to or through the Big Bend, establishing presidios and churches and missions, until in March 1729 Captain José de Berroterán had to give up his attempt to follow the Rio Grande when he encountered what he called in his report an impassable "labyrinth" and could not go on. In fact, he had found Santa Elena Canyon. He was stripped of his command for the failure. It wasn't until 1747 that the Spanish actually made it to the heart of Big Bend. The governor of Coahuila, Pedro de Rábago y Terán, when faced with Santa Elena Canyon, understood that his predecessor had been right. But instead of plunging into it, he climbed the Chisos Mountains and crossed over to Terlingua Creek, then found his way back to Mexico by the present-day Lajitas, Texas. By 1760, with the completion of a presidio on the flank of Big Bend, the militarization of the area by the Spanish had begun in earnest.

In 1766 the Spanish royal engineer traveled seven thousand miles through the area, starting at Mexico City, in order to fashion a grand plan for Spain's military installation in the region. He proposed that a line of presidios be built along the Rio Grande and the thirteenth parallel. As other European nations moved into the area, it became even more urgent for Spain to defend its West Texas frontier and occupy it. With the Treaty of Paris in 1763, Spain had the luxury of a caesura in which to commit its entire military might to a full-scale genocidal war of extermination against the Apache. But the country of Big Bend was so confounding that the effort was to take another 120 years.

In early 1775, the Spanish launched a well-organized attack on the

Mescalero and Lipan Apaches' stronghold in the Bolson de Mapimi, an area 100 miles south of Big Bend, measuring 300 by 150 miles. They drove them all the way north to the Guadalupe Mountains and surrounded them. But before they could finish their business, an even more vicious and grotesque deputation of killers materialized out of nowhere on unshod wild ponies painted head to tail in colored devices (hand, fish, sun) and playing on flutes carved out of human bone, bearing mirrored shields of mosaic glass to blind their enemies, feathered, helmeted warriors wearing the uniforms of slain soldiers; bringing along with them a wall of boiling desert dust, they killed with lance and arrow and knife more than seven hundred of the Apaches, who quickly came to realize that negotiating with the Spanish was preferable by far to fighting the Comanches.

When the desert heat and the clamor of the truck became too much, sometimes Maria and I would put on our packs and walk up into the Chisos Mountains, where the Spanish had repeatedly chased the Mescalero Apaches. Tyler Wickham Chandler, an engineer with the US Army, described this place in 1852: "a cluster, rather than a range, of mountains on the American side, known as 'Los Chisos.'" Actually a volcano, or the signature thereof, now weathered to a mellow softness and covered in forest. Climbing on foot out of an area known as the Basin (with a real road, a motel), we quickly left the desert behind and entered steep trails through shade trees and mountain meadows of bunch grass. The sloping forest floor was covered with yellow leaves of deciduous trees, and although the water there did not rise to the surface, this new place was shockingly green. Mountain lion and bear roamed freely. A lion had recently descended into the motel parking lot, killed a deer in front of a clutch of horrified tourists, and dragged it into the canyon to feed it to her cubs. It was the drought, Maria said. The lioness was under stress, or else she never would have come that close to people.

A short but strenuous hike of a couple of hours led us straight up by switchbacks to the highest point in the park, Emory Peak, named for the chief astronomer of the American Army Topographical Corps, Brevet Major William Hemsley Emory, a colonial aristocrat from

Maryland. In the wake of the Mexican War, his party surveyed the Texas-Mexico border. High in the Chisos, standing within feet of the rocky crags that we'd seen from far below, it was difficult to accept that we were in the heart of the Chihuahuan Desert. For a long time we just sat in the shade of a tree, felt the cool breeze, drank water, and ate fruit. The smells of those places were the smells of my youth, cactus flower and mesquite. Up there in the Chisos, the pine resin rose in the heat of the day and mingled with the scent of dust. The effect was reminiscent of burning incense.

Hiking up a long series of hairpins on Pinnacles Trail, we entered a forest of pine and oak, which opened to more meadows of grass studded with enormous boulders, some of which had century plants growing right out of their seams. We passed a German man hiking in shower clogs with no shirt, no hat, little English, and no visible source of water. He carried a plastic shopping bag. He seemed cheerful and jaunty and passed right by us, nodding and smiling. There's one in every wilderness.

As we pressed on, Maria reached out and took my hand and pulled me back. I thought she was being affectionate. Then I turned to look at her. "What?" I asked.

"Listen," she said. If I hadn't been in a stupor, I'd have noticed the blue jay sitting in a tree screaming at the top of her lungs. "Her baby," Maria said. And holding my hand, she pointed with her chin. I followed her gesture down the trail. A rattlesnake had just eaten a baby bird. The mother jay was warning everyone. Perhaps the baby had been blown out of the nest by the big winds last night. At first I believed the snake was dead, for it wouldn't move.

"Is it alive?" I asked.

"Yes," Maria said. "It's just full and doesn't want to move." We waited a while and at last, beset by birds and now by our presence, the rattler slithered off the track onto a flat rock, and we passed up the trail. While rarely fatal, the bite of a rattlesnake can gravely complicate a trip.

At day's end, Maria and I hiked down to the hot springs near Rio Grande Village on the east side of the park. J. O. Langford built a resort around the hot springs in the early part of the twentieth century but was driven out by the Mexican Revolution. The hot springs was a ruin by the time we reached it, but the 105-degree water still gushed from its volcanic source inside the earth. The low collapsed walls of the bath that Langford built still contained enough water for our purposes. Maria and I had bathed each other just once so far, at one of our campsites a few days earlier. We'd accomplished the feat by spraying each other with water from the ten-liter Dromedary bag.

The Rio Grande ran all around the ruins of the bathhouse, dithering over rocks and making eddies against the walls. I watched Maria strip out of her clothes. She undid her bound-up sandy blond hair, now going to gray, and let it fall to her waist. She shrugged off her shirt and stepped out of shorts and stood there, regal, powerful. She had the body of a woman half her age, pale skin rich with freckles. She was a sight in any setting but was a revelation in those overgrown ruins. I undressed and sank into the hot water with her. We lay side by side, watching Mexico across the way. It was only then that I noticed a lone Indian, watching us from the other side, his face cloaked in the shade of his cowboy hat. I pointed him out with my chin.

"What the hell," Maria said. "Let him look."

We lay for half an hour and then rose and scrubbed ourselves, taking turns with a washcloth. When we rose from the water and toweled ourselves dry and dressed, the Indian lifted his chin in acknowledgment and waved, as if to say: *Yes, we are still here, Señor.*

———————

One of the great pleasures of the desert is to watch the furnace of the day get sucked down into the maw of the earth, as the volcano takes back its empire of flame. Then to watch it reappear in the morning, to sit from light to dark and then to sleep in a nothingness sketched out of lightning, then to sit from dark to light again. The only force that truly dominates the desert is night, which tames it. But night goes round the world, running ahead of the volcano, and now the desert wakes again with a slow grin aflame on the hill.

Night is the question. Day is the answer.

We sit in a bowl of rocky hills with a crack in the crockery through which to view the Corrazones Peaks materializing out of the smoky mist. Prickly pear all around, yellow, green, and purple. A forest of low creosote and dwarf honey mesquite, candelilla, sotol, ocotillo, and yucca (of which there are one hundred varieties here, said Maria). Mars and Venus burn, trailing the waxy meltings of the moon. The first pyrrhuloxia, southern cousin of the cardinal, calls and is answered by its young. Freetail bats flicker and dip like butterflies. Crickets are busy sawing all around. But still no stars have shown their faces. Mexico City, Carbon I and II, the coal-burning power plants across the Rio, even the industry of Houston, all contribute to the smoke. And that is how the stars at night went out deep in the heart of Texas.

They say that to get a driver's license in Texas, you must demonstrate an ability to parallel park while holding an icy bottle of Lone Star beer between your knees. At least that's what I heard when I was a teenager, growing up there. I'm not sure I believe that anymore, but at Terlingua the people who arrive in their trucks and alight on the porch of the general store would seem to confirm the notion that practice makes perfect.

If you were to die in your broken car on a bareback road in the heart of Big Bend, a paradox would attend your passing: that you'd be only half an hour's drive from the nearest bar. The park is small. So on more than one night Maria and I drove out from camp and joined the drinkers at Terlingua. We sat on the long flagstone porch under a corrugated steel *finca*, overlooking the ruins of a mercury mine, once the economic basis of that town. The shaft was still there and seemed to drop deep into the center of the earth. The Texas Railroad Commission put a grate over it because people kept falling in.

Crude wooden benches were set up against the flank of the building, and the bartender, Tony, an aspiring guitarist, had settled down there to pick and strum his battered Classico. On the other side of us, a long-haired man with a Carta Blanca held between his knees rolled a cigarette. A wooden ceiling fan turned inside the store. A sleeping dog groaned, his legs running in the unknowable dream of dogs. The town was a ruin, made up mostly of exploded stone foundations crushed by the pile-driver sun. The Chisos Mountains formed a jagged line through the wildfire smoke. A turkey vulture turned in slow circles on a rising thermal, and twisted mesquite formed the only sprays of color in the entirely yellow landscape. A few tin-roofed structures marked the lonely habitations on the hill behind the general store.

Below us was a small Mexican graveyard. It, too, was in ruins, with its nailed crosses of crude lumber, all dry-rotted, cracked, and thrown back on the elongated heaps of shale and mudstone, which were unmistakable as the humped outlines of human forms rising from a long-shadowed land. More elaborate graves were built to resemble rough cathedrals of rock, ending at the head in Moorish domes topped by crosses. Rank creosote bush. A barbed-wire crown of thorns. A lizard tabernacled in the nave. A baby buried in concrete and surrounded by a low wire fence, its wooden posts eaten by ants. *JuMaria 7-1929-7-1929*, her life no more than a shadow that crossed the sun. Who placed this rotted basket containing a pink paper flower and a candle in a plastic cup for the seventy-year-old infant? Who still cares enough? Those Spanish missionaries sure made their mark.

Once the area around Terlingua Creek was rich with cottonwood. Then the Chisos Mining Company came. It was supplying a fifth of the nation's mercury in 1905. It employed indentured Mexican laborers to run its two ten-hour shifts. They were paid less for their labors than any other workers in the state. Moreover, they were not paid in cash but given a punch card good only at the Chisos Mining Company store, where prices were inflated. The smelter ran nonstop and burned cottonwood for its fuel. James B. Gillett wrote in 1933, "The Terlingua was a bold running stream, studded with cottonwood timber and was alive with beaver. Today there is probably not one tree standing on the Terlingua that was there in 1885."

Maria and I arrived on a Saturday evening. The people referred to their weekly gathering as a porch party. A young guy in a dirty red sleeveless T-shirt, red seed cap, and red sneakers bought three Budweiser beers, and carrying them in their plastic six-pack holder, he squatted against a peeled mesquite pole on the porch and drank them in succession while expounding on a variety of subjects. The kid talked about turning his father's defunct junkyard into a campsite for tourists or perhaps using the vehicles for personal storage lockers. The man he addressed said the junkyard was just an eyesore and needed to be cleaned up. The kid seemed to be one of those boundary-less souls doomed to remain forever alone, because the desperate urgency of his need for contact frightened away anyone who might have considered being his friend.

A big bearded man arrived with an armload of antique books on beekeeping and distracted the kid from his ambitions. For a while the kid was buried in his researches, nervously sipping his beer.

Many of the people on the porch were discussing the forest fires, which had spread the pall of smoke over the area. Fires in Chiapas, fires in West Texas, the whole world seemed to be on fire, they were saying. A wall of black clouds had formed in the west, and at five-thirty it was already starting to get dark, though the sun would not set until nine o'clock. Some were spinning theories that the Mexican government had set fires in Chiapas to drive out the Zapatistas. Maria asked one man where he heard that, and he said it was on the ham radio. A local survivalist picked it up from someone who operated out of a booth at a Denny's restaurant in Michigan. They believed that the world was coming to an end. But they were prepared.

"Anyway," the kid said, "it wouldn't be the first time."

"The first time for what?" Maria asked. But the kid had no answer.

Others were saying that the particulates in the air might break the sixty-day drought that had the region in its grip. Terlingua Creek was dried to a smudge. Indeed, as we talked, thunder and lightning began to shake the tin roof. At first everyone denied that it was thunder. They laughed when I said the word.

"It never rains here," somebody said. "Maybe they're blasting."

"On a Saturday night?" Maria asked.

They seemed more willing to believe that it was another Mexican revolution than rain.

An hour later drops were falling, and I led the kid out into the dusty gravel parking lot and showed him the drops on my windshield. "That's not rain," he said.

We stood with drops falling around us, and he steadfastly refused to discuss the possibility that it was raining. Instead he talked about what it was like to live in Terlingua. "It's just *being*," he said. "You don't *do* so much here, you just exist. It's a different kind of life." He looked around, squinting at the place where he had grown up, which was cast in an eerie, almost greenish light, as if the mountains were being projected by a broken lantern. A jagged scrawl of lightning creased a black reef of cloud and left green motes of light gleaming in the air.

I understood what he was saying. Our tendency is to *go* and *do* and get out quickly. But the core of true experience is to be still. One of the greatest wonders of Big Bend was the silence. It was a place dedicated to solitude, the exact opposite of America. I felt a sudden urge to flee that tiny urban spot and retreat to the wilderness again.

"Now it's different," the kid was saying, sounding like an old-timer, though he couldn't have been more than twenty-two. "The tourists came and ruined it." We looked around. Five local people sat on the porch and a couple who looked to be from somewhere else bought gifts in the shop. No one else in sight for twenty miles. But I knew what he was saying: even those few pilgrims seemed too much of a crowd.

Next door to the store, sharing the same porch and benches, was the Starlight Theater. Lyle Lovett was playing on the stereo when Maria and I walked in. Cattle skulls with red Christmas ornaments in the eyeholes hung above the curved mahogany bar. A concert stage backed by a mural of a cowboy campfire. An upright piano. Dried century plant blossoms twelve feet high. Buckling green carpet. Tony the bartender told Maria where to stand to get reception on her cell phone, just one spot across the highway by the historical marker. Maria shrugged. She didn't want to talk to anyone. We sat inside the adobe walls beneath a high-beamed ceiling and ate pork chops and beans with chipotle sauce and watched through the open door as dry lightning frightened barn swallows in their wild veerings. A fresh breeze lifted our tablecloth. In the distance the mountains were wreathed in smoke. A whirlwind of dust came off the road outside and right into the restaurant, and we ate the dust with our meal.

Coming out of the Starlight Theater after dinner, we found the evening so hot and bright that I felt I might faint from the pressure.

Driving back, we saw lightning in the Chisos. The road was dark with vanished rain. We could smell the dust rising. We passed bicyclists with their headlights on, laboring up the hill, spectral in the falling mist.

BIG BEND

Darkness was coming on rapidly by the time Maria and I pitched our tent at Paint Gap, a thin arroyo. We lifted the metal poles to blasts of thunder and displays of lightning coming out of the valley to the northwest. Despite the urgency of getting into the tent, Maria put her hand on my arm and pointed. We stopped and stood in the wind to watch a Lucifer hummingbird make one last trip to the magenta cactus flowers. We crawled inside, and I laid my head in the cradle of Maria's pelvis, but we couldn't sleep for the violent storm that raged for several hours, as rainless and dry as a coughing fit. It pulled our stakes until only our bodies held the tent down. We adjusted our positions, and Maria laid her head in my lap. The wind howled and sent the desert sand smoking across the open spaces the way snow does in the Midwest in winter. The coyotes yipped and cried all night. But as the kid had predicted, not a drop of rain fell.

In the morning all was still. We found ourselves in a relatively lush place surrounded by low hills and prickly pear, looking out to a beautiful view of the Corazones Peaks.

Lightning began again the next night. Maria and I laughed, remembering the kid's pronouncements about rain. We ignored the storm. We were sound asleep when the rain began. Maria sat up and said, "What's that?" I reassured her, for not even the drops I had showed the kid on the window of my car were real rain. Just a phantom. When the sky cracked open and downpour came through the mosquito netting, drenching us, we leaped up, remembering that we were in a tight arroyo, remembering Burro Mesa Pouroff and the smooth polished rock, which had been fashioned by rain right here in this desert.

It was half past midnight as Maria and I, naked in the darkness, dragged our gear to the truck and went lurching up the road, headlights bouncing through standing water a foot deep in the roadway. But halfway out of the canyon to the main highway, the rain stopped. By the time we reached blacktop, Maria had struggled into shorts and a T-shirt, but no rain fell there. The road was dry. We just happened to camp underneath a thunderstorm cell. Another cell hit Terlingua, we'd later learn, and hailstones fell like blind optic spheroids out of a night bombardment.

We drove back, and on the way we saw a collared peccary flee our headlights, a mule deer freeze in them. A coyote crossed our path, and a thousand jackrabbits scattered. "We should go out at midnight more often," Maria said.

Four days later, Paint Gap would be crazed with summer blooms from that cloudburst.

Geronimo surrendered to General Nelson Miles in the fall of 1886, and the great war of extermination ended more or less forever in the most fabled stronghold of the Plains Indians, Big Bend. It had taken the Spanish, the Mexicans, and finally the Americans more than three hundred years to do the job, making it one of the most protracted genocidal efforts in history. No sooner had the Indians been subdued, though, than the Mexican bandits turned around and began raiding deep into Texas, slaughtering farmers, ranchers, and miners.

Early in the twentieth century, Big Bend was under military occupation. By the end of World War One, the Eleventh Aero Squadron was patrolling the border in DeHavilland DH-4 fighter planes and shooting down bandits with mounted .30-caliber machine guns as they fled back into Mexico after their raids. Not until Pancho Villa was assassinated in 1923 did the US War Department feel it was safe to pull out and leave the Texas Rangers and local authorities to fend for themselves. So in essence, from Cortez to the Great Depression, Big Bend was more or less an armed camp, an indefatigable wilderness that admitted as its masters only the most savage among us and made a mockery of those who would civilize it. In declaring it a national park we were simply saying: All right. We give up.

We came upon a place called Ernst Tinaja, a dry rock bed where once a tremendous white-water river flowed. Great uplifted plates of blanched stone led up the drainage like the tilted steps of a collapsed cathedral. The canyon that was cut by churning sand and silt rose sharply on both sides in angled slabs of shale and limestone. High yellow grasses grew sparsely there, waiting for rain. The layered walls were easy to climb, and we found our way up to a cave and sat to watch. The wasps' nests were as big as pie plates. The wasps themselves were yellow and bold, and Maria warned me that they might swarm us for reasons unknown.

Advancing up the river course, a world of complex formations emerged where the water, as it came crashing off the overthrusting crest, polished deep holes in the rock. The pressure of geologic movement melted and bent the layers of those walls into horseshoe shapes so complex and studied that they seem to conceal a mad intelligence, the ventricles of some ancient works. We could see the power of that water in the white boulders tossed here and there and rolled to a lustrous smoothness. Those lunar formations led back and back for miles up the dry river canyon and only became more confounding as they went.

A *tinaja* is a jar for water, and the reference in the name of the place was to a deep hole where water stood year-round. We found it surrounded by slick, polished rock. Imagine that lioness, exhausted from thirst, coming upon this limitless cool cauldron of water standing in these million miles of rock. She leans closer but cannot reach it. The rock is smoothed to a metallic sheen by the white water that once thundered here. She dips, she leans, she starts to slide. Instinctively, she extends her claws to stop herself , but all instinct is against her here, for the claws merely make better runners for the sled she has become. She hunkers down to stop, tightens her haunches, but her slide continues, and she launches off the edge of the chute and splashes into her own reflection, shattering it. She has all the water she wants now. That's where they found her last year, drowned in that selfsame hole where Maria and I now stood, wary of going any closer.

The ranger told Maria that Old Ore Road was "our worst road," and so she naturally urged me to head for it early one morning. A speed of between forty and fifty miles an hour gave the right sense of catastrophe to the ride, crashing through arroyos and dry washes where thunderstorms had cut the road to bedrock. Those roads made a big sport utility vehicle handle like a dirt bike, leaping and jolting and sometimes lifting Maria completely out of her seat with nothing but the seatbelt to hold her. Then I stood on the brakes to manage a steep and rocky section. Then back to forty with cactus slapping the mirrors on both sides. We crested a rise in the land, and I stopped the truck. Maria got down and stood watching as I climbed onto the roof to have a look around.

"You want a piece of this?" I asked. She reached her hand out to me, we locked wrists, and I pulled her up beside me.

A wide valley opened its legs before us with the Chisos making a dark triangle in the background, a central thatch of deep green. The flanks were hills and mesas. To our right the land dropped away to a steep arroyo and cut back toward the Dead Horse Mountains. Steep lime and sandstone cliffs formed dense striations against the low eroded volcanic peaks on the western rim of the earth. A low flat plain stretched away, fixed and finite, to a place where spalls of sunlight cast up imagined beaches.

Back in the truck, Maria urged me to see if I could get all four wheels off the ground at the same time. Four-wheel drifts through the corners. The sense she wanted was that of the comers here, that sense of dominating the indomitable land, of cracking its internal code. All efforts failed. The cattlemen overgrazed the lush grass until nothing held the soil, which blew away, forcing the springs underground. The grasslands died. Cattlemen and goatherds shot the little wolves out of existence. The farmers who came didn't understand the give and take of the Rio Grande. They irrigated in places where the river's yearly flood couldn't reach to leach out the salts. The accumulating salts destroyed the soil so that nothing would grow. They brought in a false willow tree as a windbreak, but it sucked up all remaining water, killing native plants and converting the land to naked desert. The miners ran their smelters twenty-four hours a day and cut every tree on every riverbank in the region until not a stick stood upright, and then they burned coal. When Roosevelt announced that the land was going to be turned into a national park, the remaining ranchers brought in as many cattle as they could to eat the last little tufts of grass and put the finishing touches on their depredations, leaving nothing but stone.

It's difficult to place blame. People who see cities look for cities, and where there are none, they see nothing. We will probably be remembered for the interstate highways that take us to the wilderness, not for the land around them that we try so hard to worship.

The problem with our intrusion here was this: when we stopped the truck and got out, the sun hit us like poison gas. The heat was asphyxiating. The place reasserted itself. The road lay unchanged from our savage passing, shimmering like a snake in the light below, bright as an overexposed Kodachrome. Maria and I knew that we could not beat that place with the tools we had. We'd had our momentary illusion, and before our dust had settled, all was as it always had been. We were never even there. We only dreamed it.

I stopped again, and we got out. I cupped Maria's rear in my hands and pushed her up onto the roof of the truck. I climbed up next to her, and we looked around again to see how far we'd come, how far we had to go in that ever-changing *malpais*. I knew Maria. She wanted to be everywhere at once, and the closest thing she could get to it was our futile racing back and forth. That land admitted access like no other place we'd been and yet denied it in the next hot breath. Slowly, coming into the park over days and days of struggle, we saw at last the wisdom of the kid in this place of solitude. Maria and I began to do nothing, too. Our assaults slowed down. We settled on one campsite. Maria knew the wisdom of the snake, the stillness of the lizard, and the way the wind lay in the shoulder of the valley, waiting out the day, giving night full dominion before it moved. The wind was a night creature. So the only way to regain that land was to come into it, to do nothing there, and to try to recapture if only for a while what it was like to be a Human Being.

———————

Going home, we drove through naked flats of a blinding white pumice. The rummaging of flame and time had turned up heaps of scoria four hundred feet high. I stopped the truck, and together we walked out into the white hills under a scleroid sun. My boots, Maria's sandals, were covered with the white powder, fine as talc. Our shadows burned white, and we turned white like shadows of shadows. In a few moments, we were snowblind in the one-hundred-degree heat. That was the handicraft of the old volcano.

Driving again. Around the next bend, alluvial fans of an ancient watercourse. And then the green river valley heaved into view, and a great undulating plain that had once been grass, bordering against the escarpment. Over there, Mexico.

We slept the night in a real bed in a resort hotel room in Marathon, Texas, and awoke to the sounds that I grew up with in that land. The rooster at dawn. The far-off barking of a dog, who was merely bearing witness to the terrible struggle with darkness in which the light had won another round. I sat up to listen and remember. I watched my great-grandparents wedded into stillness in that land and then put under it. I watched my grandparents, too. They were still in those hills, in warring rock formations, their bones buried in canyons of stone. Maria woke and sat up in the bright room.

"Are we there yet?" she asked.

"Yes," I said. "We're there."

FIRE FIGHTERS

When the lieutenant at the firehouse gave me my turnout gear, the first thing that caught my attention was the hat. I think that's what gets us as kids, isn't it—the hat? When Lt. Bob McKee of the Chicago Fire Department handed it to me, I was surprised at how heavy it was, as if it had a steel liner. As I looked it over, I just knew it had a tale to tell. The fire hat is no mere hat; it is a protective machine of black reinforced battering-ram material, bristling with the bolt shafts and nuts that hold its parts together. The cracked white shield on the front was emblazoned with "Squad 1," and the regal brass topknot was bashed in from what must have been a stunning blow. The flip-down eye shields were smoked over and smeared with a black paste like dried India ink. The dense black crown and brim of the hat were spattered with melted tar and plastic and solder, as if its previous owner had been walking through a wall of burning pay phones.

There was an inner lining of webbing and leather with soft Kevlar fabric earflaps that could be turned down (against the cold, I assumed) like that cap my mother made me wear in the third grade. But when I got inside my first real fire, I found out that the earflaps were meant to be turned down against the heat. At one point I took off my gloves, and the heat burned the hair off my hands. Hair is always the first to go, and it goes in a flash—eyebrows, eyelids, flat top—and if you stick around, then the ears themselves burn off. I heard the men talk about the Greenmill fire, in which a firefighter got caught in a stairwell when the stairs burned out from under him and left him hanging by his fire coat up there, turning like a pig on a spit. One officer told me, "When we got to him, his head was the size of a cantaloupe." He lived.

Running at night, then, with those thoughts clear in my head, I became acutely aware of how alone I was. My children were at home, covered and protected in bed. If anything went awry, they wouldn't know. One night we ran to a fire at the Drake Hotel, and when we got there the smoke was so thick that we couldn't see down Walton Street. I had eaten many business lunches in the plush lobby of that hotel, and now I was going in with turnout gear as the guests were being evacuated. It was eleven at night, and some of the women we saw were fresh from the shower, loping down the main lobby stairs in their beige Drake Hotel bathrobes, with wet hair and the startled look of ponies. My black Kevlar coat was heavy on my shoulders. I felt the iron weight of firefighting equipment in my leaden gloves. I saw them look at us in amazement as we went (Lieutenant McKee and I and big Bob Kuehl and others) down a stairway to the basement and passed incredibly into a thick shroud of smoke that smelled like electric death.

Down there all was quiet. The walls were light-colored tile. It was a service corridor, but it looked to me like morgues I'd seen. Lights flashed through the smoke. I could hear the pry bars and pike poles clanking. Dull explosions in the distance made the hair stand up on my arms, and I was sweating in waves beneath my coat. We were all coughing, trying to see, but there was only smoke and the tile slabs, which seemed to close upon us, and room-service carts to trip us, and a terrible maze, where every sign points the wrong way.

When Bob Kuehl, six feet six inches, 265 pounds, on one side of me, and the muscular black man named Al, on the other side of me, were both taken to the hospital, overcome by the toxic fumes, I understood how serious the trouble was I had gotten myself into. The old Irish firefighter named Red began screaming at me, saying I should never have come down, and who the fuck did I think I was, and who was going to carry me out if I got killed—and of course, he was right, but there I was. I wondered how I had gotten in so deep so fast, but the answer was alarmingly simple: one step at a time.

Although it involved dozens of pieces of firefighting equipment and hundreds of people, the Drake Hotel fire, in the end, was not the one, not the big one. It was a mess, to be sure, but it was not the Moment of Truth. For each man and woman that moment is a different place, a different time, and it comes in a form we cannot imagine.

Each of us dies differently, as each of us lives differently. I could see it at night, at the long picnic-style table in the firehouse dining room. Firehouse corned beef is a Chicago classic, with boiled potatoes and cabbage and carrots. Lieutenant McKee refused to eat "that Irish shit" and instead piled boiled potatoes on his plate and mashed them with a quarter pound of butter. A young firefighter took a look at the slices of corned beef to try to figure out what it was, then took two pieces of rye, added mustard, and had a sandwich. A big paramedic piled his plate, twice, with everything, and ate half a head of cabbage. As I watched them eat and talk and laugh around the long table with the television blaring a pre-season football game, I could see the death in each man, just as I had seen it out on the bulletin board up near the business end of the firehouse. The men passed that bulletin board each time they went out on a run.

The bulletin board (behind dirty glass in a painted wood frame in a corner by the old radiator) contained departmental memoranda with bad Xeroxes of the haphazard Polaroid IDs taken in harsh light with sharp shadow and coarse grain. The faces all had that shocked, dumb look we have when they snap our IDs, that stunned moronic look of gaping solemnity that we get from waiting in line. And beneath each photo was the canticle: "It is my sad duty to inform you . . ." followed by the name and company and the location of the fire at which the man died and a date for services. They were not all grunts, either. There were lieutenants and captains and even the occasional bigwig in there. Tommy O'Donovan fell off snorkel #4 on a still alarm. Both Mike Tally and Mike Forchione died at 2847 North Milwaukee on February 1, 1985.

Big Bob Kuehl and Lieutenant McKee each lost an uncle in the same fire on the same day by a freak accident. The two men older were fairly high ranking: one at the academy and the other in charge of investigations. They heard about a fire while they were having lunch. They did not have to go, but a good fireman lives to get to a fire, and so they went. They were the only two men who died in that fire.

Each time I passed that bulletin board I wondered: Why do they do it? Each photograph showed a man who died at the peak of living. Not many people get that opportunity. Most people die in bed.

But one of the most telling facts I learned about firefighting was that on each day of the year, on each run, each man must renew his pact with the element of fire and his dedication to his work. It is not like the military, where someone puts a gun to their heads, literally, and says, "Charge!" No officer tells the men to go into a fire, and if one does, Kuehl said, "You always say, 'Teach me, Sir. I don't understand. Come in here and show me.' And if he won't go with you, you don't go either." And so for every moment of truth in that great big tinderbox world, there is a moment of transcendental truth for each firefighter, in which he must decide for himself: Is this the fire of all fires? Am I the chosen one for this fire? Can I go in there and live? And if there are children in there: Am I willing to die for them? The truth—the deepest and most amazing truth I discovered—was that Lieutenant McKee and Bob Kuehl could always answer those questions.

More than once Lieutenant McKee told me that he was bothered by the fact that civilians (as they call people who are not firefighters) think that the fire department is always wrecking things. "We come in and break your windows and wreck your roof, that's what people think." They don't understand, he said, that in order to fight a fire, you have to ventilate it. "The fire has to go somewhere, and if you don't let it out the other side, then it's going to come back on you. Windows are the cheapest things to replace."

More important, the civilians don't understand the gestalt test that a fire is. We see what we want to see in a fire. The resident sees his home burning up, and when a fireman breaks a window, the homeowner sees a man breaking a window. But the fireman sees a dangerous puzzle, and when he breaks a window, it is like a chess master moving a pawn.

———

The firehouse I was assigned to, Engine 5, was built in 1928, in the days of Al Capone, under Chicago Mayor William Hale "Big Bill" Thompson. It was a downtown firehouse, set back in a light industrial neighborhood west of the Loop, an architectural treasure of stone and brick with overhead doors and a brass plaque in front. The inside walls and supporting pillars were faced with a gleaming, glazed, sand-colored institutional tile all the way up. The ceiling was elaborately decorated in the grand

Chicago style of the day, with impressive moldings and dentils in deep patterns, each ten feet square. But decades of wild-growth technology had brought in the makeshift modern age beneath layers of telephone wire, jury rig, new paint, gaffer's tape, and conduit that made up the routine necessities of firefighting in the big city. Unit performance awards were stuck haphazardly behind the conduit that was hammered into the old concrete walls. The pipes ran up toward the ceiling, changing from silver to white where the ceiling paint took over. A cheater speaker hung on a nail above the red phone, and a faded old decal above the lieutenant's desk said: Up Your Chimney!

At the front of the house, near the lieutenant's battered gray metal desk, were the communications lines by which the company and squad were called to a fire. There were several telephones, several speakers, a radio or two, and the joker line, all above a makeshift formica counter with bundles of wire hanging down in hag-brown, tangled tresses. Nearby was the dirty old army-green steel card catalog listing the alarm boxes around the city and outlining which engines should respond to them and in what order. The card file was desk-high, and its top was made of blackboard slate. Whenever a call came in, someone (whoever was near) wrote the address of the call on the blackboard, held down a button that prevented the firehouse bell from ringing (it rang automatically unless someone was there to stop it, a safety device in case everyone went to sleep at once), and then decided what code to ring, if any. Three bells, for example, would send the ambulance.

The whole operation had a temporary, thrown-together quality about it, as if we were just making do, just barely holding the rising tide of chaos at bay, just enough to get our shift done, until the experts arrived. I had the feeling at every moment that our position was embattled and that we were about to be overrun by the enemy. But who was the enemy?

There had been attempts to modernize the Department, but it had resisted change. Perhaps it's better this way. The original system, still in use, was elegantly simple: A man in the central alarm station would press a switch that said "Engine 5" and he would talk into a microphone. Then a big speaker right above the telephones in our house would carry the words directly to the man on watch. "I always knew who I was talking to," said the officer at the alarm center. A backup system called the joker line operated at the same time. If one system failed, the other would get the message through. Hundreds of miles of cable underneath the city carried the signals. A few years ago the Chicago Fire Department contracted Motorola to build a modern computer system for communications, which they did for many millions of dollars, and as the man on alarm watch told me, "It didn't work worth a shit. I never knew who I was talking to, and it took twenty-five seconds to get the thing cranked up."

Half a minute might be forever in a fire. So now the Chicago Fire Department has a building with $7 million worth of unused computer equipment in it, and alarms are sent the same way they were sent over one hundred years ago—and the system works pretty well. When the call came in, we heard a human voice, and all it said was the address and what type of call it was (for example, a still-and-box alarm).

The first time I heard a call, I nearly missed the whole thing. Lieutenant McKee was sitting at his metal desk at the front of the house. It was summertime and the overhead doors were open. Some of the guys were sitting on black Naugahyde chairs outside, nearly in Des Plaines Street, with the downtown traffic rumbling past. The garbled voice said something over the speaker, an address, and then the joker line clacked out its series of numbers—5-5-1—and Lieutenant McKee stood up slowly and said to me, "We're going. That's us." The way he said it was so casual, so matter-of-fact, that I didn't know what he meant at first, until I saw a couple of men getting onto the rig, and I understood he meant going in the fire engine. I had somehow envisioned a scurrying of rubber boots, men sliding down the poles they kept so meticulously polished, the rush and noise and urgency that people in a burning building must feel.

I shrugged into my turnout coat, which felt like it was made of tire chains. It had reflective yellow stripes running around its girth so they could find us if we passed out in the smoke. The collar was soft corduroy. I kicked off my shoes and jumped into the hip-length rubber boots that were turned down to the knee, and I put on the ten-pound helmet and the gauntlet gloves. When I went to climb onto the rig, I realized how very heavy I had gotten. I had to pull myself up, like hauling a sack of sand up a rope; and then we were starting out the door, four guys in the back with me. Lieutenant McKee was in front with the driver, big Bob Kuehl. And we were lurching and bouncing down the road with the immense diesel engine strumming the steel beneath us. A strap hanging from the ceiling operated the big air horn, and Lieutenant McKee kept it busy—a great, grand, irritating, bleating, squealing bellow that fell like Armageddon upon the sleeping buildings of the city.

Running in the city, there was not so much a sense of speed and emergency as there was a sense of mighty, unstoppable momentum. The big red engine was forty feet long and carried a long silver ladder and a snorkel basket on top, and the interior cabin of steel and black upholstery, where I sat with the firefighters, was the size of a respectable Manhattan living room. Our seats were each backed with an aluminum rack that held the yellow-painted steel air bottles and breather masks we would use inside of fires. In addition to that, the truck was laden with miles of hose, dozens of pike poles, axes, sledge hammers, pry bars, and every manner of rescue equipment from cutting torches to "Jaws," a pneumatic device the size of a shark, which could be used to open an automobile like a sardine can. All this, then, was sent hurtling down the street at forty miles an hour, diesel-powered, air horn bleating furiously, its cries echoing off the glass-and-steel cathedral towers around us, as morning traffic dipped and swam in the windshield. I had the distinct sense that it mattered little if those high-colored fishes got out of our way or not: Moby Dick was coming through. I remembered Bob Kuehl, who drove the engine, telling me about a guy in a Lincoln Continental, blocking the way to a fire one day. Bob leaned on the air horn, and the driver gave Bob the finger. Bob just rolled right over the Lincoln and pushed it out of the way. The insurance company called, evidently not in possession of all the facts. "This man says you hit his car," they said. Bob said, "Yeah, I was driving a fire engine, and he got in my way."

But it was during those first few runs with Squad 1 in Engine 5, as I became aware of the fact that there was no real sense of urgency, that I began to understand how firefighters can go from being such ordinary people to being such heroes in such a short span of time. And the answer was: one step at a time. By very small increments. Michaelangelo carved his famous statue of Eve one little chip of marble at a time. It was just an ordinary rock before that. We get into the worst trouble that way, too. One moment we were pushing a column of noise down the street, cozy and protected in our berth, and the whole world was making way for us, and along the street all the women going to work were stopping to turn and look at us, touched with empathy and understanding. (They say no one gets more affection from women than firefighters, not even fighter pilots. I've worked with both, and I believe it.)

But the next moment we were in the blazing doorway, looking into the unknown. One more step wouldn't kill us, we always knew that. It was never the first step into the void that killed you. Was it the second step, then? Probably not. And yet, somehow, by otherwise imperceptible increments, things got worse—they always did. It was a law of nature.

Lieutenant McKee was typical in many ways. He was one of five brothers, "And only one of them was smart enough to avoid becoming a firefighter." His father rose through the ranks to become a battalion chief over a thirty-year period. When I ran with him, Bob McKee was thirty-eight and looked young. He was under six feet tall, powerfully built, with brown hair and blue eyes, a quick laugh and a knowing smile. When I'd ask him a very direct question, one that probably ought never to be spoken out loud, he would look at the ceiling and get very quiet and then smile in a certain way, like I had touched upon a secret that he didn't want to tell. But he was so good-natured that he couldn't disappoint me, and he'd tell anyway.

One night we were out under the stars on the concrete apron in front of the firehouse, sitting in old chairs, our feet up on the red fire hydrant, and I asked, "Have you brought many children out of fires?"

He gave me that look of his, but there was no little smile as usual. He just looked blank. "Not many live ones," he said.

McKee and Kuehl had worked together for years and were as close as two soldiers in a trench. In fact, they had both been Marines, though not in the same place, and now that they were together, they made something of a Mutt and Jeff team. Kuehl, an immense and powerful man, towered over Lieutenant McKee. When I'd ask either one of them a question that demanded a personal or thoughtful response, they would get around their embarrassment by telling the story to each other instead of to me, so that I could listen in. But like so many men I had met over the years who were in naturally hazardous professions, they did not like to speak directly of the hazard in a way that acknowledged that it was there. For if they acknowledged that it was there, then they'd have to be fools to do anything other than avoid it. But their profession was to confront the hazard. So what could they make of their lives, when its most central and definitive professional act was to do something that others would consider foolhardy?

No, certain things had to be kept at a respectful distance, and then they could be approached sideways, by small increments, until one was square in the jaws of the dragon. And when I made them talk about it directly, they told stories and they laughed and laughed, as if it had been the funniest thing in the world, to be almost burned alive.

They talked about the way you approach a fire, the signs you're supposed to see as you come up to the building. Say there's smoke coming out, dense black smoke, but there are no flames. And say the windows are black on the inside, like they're covered with soot, but there's a little glow of red deep in there somewhere. That is a fire that has burned itself out for lack of oxygen, but everything inside is superheated, ready to blow; all it lacks is some air. If you don't know what you're looking at, you might go up to the door and open it, and, like opening a can of coffee, break the seal on the vacuum. "Sometimes you can see the smoke pouring out around the window frames," Lieutenant McKee told me, "and it curls right back and is sucked back inside."

That is a backdraft.

And if you open the door unaware, it can pull you right in with it, like an undertow. As you are dragged inside, kicking and screaming, the missing ingredient, oxygen, is sucked in, too. "When you do the wrong thing, you find out real quick," McKee said.

One night, he went to a tavern that had been built on the back of a three-story apartment building. The fire had started in the tavern area and burned down until there was no air left. "When we got there, it didn't look that bad, some smoke coming out. I'd gotten the line laid out, and I was standing by the door putting my face piece on. I opened the door, and next thing I knew, I was laying fifteen feet away. I had no idea what happened to me. We went from solid black smoke to a building completely involved in flames in about two seconds. The worst thing was there were two guys going across the roof when that happened. That was not a great day." Luckily, the two men had just gotten to the three-story apartment building when the roof vanished beneath their feet and flames shot into the sky. They scrambled up a fire escape.

Each type of building, each type of fire, has its own way of killing you; and just when you think you understand them all, one turns on you with a new trick. Like the lion tamer in the cage, the firefighter must approach a fire with the knowledge that it is never tame. You can make it do tricks, but you can't turn your back.

Those big old brick industrial buildings, three or five or seven stories high—every big city has them. They were constructed out of immense pine timbers that used to be available before we cut down all the forests, virgin growth out of prehistory, dripping with resins. When they burn, they go fast. The sappy wood burns bright and hot, like nature's own acetylene. The firefighters are aware of the irony of the rehab business, in which old factories are converted into dwellings for the over-privileged. Those buildings are firetraps. Even if he had the money, no firefighter would live in one. They're too dangerous.

Once the timbers get going, the load-bearing walls of brick and mortar come crumbling down around the fire engines and men. Lieutenant McKee's brother was buried by a collapsing wall. He was working with Bob Kuehl at the time. "And I just happened to walk away at the right moment," Kuehl said, "and he didn't." He miraculously survived, although, as Lieutenant McKee said (putting his hand out three feet above the floor, with that little smile of his), "He's about this short now."

We were sitting around the firehouse one day when the battalion chief came by and chewed out the lieutenant for leaving a fire. "But you told us to leave," McKee said. And the battalion chief blew up, denying that he had released anybody. McKee, a sensible officer, said he was sorry,

FIRE FIGHTERS

but when the battalion chief left, he and Kuehl talked about how the chief had been acting a little strange lately, ever since the tire fire.

"The tire fire" was the way they referred to a big industrial fire at 2416 South Archer, which had involved three buildings and shut down the power to Comisky Park during the Chicago White Sox season opener and delayed three railroads. It was overshadowed in the news, because the very next day, while the tire fire was still burning, a landmark Sullivan building, housing numerous art galleries and millions of dollars' worth of art, was torched in Chicago's fashionable River North gallery district, and it was one of the biggest fires since the Chicago Fire. During the tire fire, the battalion chief had gotten himself in a bad spot and ended up in the hospital.

"He damned near got himself killed," Kuehl said.

"What happened?" I asked.

"He panicked," Lieutenant McKee said. He explained that the problem is that in big industrial buildings, it is very easy to get lost. In this case, there were two buildings of several stories each, with a mountain of old tires between. The tires were burning, setting both buildings on fire. It was a very big fire. The fire boat came up the Chicago River to help put water on it.

The chief had stormed through one building with a line, a hose, and came up, actually underneath the fire—in one building but below the level of the burning mountain of tires outside. When the building on the other side of the tires collapsed, it blew the fire back at him, sending him back into the building. Evidently, he lost his grip on the hose at that point. He went up a flight of stairs to the next level, and then he was lost.

"You ain't gonna burn up if you got a fucking hose in your hand," Lieutenant McKee said.

"The first thing they teach you in the fire academy," Kuehl said, "is that the hose is going to lead you to one of two places: On one end there's water, and where there's water, there's also air. You can actually breathe the air coming out of the end of the hose, and you can fight the fire with the water. On the other end is how you got in, so you can get out. So you never let go of that hose. It's your life."

"What happened to the chief then?" I asked.

"Fuck if I know."

"He panicked."

There were two of the chief's men down, critical, before it was over, and one of them wound up high above the fire on a balcony. They said the chief had been flaky ever since, blowing up at people, giving contradictory orders, forgetting that he'd released people from fires. It happens. You get too close to the flames too many times, and not only can you get burned, you also can get flamed out.

Lieutenant McKee and Kuehl were still young and cocky when I met them. They had been saving each other's lives for years. It's enough to make you think you have nine lives, like a cat. At one fire Kuehl looked around and saw McKee standing on an 800-amp live wire that had been knocked down. "What do you say?" Kuehl asked. "He's got both feet on it. If he takes one off, he's going to touch the ground and get fried."

So he quietly, very softly, said, "Don't move. Now look at what you're standing on. Now jump with both feet at once."

A moment later McKee was going to go down a gangway when Kuehl saw the chimney above falling. "Don't go down that gangway," he said.

"Oh, I can make it," Lieutenant McKee said, and he ran as the bricks rained down behind him. As they told that story, McKee and Kuehl laughed and laughed until I thought they'd fall out of their chairs. "We saved the attic," Lieutenant McKee said.

"Yeah, but the first two floors burned out from under us!" Kuehl said. And they doubled over with laughter.

But after all the laughter, Lieutenant McKee admits that it bothered him that the battalion chief yelled at him, no matter who was right. He prides himself in doing the job right. Besides, his father was a battalion chief, and he knows that some day he'll probably be one, too. And although he knows he must rise through the ranks, as his father did—because it is his destiny and he was born to it—still he does not relish losing the familiarity of being one of the boys. "I'm just a poor boy who wants to go to a fire," he told me. "I don't want to sit behind a desk."

Late at night I found him at his desk with the big, black, red-cornered Squad 1 logbook in his lap, scribbling entries. Rock music, turned down low, played from a small plastic radio on the gray metal desk. Lieutenant McKee's chair was dirty and orange and ratty. He drank coffee from a heavy, old, chipped white ceramic cup such as the ones you'd find in a railroad dining car. His telephone was fire-engine red. The Sears Tower blinked from above us in the streaming August rain. If that tower ever burned, it would be Lieutenant McKee's fire: the tallest building in the world. He'd never even seen the inside.

This is probably the biggest secret in fire departments around the country: The real reason people become firefighters is to help other people. That is hardly ever spoken. It's almost a sacrilege to say it, because it sounds, well, it sounds kind of sappy, like you're some kind of do-gooder.

I asked him one day why he wanted to be a fireman, but it was a stupid question, and I knew it before I asked. Lieutenant McKee looked up from his book and said without a smile, "I like to wreck things."

———————

We'd always get a run in the middle of something. We'd be talking or doing a chore or eating, and the call would come, and then we'd get into our boots and coats and we'd rumble out onto Des Plaines Street and down the avenues of the city. We were running one day to the Chicago Hilton Hotel, and in the cab of the fire engine there were two young guys on my left and two old guys on my right. I knew the older guys, Bernie (the Irish guy they called Red) and Wally. They were there all the time, had been for years. The two younger men were from other houses, temporarily assigned to Squad 1 while someone was on vacation or out sick or (in this case) injured by falling bricks in a fire. I noticed that whenever we ran, the two young guys and I got all dressed up right on the way out the door. We snapped the hasps on our Kevlar coats and did up the Velcro closures. We got our air bottles all strapped on and put on our gloves, and we were ready. But Wally and Bernie just hung there on the seats, heads down. Bernie would chain smoke cigarettes, and Wally would just sit and look out the window, as if he were on a very long train ride. Every once in a while, Bernie would enliven himself and scream something out the window, especially if he saw another firefighter or a pretty woman. He was a wild red-headed Irishman with a foul mouth and a crazed glint in his eye, and a typical Sunday morning greeting to a brother firefighter might be, "Hey, motherfucker, lay off the cocksucking cheeseburgers!"

It was the middle of the afternoon, but we had obviously gotten Bernie up from his nap, what with the bells and all. Kuehl commented that Bernie could sleep just about anywhere, and Bernie said, "I could sleep with my dick slammed in a door."

The Hilton wasn't really burning, although maybe a trash can was, and we sat in the rain for a while, smoking and joking, and then we were dismissed and rolled away into the city smoke and haze. As we left, Bernie leaned out the window and screamed at one of his fellows in a shrill voice, "Ah, they'll make anybody a fucking engineer!"

Rolling down the avenue, Red caught sight of the chief in his red LTD Ford with a firefighter for a driver, and he yelled out the window at the firefighter: "Hey, how's the chief's golf game, cocksucker? Maybe we can get you a job as the chief's caddy when you get shit-canned outta that buggy." The derision was not aimed at the man but at the fact that he was driving a red Ford with the battalion chief in it. He was not in a fire engine, and he was not going to walk into a fire. He was going to sit in a buggy with the chief. I understood: Riding in that silly little red LTD was, well . . . degrading. Riding in the fire engine was the thing. The real thing.

The fire engine was an amazing object of art and engineering: It was, for one thing, as big as an old-fashioned locomotive. But it was also worked into a blazing red luster of enamel and filigree with chrome fittings and brass pipes, and then hung all over with buffed steel attachments, battlements, and gear, so that it looked like a rock-and-roll battleship when it went clattering down the lane. Now, leaving the Hilton Hotel fire, this amazing machine pulled up next to a UPS truck. The driver looked over, and we were just about face to face with him. Our windows were open. He smiled and said something in greeting and then lit up his cigarette with a Zippo. When the flame appeared, Al, the young black fireman sitting across from me, screamed at the top of his lungs, "Fire! Fire! Fire!" The UPS driver was so startled that he dropped his cigarette in his lap and turned pale, and the firefighter across from me laughed and laughed as we pulled away from the traffic light, our diesel engine churning up the wet air with an oily soot. "I done scared him," he said.

———————————

Firehouse humor: They call the big beer cooler the Baby Coffin. And they have different names for different kinds of dead people. Dead ones they find in fires are Crispy Critters. Ones that have been dead for a long time, like gangsters in somebody's trunk, are called Stinkers. There are Floaters and Headless Horsemen and Dunkers. McKee and Kuehl were reminiscing about the times when they were lying around or swimming (they can do that because the squad has a scuba team, and so the whole squad can go swimming on the excuse that they're practicing scuba diving) or doing something else sinfully lazy in the middle of the mean work week, commenting to themselves how the regular working slobs were out there getting their asses packed on the rock pile, and they all smiled and laughed at one another, saying, "What a fucking great job," when the call came in: Assist police. They dreaded that call: Assist police. That meant do the dirty work for the cops. "That is a definite shit detail," Kuehl said.

The police were down on the first floor in the apartment building, and they didn't even want to go near the apartment. So Kuehl and McKee went up. They were those kind of guys, the Special Forces of fire-fighting: They'd do anything. There was a stinker in the bathtub, and he'd been there for a while. The soup in the tub was green, a kind of green that's not on the Sherwin Williams color chips. So they wrapped the corpse in a tarp—which in itself was no easy task, because his arms and head were falling off like a chicken that's been in the pot too long—and then they put it in the elevator and pushed 1 and let it go down alone: Little present for you, guys.

The firefighters have to risk their lives fighting fires, but they also get the lowest shit work in the city, like picking up the dead. Kuehl picked up a lady one day who had crossed against the light, in front of a truck. She slipped, and the truck ran over her head. "When I grabbed her hair to pick up her head, it was actually stuck to the road with suction." And then he made this suction cup sound with his mouth.

They get called to the highest places and the lowest. They get called when someone has jumped or wants to jump. One morning the call came, and we all got into our turnout gear and jumped into the rig and wound up in the lobby of the Leo Burnette Advertising Agency, a brand-new building in Chicago's Loop. Beautiful women in expensive clothes and guys wearing silk ties and eighty-dollar haircuts swished past us as we clanked in our bulky protective clothing there in the green-marble lobby with its buffed chrome fittings. We were like sooty armored animals who had stumbled into the china shop. We smelled like high noon in hell, and the women who passed us smelled like heaven. They looked at us with this mixture of awe and shock, respect and disgust, for they knew they were looking at the only real heroes left in America, but we were so grubby and awkward, our appearance so rude, it just didn't add up. This was definitely not what the Leo Burnette Agency would do with a fireman's image.

We went to the roof and did a hero-like thing. There were two window washers on high ladders, and they were stranded on the side of the building, forty-eight stories above the city, and the Chicago Fire Department saved their lives, pulling them off with ropes. As I hung over the side of the building, I saw the look on the face of the worker who was being hauled up to safety by the firefighters. He was dangling there on what looked like spider web, five hundred feet over the street, a straight drop, and the city beyond was wreathed in the summer green of the park by the glittering blue-silver lakeshore. The tops of office towers floated ghostly above the pointillist city, and in the middle of it all, like Breughel's Icarus, was this redneck window washer, his face as white as a lamb. I could hear the electric commuter train rattling past in the loop below, and I could see our red fire engine like a match-box toy with the firemen in black with yellow hornet stripes, walking briskly in the mist. The lake and the park fell away into haze, and the single man dangled like a doll on a yellow thread with five firemen holding the end and nothing but the moist and empty air to catch him if it all came suddenly unwound. When they pulled him clutching and gasping onto the roof, ten hands were on him—nobody here was going to let this one get away—and the window washer stood pale and shaken and thin in his seed cap and green T-shirt. He stammered, "Thanks. Thanks, guys." And that was all.

FIRE FIGHTERS

When we came back down through the lobby, it was strange to see this other side of life, the luxury, the opulence, the riches, the goodies of society, and know that it was forever out of reach. Firefighters save all this for the rich people. They save it equally for the poor. They save your life just the same if you are the president of Leo Burnette or the window washer. Yet the biggest rewards of society are forever out of reach for them.

More than once Lieutenant McKee thought his life was over. He has come near panic, he said. The worst time was in an old industrial space, one of those old firetrap buildings of exterior brick and timber joists. Lieutenant McKee had gone to an upper floor to reconnoiter while the others fought the fire down below. He wanted to see if the upper floors were involved so that they could plan their tactics. But then the upper floor was engulfed in smoke, and when McKee had gone in far enough to look around, it turned out to be one of those new office mazes divided into cubicles, with desks and computers and false walls, long zigzag corridors, and dead ends. Before he knew it, he became turned around, and he was lost in the labyrinth. He understood, yes, this is how it happens: You get into the worst just the way you get into the least, one step at a time. And at each step he took, he knew he was getting in deeper.

The smoke was rolling over him. He had started to hear the crackling of fire, the tinkling of glass, as things began to break. There was heat coming from over there in the darkness. The smoke was choking him, and he heard human voices, possibly from an air-conditioning duct—somewhere. He had no line to follow, no hose, and he could not even find a real wall to follow. It was all fake barriers that came apart in his hands, and he fell over them as he blundered this way and that. It was then that his superior breeding—son and brother of firefighters that he was—came to the fore. He told himself to calm down, to take charge. Panic has no place in a fire. There are always clues, if only we can read them. You have to think your way out like a detective. Okay, no hose to follow out. How else can I tell which way is out? Something must tell me, something. Smoke was all he could see. All right, how about smoke. Smoke has to go somewhere, right? It has to go out. And how does it get out? When I approach a fire, I see it pouring out the windows. That's it!

He looked to see which way the smoke was going and followed it. Soon, he was at a window, and in another minute he was off the floor and had been reunited with his company. Another man might have panicked and died in there.

Firefighters talk about fires the way musicians discuss the symphonies they have played over and over. And the fires are different the way the symphonies are different in the hands of different conductors. "You know that place where it's allegro and there's a key change? That always screws me up."

Then there are attic fires in frame houses. Old frame houses in big cities are almost always made with hollow walls, so the fire can start in the basement—or anywhere—but it's going to go to the attic, because heat will rise through the hollow walls. And it's such intense heat, that it starts a fire up there early on. So Lieutenant McKee and Kuehl always find themselves, sooner or later, trying to save an attic. It's a part of their lives, and they pride themselves in their ability to save attics (not that the attics are worth anything, or serve some useful function in society once they are saved; these acts are pure, without ulterior motive—in their own strange way, they are sport or even art). McKee and Kuehl have a technique. They feel they can read the fire, sense its moods, and outfox it.

One day they arrived at a fire. Another company was already there and had lines all laid out, but no one was going in. As Lieutenant McKee and Kuehl came up, the other company officer told them, "You can't make it in there."

Lieutenant McKee took a look at the fire and said, "Let me just get by you here for a second and see what I can do." And he and Kuehl went on in, Kuehl holding the pipe, or nozzle, and Lieutenant McKee holding the hose behind him. One technical note: They didn't have their breathing masks on. They had air bottles, but they were wearing cheaters, which are simply mouthpieces like scuba regulators and offer no eye protection. (Strictly speaking, cheaters are forbidden by the Department, but there are always three levels to every institution: the administrative fantasy, the staff reality, and then there's how ordinary people really do things.)

Later McKee would say, "Those little frame houses are small but they're hot." And he and Kuehl would laugh and laugh, sitting out under the stars and sipping coffee. They nearly lost their eyesight from using cheaters.

"We showed them, didn't we?" Kuehl said.

"Yeah, we showed them. We put it out, but it nearly put us out."

"It was either put it out, or resign from the Department after that."

They crawled into the attic, literally on their bellies, and the fire flashed over their heads and got behind them. "It took about two years to crawl thirty feet that night," Lieutenant McKee said.

"Yeah, Bobby Hoffa got burnt up that way. He walked through the attic to see what was up, went to the far window, and yelled down for them to send a line up. When he turned around, it was nothing but fire."

"Yeah, I'd like to hear the real story-story on that," Lieutenant McKee said, meaning that behind every story there's something else that will kill you. Or at least that's the way they like to analyze fires. If someone is hurt, they always believe that there was something done wrong, which, if they could just pinpoint it, they could avoid in a similar situation. In other words: That won't happen to me, because I'm too fucking good. No one truly believes in death.

I asked Kuehl what we should do when we're in an attic and it flashes over. That's when the fire gasses catch and burn through the air, over our heads, and start another fire behind us. "Just lay down," he said, "and stay down. It looks like lightning over your head in the smoke," he added, reminiscing about the attic fire in the frame house. "Going through those rooms was like going through the Seven Gates of Hell. But if you stand up, it'll take your head right off you. I was in one house once where a flashover came down a hallway. This other guy comes running down the hall shouting, 'Get out! Get out!' And here's this rolling, bubbling ball of fire coming down the hall. I'd never seen anything like that before in my life. We dove down the stairs, and I mean head first. Then we went out and had a cigarette," he said with a thoughtful smile, adding after a moment, "and we don't even smoke!"

"So what happened in the attic?" I asked.

"Oh, we put it out."

They say either "we won" or "we didn't win." On one fire they described (another frame-house attic), they said, "It was over our heads, coming out of the holes we had made, coming up behind us— we burned that one to the ground."

McKee described another one, when he was just a firefighter. He was going up the stairs leading a departmental lieutenant, when he shouted, "I think this stairs leads up to the back of the house."

And the lieutenant shouted back at him, "I know where the fuck it goes! This is my house!"

"We burned that one to the ground, too," McKee said. Again, he and Kuehl laughed and laughed, kicking their feet on the fire hydrant.

The moment of truth came for me on a sunny day when we were all down at Meigs Field, Chicago's lakefront airport, getting ready to go scuba diving. It was one of those days I'd heard the men talking about, when they're all saying to themselves, "What a great job." It must have been ninety-five degrees out, and jumping in the lake sounded good. Kuehl had just gotten stripped down and was about to shrug into his scuba gear when he stopped. I saw him stop and look out over the sky-line of the city: "Hey, there's a fire," he said.

We quickly got back into our clothes and jumped on the rig and drove across the city to the place where we had seen the smoke. There, in a humble neighborhood, we found a little frame house completely involved in flames. It seemed unimpressive as we arrived. It was just a few rooms, two stories, in a row of ordinary houses, and there was a big brown Cadillac blocking the fire hydrant. When I jumped down from the engine, Lieutenant McKee handed me a pike pole with a metal hook on the end and said, "Follow me." And we walked right into the burning building.

I had never done anything quite like that before. It seemed so simple, but it was then that I realized that fire is a living thing, a wild element, a manifestation of energy that eats the air. Fire can transform itself in the blink of an eye while you're looking the other way. It is a dragon, a bird, a wolf, a shark—and this one was in a feeding frenzy.

Lieutenant McKee ran, and so I ran to keep up with him, for the thing I feared most was losing him, because I had come to trust him completely. Before I knew it, I was going up a stairway. I recognized that stairway. I had lived with one just like it when I was a little boy, narrow, with a round wooden handrail, only this one was like the bottom of a back yard charcoal barbecue grill: It was glowing. We were encased in our protective clothing, but I wondered what a little boy in his pajamas and socks would do here: Everywhere I looked, everything, the walls, the floor, the ceiling, the woodwork, was glowing embers. Coiled snakes of smoke issued forth as if the wood had rotted before our eyes and maggots filled its blackened flesh. I was hit by wave after wave of heat that knocked the breath out of me, and when I gulped to catch my breath, I inhaled something noxious. It was not air; it was some super-heated admixture of poisons. In all my lessons during all the nights and days with the firefighters, there was nothing that could have prepared me for this. I felt that I'd been dropped onto the surface of Mercury, and we were burning in a methane sea.

On and on we went, up the stairs and into the close little bedrooms where someone had lived. "Here, here!" Lieutenant McKee was shouting at me. I was coughing and trying to see what he was pointing at. "Don't look up!" he shouted, so I looked up. He grabbed my head and pushed it down. "Don't! Look! Up!" he said again. "Pull the ceiling!" I didn't understand what he wanted of me until he showed me. He wanted me to use the lance I had in my hands: Shove it up with both hands until it poked through the plaster and lathe of the ceiling. Then yank on it until the ceiling came crashing down around me. And don't look up, because all that falling plaster and burning wood could blind me. It was then I realized that the fire was burning not only all around us but over our heads as well, and the man coming up behind me with the pipe was waiting on me to pull the ceiling so that he could open up with the water and put out the fire over our heads and keep it from leaping out to eat us.

I began jabbing furiously at the ceiling, ripping and tearing with the lance, and a great shower of lathe and plaster and conduit began raining down upon the hard helmet I wore. For the first time I understood the shape of the fireman's hat. I could no longer breathe, but breath seemed a peccant extravagance to wish for by that time. I was roasting in my Kevlar coat like a potato in tinfoil, but I pulled my way through the ceiling from one end of the room to the other, and the man behind me (whom I never saw) opened up the nozzle and showered the ceiling with water. We were engulfed in steam now, steam and smoke, and I was drowning in water, soaked from head to foot and covered with a kind of black paste. I was glad, though—glad because the water was cool and because the voracious oily dragon of flame was eating oxygen and water and not us. Now all I had to worry about was the steam that was burning my face.

I moved to the next room just in time to see that the outside wall had fallen into the back yard, and I took a moment to walk up to the edge and look down—actually, I went over to steal a breath of what I saw there: clear air. When I looked down, I saw the whole back yard was aflame with the rubble of cars and with stacks of truck tires and trash, burning in mystical rings of fire. The flames seemed to dance the whole world around—there seemed no end to it—and I remembered visiting the Prado in Madrid and seeing the gorgeous and hideous visions that Bosch painted of the world in flames.

Wondering how much more of the house was going to fall into the yard, I backed away from the precipice and returned to my task with the ceilings. I don't know how long I fought in there, wielding that pike with the man behind me spraying the flames overhead, but after a while the heat seemed to subside, and I was put to work poking holes in the roof above, through the attic space I'd opened up by tearing down the lathe. There were men on the roof, and when they'd see my pike going through a soft spot (soft because it had been burned), they'd chop a bigger hole with an axe, and someone would spray out the last lingering tongues of fire with a hose.

It was finally over. The whole place was encased and glued together with black paste. I came back down the narrow staircase, which had partly burned away while I was upstairs.

On the first floor, in the living room, I looked out onto the street and saw the crowd that had gathered to watch. A battalion chief grabbed me, and because I had a pike, he said, "Square off those windows, son." He meant the windows through which I was looking at the people. So I took my lance and I shoved it through the panes of glass, breaking them, and then I ran it around each square, raking the glass away with my pike and smiling out at the people on the street and remembering Lieutenant McKee, when I had asked him why he wanted to be a firefighter, saying, "I like to wreck things."

IN THE BELLY OF THE WHALE

Maybe you don't know how oil was
formed. It was formed by things
dying and being held in the earth.

—JAMES STEWART, *Thunder Bay* (1951)

When the crew boat arrived at a little past dawn, I saw no way for us to get from the deck of the boat to the main deck of the rig, no stairs, no elevator. And yet the offshore oil drilling rig towered above us and blotted out the sun, a skyscraper teetering on three great steel pilings driven into the surface of the heaving sea. The slick pilings, shooting right out of the sea, offered no handholds, so the entire question of getting on and off the rig remained mysterious to me. I had been sleeping with the crew in rows of aqua-blue Naugahyde chairs in the darkened cabin below deck ever since we left Galveston several hours earlier. Now we had all lurched out onto the deck, sleepy and yawning, with hair matted and eyes crossed. I watched those rough and dirty men in T-shirts and jeans and construction boots carry their sea bags onto the rear deck of that ancient one-hundred-foot diesel boat and stand on the greasy wooden planks as if God himself were about to come down and lift them up to the deck above so that they could go to work.

I had been waiting to meet the man in charge, Bud Cole, but he had been asleep below during the midnight trip, and now I saw him standing on the deck ahead of all the other men, his sea bag at his feet, first in line, it seemed, though in line for what, I still could not imagine. I staggered across the planks, which were blackened with oil and worn to a supple suede by years and years of boots and gear. I stumbled over chains and wooden crates to get to Bud, and when I finally stood beside him, I gazed up at the amazing edifice of gray steel, which we faced in our tiny boat, bobbing on the open sea. A pile of brown rope lay at Bud Cole's feet in the center of what looked to be an oversized orange life ring. Its purpose, if it had any, evaded me, as everything else about this trip had so far, ever since the twinkling lights of Galveston Island had withered and vanished on the dark horizon behind our churning green wake in the dead of night.

Bud, in his blue jumpsuit, was built like a Rottweiler dog, the kind of man it would be difficult to knock over, because he was wide and had a low center of gravity. I was to learn that natural selection would favor that quality on an oil rig: a man like that is already down when he's standing up, and so he would be less likely to fall off. Bud was looking up and away from me, so I poked him in the arm to get his attention, and my fingertip met something the texture of an inflated truck tire. It was Bud Cole's tricep muscle. He glared at me as if deciding whether he'd have to fight or not. I introduced myself, and it became immediately apparent that no one had told him I was coming onto his oil rig. He turned his scowling, incredulous rage upon me: a visage that was reticulated with the complex carvings of sea wind and time, like a face on a crumpled hundred-dollar bill. He wore a hard hat, and beneath its brim were the small and venomous red spiders of his eyes, peering at me out of their agitated web of wrinkles.

"I'm a writer," I said by way of explanation.

"Oh," he said, his face breaking into the smile of a guard dog. "A writer. Just what we need." And with no goodbye or further warning, he stepped onto the big orange life ring near his feet. The rope that had been piled within its circumference straightened up as if by a magical force and created a woven basket in the air, standing by itself without any evident reason why it should. The boat pitched and rolled with the sea, and Bud grabbed hold of some of the rope that stood inexplicably among us, and three other men grabbed hands full of that same black rope, all matted and slick with grime and the secretions of some dark process. Each man placed one foot on the orange ring, and then, with the rope taut and singing in the sea wind, they all rose astoundingly into the sky, like the trapeze lady does before her circus act, a hand trailing languidly in the air.

IN THE BELLY OF THE WHALE

Because of having pushed my way to the head of the line to talk to Bud, I found that I was next, along with three companions. The man to my left must have seen the look of horrified incomprehension on my face when Bud ascended into the heavens, because he tried to explain to me how to take the ride. As the openwork basket was returning to us, empty now, I began to understand the mechanism by which we were expected to get onto the oil rig from that pitching boat, which was holding itself steady in the running seas by means of its diesel engines and the skilled hands of its captain at the throttles. Now I had begun to piece together the puzzle: I could see far above us the red Link-Belt crane, perched atop the twenty-story structure. It swiveled and ground away as it lowered the cable on which dangled the woven rope basket with the orange ring affixed to its bottom.

The man to my left was now speaking to me with the intent, perhaps, of saving my life. He was thin and wasted beyond recognition as a human being. His teeth had turned black, and his skin was creased into a mummified, corpse-like appearance, and his moustache dangled like a false moustache, fashioned for Halloween effect out of a handful of horsetail clippings. He wore a hard hat and squinted at the sun now rising higher, and he said with a Cajun accent so thick I could barely understand it as English, "Keep one foot on the deck, so you can get off if the boat pitches out from under you. You don't want to be caught up on the basket until you're ready to go. Then just hang on."

"What?" I asked. I didn't understand what he meant. But the three men standing with me had thrown their sea bags into the middle of the orange ring, which had a round piece of canvas lashed to its circumference to form a trampoline that would accommodate cargo. I saw now that the outer ring was a circle of steel pipe with orange polystyrene padding. The man who was trying to help me grabbed two hands full of rope and put one construction boot on the iron ring. I threw my bag in the center with the others and took hold of the rope. I put my steel-toed boot on the orange ring. Watching what they were doing I guessed that, contrary to my instinct of self-preservation, we were to hang on outside the basket rather than crawl inside the cage it formed, where I would rather have been.

"Now, what did you say?" I asked. But before he could answer I was jerked off the deck, up and away from the gentle lapping of the green sea, and I was swinging and floating in the air—now ten, now fifteen, now twenty stories up—over the tiny boat below and all the other crewmen down there, gawking up at me and grinning in this peculiar way I was going to learn about, a kind of detached and malicious delight at the mortal plight of another human being.

I found myself dangling high above the very rig itself. I was looking down on the chaotic angularity of the great gray derrick and the vast and cluttered Texas deck, which was strewn with sharp objects and welding tanks and hoses and drums, churning black gears and whirling red machinery, and I understood that the greasy rope in my hand and those four pale fingers that I used for nothing more strenuous than hoisting a pencil now and then—they were all that stood between me and infinity. One slip of the hand, one cough in the mighty grinding engine that lifted us, one cramp of muscle or the tripping of my boots on the ring upon which I and my three companions stood—and I would dive to my death. I understood that this was a test. The stepping onto the basket had been a profound test, one of those moments like first combat, when I was expected to reach into the dark grab-bag of my soul and come up with a big surprise—in a matter of a second or two everything will have been decided. So I was surprised at how comfortable I was up there, dangling like a toy in the sky over the jagged metal jaws of the rig. I was almost sorry when the ride was over, because it was such an interesting vantage from which to view men and the things they try to do with their breathtaking arrogance.

But when I alighted from the basket, just when I should have felt the safest, I understood immediately that I had been delivered into the far greater peril of the clanging, churning rig itself, as if I'd been a tender bit of carrot, tossed into the teeth of a blender.

———————

We were out in the Gulf of Mexico, in thirteen fathoms of water, for one purpose and one purpose only: to make money. The men were there because no one would do that kind of work unless it paid well. And the pay was good, because no one would take all that trouble if the profit was not immense. We were there to take oil and gas out of the earth, and oil is the blood of the Dragon, and gas is his fiery breath. We would arrogantly ride his back and puncture his lungs and veins and steal his fire for our petty needs and our greater glory. It's a dangerous game, to say the very least of what it is. When I put my ear to the steel superstructure of the rig, I could hear the tumbling guts, the Dragon muttering underneath its breath, struggling not to relinquish its prize.

The type of rig we were on is known as a Bethlehem jack-up rig. It was made by Bethlehem Steel, and the mechanism by which it is jacked up is peculiar to that company's design. The main deck and the entire steel structure of the thing, which is about the size of a downtown office building in Saint Paul, Minnesota, are designed to float in the water. It has three immense steel legs running through it, like the legs of a stool. The rig can run itself up and down the legs by means of hydraulic power and steel pins inserted in holes in the legs. Thus the building can, as it were, crawl up and down those legs. With the building at the bottom of the legs, the building floats, and the legs ride high over the water (like the stool inverted). In that position the rig can be towed to any location. There the hydraulic mechanism ratchets the legs down, while the building is still floating like a barge. The legs descend until they touch the ocean floor, and there they stop. Then the hydraulic power begins lifting the rig. Pushing against the sea bottom, it jacks itself up out of the water. Thus it climbs to the top of the legs and balances there, like a man on stilts standing in the waves. One man, who'd been working those rigs since they were invented, told me that when they first appeared in the Gulf, "People were scared to death to work on jack-ups." He said they just seemed too weird, this whole building hiking itself up three steel pilings in the middle of the ocean and being expected to stay there. People thought it was crazy. Some still do. Approaching those rigs out in the open sea, there is certainly an eerie sense that one is seeing an Orson Welles vision of an alien world.

Once the platform is in place and the legs are fully extended, the actual rig (the derrick we have all seen in movies) is extended out over the ocean on a cantilevered mechanism, the size of which defies comprehension. The everyday machinery of the oil business is beyond the scope of ordinary experience: everything is extremely large. Men on the rig are but slivers of skin. The offshore rig is a world of immense gravity, of moving steel in quantities that ordinary men are not used to seeing. And when the cantilevered derrick assembly slides out, it is as if an aircraft carrier has gotten under way, only it is under way in midair, with no waves of water cleaving on its prow. It glides out on gray steel tracks lapped with black grease until it hangs fifteen stories out over the ocean, and then the deck on which the twenty-story derrick sits becomes analogous to the West Texas desert floor, and drilling begins at that point downward into thin air and then farther downward through green seawater and on below that into sea mud and finally into the black skin and muscle and bone of the very earth itself.

I landed on the rig in the midst of talk and work that I did not understand, as if I had landed on the surface of a desolate and dangerous planet. The space ship crew that dropped us had quickly tossed out its contents of tools and gear and men and had blasted off again. Men were now coming off the basket four at a time and jumping down to the steel deck and tossing their sea bags off and sitting on them to await instruction, while all around us swirled the talk and the machinery, the steel and noise.

"You the new tool pusher?"

"Feels good to be home again, doesn't it?"

"I don't even know how to start an SKD-4, let alone pump one."

"You know the difference between a fairy tale and an oilfield story?" someone asked me. "A fairy tale begins, 'Once upon a time,' and an oilfield story begins, 'Now this ain't no shit.'"

Not long after I got there, someone told me, oh, by the way, there's no medic on board, so don't get hurt. It's a long wait for the helicopter. "Say, you got any gloves, or what?" It was a warm autumn day in Texas when I left. I had no gloves.

Now all around us on this topmost deck of the rig, I could see the chaos of the audacious effort we were here to undertake. The only clear, clean, and uncluttered area I could see was the cantilevered helipad, which balanced out the leaning weight of the cantilevered derrick on the far side of the rig. An orange wind sock waved high above it on a mast. Every thirty seconds I could hear the bleating of the foghorn attached to the rig. It went on like that around the clock. Near us one of the giant columnar legs of the jack-up rig stuck out of a circular hole in the steel deck floor and was shimmed all around its circumference with buff-gray aluminum wedges that looked as if they were designed as door stops for the gates of hell.

On my left and right were a matching pair of red Link-Belt cranes, one of which had picked me from the deck of the boat and had carried others from the rig down to the boat during the crew change. The offshore crews worked seven days on the rig and then had seven days off. Each man worked a twelve-hour shift, from six to six. The rig ran twenty-four hours a day. Approximately thirty-five men worked the rig when I was there (a complete crew was forty-nine).

The available deck space consisted of multilevel steel platforms, many football fields in size, open to the sun and air and connected by a maze of steel-mesh staircases like fire escapes, with yellow pipe handrails, so that, in an attempt to cross from one end of the rig to the other in a straight line, one would walk down a level, then up a level, then up another level, then down three levels, migrating in this fashion as if over mountainous terrain. All of that deck space around us, as far as the eye could see, was cluttered with the mess and wreckage of the oil business. Mesh baskets the size of Lincoln Continentals, formed out of red-rusted steel, were filled with trash, pipe, wire, hose, paint cans, and discarded styrene coffee cups. On a lower deck I could see skids of chemicals and sand and cement in brown paper sacks, all wrapped around in clear plastic sheeting against the weather. Red oil drums with black grease streaks sat here and there with no apparent purpose. Cooling fans in heavy sheet steel cases that protruded ten feet above the deck seemed to ring around us, breathing hot air and a constant roaring noise that made it difficult to talk. Everywhere I walked, dirt collected, mixed with grease and oil, and formed a black coating on my hands and clothes and boots, which stuck to the surface as I walked. The incessant wheeling roar of machinery stalked me, and foul odors amplified the hugeness of the rig and the odious purpose to which it was bent. At the highest dizzying point of a catwalk, I turned a corner and found myself face to face with a ten-foot-tall blue fan creating a cyclone of air and trying to blow me off and hurl me fifteen stories to the waves below. Lines of pipe lay on a wooden platform below, and ropes and hose were everywhere distributed in chaotic coils and heaps. From one side of the rig, great blast-furnace exhaust stacks belched smoke into the air of the Gulf, while blue cooling fans roared beside them, and black tanks of hydrochloric acid below gave off a smell like electricity. Everything—whether tank or pallet or pipe rack—had clevis holds for attachment and was moveable by crane. All that I saw had been disgorged here temporarily, for the purpose of work, and it would be taken away when the work was done.

I had come onto the rig at an interesting time. Some rigs drill and drill and never find a thing, and then they move on and drill some more. This rig had actually located a well, and the morning I arrived they stuck an explosive charge down the hole and fired it, perforating the well casing, and actual natural gas came back up. This was the modern-day equivalent of a gusher. It looked as if, for all its trouble, the parent company might actually see some profit out of this project. The derrick, which looked like all oil derricks everywhere, was a relatively small part of the whole operation. It stood like a rusty Christmas tree in all its flexing and ringing steel glory out on the plate steel floor of the cantilevered platform, suspended fifteen stories over the ocean, which was slowly licking the yellow-painted pilings below like the soundless green tongue of a giant dog.

Now I walked out onto that platform and stood between the legs of the derrick to watch the three roughnecks working over the pipe and the winch man operate the levers and the derrick man ten stories above us perform astounding feats, which made the Flying Wallendas' high-wire act look as simple as the jitterbug. A thirty-five-thousand-pound yellow steel block and tackle was lifting pieces of pipe up out of a hole in the platform floor. The roughnecks danced around it with their eyes wide, three ordinary young men, who might have been mistaken for fraternity brothers if they hadn't been covered with oil and mud, if they hadn't been in the middle of the ocean sixty miles from the nearest land. When they attached a section of pipe to the block, it was whisked high into the air, where the derrick man, ten stories above us, had to catch it and put it into a rack. As the block turned the pipe loose, the derrick man lassoed it with a piece of rope.

Everything was done at a rapid pace, the way football players run scrimmage at practice, blocking dummies and crushing bone. But the roughnecks on this rig were playing without pads, and they were playing against steel, not flesh. While all that action was taking place, every-thing was moving in different directions: the entire platform swayed back and forth with the wind and the force of the waves against it, and so the twenty-story derrick was moving and twisting and torqueing all the time. The block, which the winch man raised and lowered like a conductor directing an orchestra with the baton of his lever, was always turning, swinging, and making lengthy excursions up and down upon its cables. The men were continually setting and removing the slips, which were like steel shims that had been hinged together to fit around the pipe so that it wouldn't slip down the hole and fall into the sea. (In that way, while a length of pipe was fixed in position with slips, the crew could remove the elevator jaws and reposition them for the next pull.) But everything was always moving, and the men were mov-ing, too. The work never stopped.

Each time they pulled a section out of the hole, a many-ton piece of pipe ten stories tall was set free. It literally came alive, writhing wildly in the air, wrestled into its cradle by nothing more than the tiny man and his greasy piece of hemp rope high up on the derrick. . He hauled on his rope, and the pipe struggled and whipped away, and I saw him come way out over the side of his little perch up there. For a moment, I thought he was going to take a ride on the end of that pipe like a miniscule pole vaulter, out into the blue air. The metal whip made by the pipe could flick him like a speck of snot into the sharky sea without even slowing the pace of its gyrations. But the man was working with the forces contained in the pipe. He was playing the kinetic energy of the pipe against its own weight, I could see that now. He wasn't fighting the pipe—he knew he'd never win. He was gentling it over, over, and it almost walked now, the way a fisherman plays the fighting tuna with a piece of string, and then when the propitious moment came, he reeled in his rope and the pipe was landed and clamped securely in its rack.

Now once again, the tip of another length of pipe protruded from the hole in our platform floor, held in place by slips, and the rough-necks wasted no time in fixing the elevator on so that the whole ballet of steel and energy could repeat itself again and again, until all the pipe had been drawn out or until the shift had run its brutal course.

While I was watching this ballet of forces, of steel and flesh, I had noticed the eyes of the roughnecks as they handled the metal. Theirs was a dance within a dance. They had, in effect, thrown themselves into the live and moving jaws of a marvelous and terrible machine, and their job was to stand on its tongue, as it were, and to pick its teeth while it chewed, like tiny birds that groom a beast.

A fellow came to stand next to me as I watched. His name was Dave, and he had advanced up the ladder from roughneck to rig mechanic. He now had a pretty good job, and he laughed softly to himself as he watched those young men dance. I noticed that he was missing a finger on his right hand, and I asked how he'd lost it. He smiled and cut his eyes in the direction of the wellhead. "Doing something just about like that there," he said. And so as they worked, I understood that what the roughnecks avoided was more important than what they met head on. They did not have to fight so hard and close to the moving metal, but they did, the way a bullfighter fights close to the bull, and their feet and fingers were always in play, as if all day long they cast dice, betting with their very bones. Occasionally the pieces of metal came clanging together in an unhappy way, by an accident of the many motions that were all in play at once—the sea and wind, the derrick and gravity, the winch cables as big as my wrist, writhing like a pit full of electric snakes, and the swaying of the block—and all this now and then added up to the great ringing of the gong, which made for grisly results if a man was not paying attention to his job.

At one point Bud Cole, the tool pusher, came up to the floor. I learned that he had been working on offshore rigs for twenty-three years. I would have thought that feat of endurance humanly impossible. In a boat, your very progress through the water makes for a kind of variety. One piece of ocean real estate can look so different from another that it can be as varied as driving through the countryside. You can anticipate the appearance now and then of dolphins or perhaps the far-off sight of an unknown bit of land. But on the rig, we were marooned, and not even the idea of motion was there to relieve the monotony of the blue and infinite sky, which seemed locked in a neatly ruled line against the green and moody sea. We could take no comfort or distraction there in those two desolate hemispheres. We could not even entertain ourselves with the hope of change, because any change in sea or sky would be a change for the worse (weather being one great enemy of the precariously balanced rig). So as Bud observed a gyrating ten-story section of pipe, I watched him with a certain respect for and wonder at his tenacity on this harsh and lonely job. He wore yellow-tinted safety goggles and an aluminum hard hat, and he squinted up at the wild black pipe, standing on its point and undulating like a licorice stick. He admired it for a moment and then grinned at me with the most malevolent enjoyment I had ever seen.

"You got that book wrote yet?" he asked.

Dean Reeves was in the film *Thunder Bay* with James Stewart. In 1951, he happened to be a roughneck on Kerr McGee's Rig Number 37 when the film crew showed up. He worked with that thirty-five-thousand-pound steel block and the ninety-foot lengths of pipe in the boisterous, swinging song of metal against metal. When I found him, he had risen to the rank of "company man," and he was sitting in his office on the oil rig, which was part of an enclosed area within that city-on-the-sea. The indoor area contained the galley for feeding forty or fifty men, the sleeping quarters, showers, recreation room, other offices, copiers, file cabinets, fax machines, telephones, and the like. Reeves's office walls were painted a sort of corpse beige. The floor was covered in brown speckled linoleum, Gray steel lockers stood against one wall, his bunk against another. Reeves was a heavy man with a broad beam and a nose that reminded me of W. C. Fields. His hard hat was hung on the side of a locker. It was covered with stickers from the companies that supply equipment and services to oil rigs. He sat at a steel desk with a phone at his elbow, and he was chewing tobacco and spitting thin brown streams of what looked like molten brass into a tin vegetable can from which the label had been removed, a metal man in a metal tower, drooling metal like a gargoyle.

"I lost a man in the early sixties," he told me. "He was inexperienced. He had just started. He stuck his head in the wrong place." The very hunks of metal I had seen those roughnecks dodging up above on the Texas deck—block and pipe and elevator and slips—two of them had come together, and the man's timing was off. He was not in step with the dance, and his head was crushed flat in no more time than it takes to draw a single breath. "He was dead before he hit the floor," Reeves said, spitting into the can and shaking his head sadly, as if it had just happened yesterday. "And there was nothing you could do about it. It's just an empty feeling . . . blood running out of his ears." I asked if it was inexperience that got most people in trouble on these rigs. "Your best hand is the one that gets his fingers cut off and what-not," he said. He learns a lesson early and never forgets. Of course, "the guy who stands back with his hands in his pockets, he's not going to get hurt." I felt a certain sense of relief in hearing him say that, since it described precisely what I intended to do with my time on the rig. But his reminiscence seemed to get him talking about the dangers of the rig, and he went on.

"I had one old boy was walking around on the Texas deck, not looking where he was going, and he fell through an open hatch. Fell eighty feet to the deck below. And he lived." I asked how a man could survive an eighty-foot fall. "I don't know. The waves were lapping over the lower deck, and maybe he hit it just right, but he was holding onto the bars when we got to him. He never worked again, though. He was pretty badly busted up." The main equipment deck on older-style rigs was called the Texas deck, because it was so big, and perhaps because, like the state of Texas itself, if you could find a way to drill far enough through it, you'd probably strike oil. On newer rigs, all the equipment is scattered about on different levels, pumps, generators, mud room, Haliburton unit, and pipe racks. There's no actual Texas deck, though some people still use the term.

It goes without saying that while working or even walking around on the decks, it is very easy to get hurt in so many ways that they are impossible to catalog. (Reeves told me about a scuba diver who was poking around a capped well below the surface when they pulled the cap off by a cable from above. "The oil level had dropped and created a vacuum," he said. "And when they pulled that cap off, it just pulled him right down. Sucked his guts out. It was terrible.") As the newest man on the rig, I was most vulnerable, and no one volunteered to tip me off to the very special dangers that lay waiting. Everywhere I turned, the yawning drop to the sea confronted my movements, and often nothing more than a flimsy piece of chain hung between me and the downward plunge that would prang the deck with my bones. The highest catwalks were made of metal mesh, like fire escapes, and always through them I could see the dimensionless ocean ten or twenty stories below.

And yet graver perils still threatened, and they were all tied up in the very nature of our endeavor here: to draw gas and oil out of the earth. Pockets of gas and oil don't just sit down there in neat geological formations, waiting to be sucked up. They are under tremendous pressure—ten thousand pounds per square inch was a figure I heard bandied about. The pipe that was lowered into the hole was hollow, and a chemical preparation called mud was pumped through it to create enough weight to hold the pressure of the gas or oil that would otherwise come spewing up the wellhead. The more pressure the gas or oil exerted to get out, the more mud one had to pump in to hold it down. It was that balance of the natural pressure from below the earth and the artificial pressure from above that allowed control of the flow once the surface was punctured. Once it was drilled, the well was essentially a casing, or a hollow pipe, down into the earth, like a straw sticking into a coconut. It was the straw that was filled with the chemical mud, which was made from a substance called barite, a white powder that crept around the rig and got on our skin and caused itching and burning and ate leather like acid. One worker, looking at my feet, said, "It'll make the toes of them boots look up at you and smile." Concealed within the bowels of the rig was a great machinery for concocting and storing and pumping the mud—I walked across the metal mesh strung over it, a dark, noisy room that smelled as if we were being dissolved by the very contaminated air itself, and below our feet, licking at us hideously, was the brown swirling gorp of barite, acres of it, like a death-swamp in a science fiction film. But this was the lifeblood of the rig. Without mud to hold back the gas and oil, the alternative was a blowout, the wild, uncontrolled spuming of gas and oil out of the ground and into the air, a gusher like in the movies. In movies, people always get happy when the well blows. In real life, they would dive into the ocean rather than stay on the rig during such an event.

Sometimes a blowout just happens. The unimaginable pressure of gas will simply cut through the steel casing or a ring gasket, and then there will be the sounding of the great whale of commerce, and it will go down burning. In fact, for all the safety briefings I did not receive on the rig, they did tell me one thing: if there's a blowout, you've got about four minutes before the steel pilings and girders melt down and flow into the sea. The man named Dave had told me that. "So get in the life boat if you hear the general alarm," he said.

"I'd leap over the side if it came to that," said Reeves, who had experienced numerous blowouts in his time. Sometimes the tool pusher can cause a blowout by hurrying, pulling the pipe out of the hole too fast and creating an effect they call swabbing. As the pipe comes out, it causes suction below. If the suction starts the mud flowing upward too fast, it can draw gas up after it, which begins the blowout. Even a small amount of natural gas, once ignited, will provide sufficient rocket power to start the whole well going. "Then you got a burnt-up rig," Reeves said. Shallow gas wells, he informed me, such as the one on which we sat so pleasantly chatting at that moment, were most susceptible to the swabbing effect.

"We lost one at Chesterfield," he reminisced, "a little old shallow well like this. Swabbed it in, but it didn't catch fire for some reason. They called me, and I said, 'Keep your suction and pump your heavy mud. I figured it would slow it down and the water mixed with the gas would lessen the chance of catching fire. We finally killed it with heavy mud." That blowout had started because the pipe going up and down had simply rubbed a hole in the side of the well casing.

"I lost one in Dilly," he went on. "Shut in and locked up and we had a leak, a small one, and about the time they got ready to pump it around, one of these little old Texas lightning storms come up and set this thing on fire."

"What did you do?' I asked.

"Got the hell off of there," he said. It burned his rig up.

He told me about another incident in the late sixties in which "we'd run out of mud and had one bottled up and leaking and nothing to pump. Everybody was running around with life jackets on. It was pretty tight there for a while, until the boat came with more mud."

One of the worst disasters, Reeves told me, could result from a salt-water flow. Sometimes gas wells contained a lot of salt water under

IN THE BELLY OF THE WHALE

extreme pressure, and if that got away from you, it would be like tapping directly into a volcano. First the salt water would come out like a rocket—uncontrollable by mud or any other means. Then the steel well casing the men placed in the hole would simply fall into the yawning earth. Then as the salt water gushed out of the lower bowels of the earth, it would drive the sand of the ocean floor away, creating a larger and larger crater, until the very foundations of the rig were undermined and the whole platform, legs and all, fell into the sinkhole created in the floor of the ocean. In other words, for their audacious affronts, the Dragon of the earth would swallow them whole, as men, machines, ambition, and all go tilting into the sucking sea.

The phone rang at Reeves's elbow, and he picked up his tin can and spit into it, then set it down and answered the phone. "We got it killed," he said to someone in Houston, "and we eased on out of the hole with that packer and I'm just getting back in the hole with a scraper now and of course we had a crew change right in the middle of all that. I'm fixin' to go to two-and-a-half dual round." When he hung up, he told me he planned to get a gravel pack in there and then put the Christmas tree on it, and for the first time I understood the mechanics of an oil well: it was like giving blood, a metal hypodermic stuck in the tender flesh, held there by friction. The gas or oil follows the path of least resistance, through the tube rather than around it. A gravel pack around the tube assures no leakage. And with a flow manifold on the end of the tube (the Christmas tree) one could then turn the gas on and off and meter it and steal it away and sell it, like blood.

On the Texas deck one day, several men stood beside me. A pause in the action. I had taken out my black notebook to write something, and I noticed the men looking at me in a peculiar way. They didn't say anything. They merely watched me as if I was some kind of curiosity in their otherwise routine day. I don't know what made me turn around, perhaps it was a flick of their eyes. Perhaps I noticed that they were watching not only me but something behind me as well. For whatever reason, I looked around and saw a crane load of pipe, moving slowly but implacably toward my head. A closer call than I would have liked. I stepped aside, and the four-ton rack of pipe went past and was set on the floor, and that was all. I looked back at the men, and they weren't laughing, but one of them glanced at me in a peculiar way, with a little smirk, like: *Well, it didn't get you this time, but maybe next time.* Maybe I was just getting paranoid from all the noise and the stories of death Reeves told, but I understood at that moment how truly grave the danger was on that rig. For not only was the rig terribly risky to life and limb on its own, but the men themselves were a potential source of peril. And I understood something important about the men and their work. They were finely honed with grim intent. Nothing escaped their vigilant notice, not a shift in the wind, a chance remark, the tinkling of machinery, a sudden odor from somewhere. Because all of those things could signal the beginning of the end, and the man who noticed what was going on first was the man most likely to survive it. Men, machines, nature, they knew from hard, sometimes deadly, experience, were not to be trusted. Fate was a handmade affair, knocked together and roughed out ad hoc from whatever materials were at hand. The rule was fixed: Opportunity plus Will equals Fate. And to the extent that I was a new and unknown force on the rig, they regarded me as coldly as if the magical Link-Belt crane had lifted another rack of pipe off that boat and set it on the deck for them to trip over and fall to their death. I understood why Bud Cole had been so displeased to find me on his rig. I wasn't helping, so I was a liability. I was ignorant and could get someone killed just as surely as someone could let me be killed.

Each man on that rig was working hard every moment for his own survival. They did not have the energy or the time for poses, for subtle or clever deceptions or for social gamesmanship. Each man pitted himself against something that would kill him if he did not dominate it now and without any protracted analysis of his strategy. Everything on the rig was a test, and the men had to react instantly. I saw in those men raw nerve and muscle, all on the surface, with no leeway for deep thought or introspection. I don't think those men were actively trying to get me killed, but they were not very actively interested in preventing my death, either. They didn't have time. They shouldn't take the time, or it might cost them a life. Moreover, I had the distinct impression that they would have been mildly amused if I had been maimed by my chance meeting with the moving machinery of their lives.

On the other hand, I had to remember that they were doing something that no one else would do. They were risking their lives so that I could be warm. This gathering of oil and gas was itself a battle for survival. We need oil. Oil is heat. Oil is motion. We are clinging to a rock in the sea, quite literally to save our lives. Those men are the forefront. Their savage wage is fear, and their sacrifice is something I have to acknowledge. If I had been them, doing what they did in twelve-hour, mind-killing shifts, day after day, month after month, I might well be amused to see someone like me get his arm cut off. But finding empathy in my heart for them made me no less eager to get off their platform and let them get about their work. I found myself standing high over the ocean on the white cantilevered helicopter deck, staring at the horizon one breezy cool October evening out in the Gulf of Mexico, watching the black dots that moved here and there among the rigs, trying to see which one was going to turn my way. I had developed a more practiced gait to step around and over and through the pipes and hoses, the coiled wires that grabbed at my ankles as I passed by the sheer drop to the sea.

When the helicopter came at last, so many people wanted to get off that rig that the pilot wasn't sure he was going to be able to take off, so he counted the luggage again, and then he counted us once more and decided to give it a try, hauling back on the collective, the skids just clearing the deck, as we wheeled out over the ocean. I don't know what state of mind I must have been in, but it didn't seem at all odd to me at the time to risk crashing into the sea in order to get off that oil rig. Several mainland office types had boarded the flight with me. They seemed to agree that anything was better than staying.

As we flew away, I glanced at the instrument panel to make sure we had a positive rate of climb. The pilot managed to get us to five hundred feet, and that was good enough for me, so I breathed a sigh of relief as the rig receded behind us. When the crew boat had brought us out to the rig, I had watched that tower grow on the horizon, until it became real and menacing in the running seas, a dark and forbidding torture chamber, a dissonant unity of the cruel will of man to defy the elements in all his baleful audacity. Now it was with great relief that I watched that same device shrink back to insignificance where I could no longer see the details, the whirling dervish of peril upon its slick and dirty decks. Soon it had shrunk to a simple geometric shape, mysterious and theoretical and far enough away to contemplate. Before it disappeared altogether, it had been reduced to nothing more than a ghostly finger sticking out of the ocean mists, like that universal hand signal of brotherly disaffection.

NO MORE IMMELMANS

In the photograph, Tom Cruise has his arm around Randy. He's grown a beard and left it untrimmed, and he wears sunglasses and a bandanna tied around his long hair. Even so, it's impossible to mistake him for anyone else. That smile. Tom is short, but Randy is shorter. Tom is thin. Randy is stocky and wears his dark blue flight suit and a straw hat, and they're both laughing. Not just laughing. They're laughing hard. I know about that laugh. You come down from those flights so pumped up, physically, mentally, yes, even spiritually. And everybody laughs like that, with the airplane tabernacled in the hangar, still hot, almost a living thing among us. We crack open a few beers like some latter-day fighter squadron of hell-bent irregulars, and inevitably someone says, "Cheated the devil again, eh?" Yes (that laugh seems to say), we went up and stole something and got away scot-free.

Behind them: Tom's Pitts S2-B. It's a white biplane with red trim in a kind of reverse Marion Cole paint job. We've all seen them at air shows, pulling snap-rolls on takeoff, flying upside-down close to the ground, or doing crazy tumbling maneuvers that seem impossible for a craft that demands to be pulled through the air nose-first in order to stay aloft at all. Randy taught Tom to fly it. And in one just like it he taught me, too. Randy had been my teacher for a year or more when I heard that Cruise had come into the fold. The next year Randy was teaching Harrison Ford to fly his new Christen Husky. Randy's students included Patrick Swayze, Treat Williams, and Tony Bill, the producer who took an Academy Award for *The Sting*. Tony and I flew the same Pitts S2-B in competition, N260AB, Randy's plane.

Although Randy acquired a small stable of celebrity students, nothing really changed. He had the same cramped office at Van Nuys

Airport just north of Los Angeles. The same clutter. During pre- and post-flight briefings, Randy would sit behind his desk, chain-smoking Marlboros with true pilot style, grinning as if to say, "Yep. I'm on fire, and I don't even mind it." I had come to know his furtive outlaw comportment, those sidelong, surreptitious glances, as he lit his cigarettes with hands cupped against a wind that no longer blew. A habit from his barnstorming gypsy days of sleeping in the wheat fields. From the first, I could see something in his eyes, a shadow beyond the laugh. I could see Randy running from something. He laughed a lot, and I laughed with him. But he followed each laugh with a stolen look, as if he knew that something was gaining on him. What was Randy going away from at such a furious clip?

October 25, 1997, Randy Gagne was killed on an aerobatics training flight with his student, a Southwest Airlines pilot named Heidi Cayouette. They dove straight into the ground at a terminal velocity in excess of 250 miles an hour. I loved Randy. The news of his death sucked the wind out of me. It wasn't even so much that Randy and I were friends. I knew his wife, Sheree, but I had never been to their house. Our life was in the cockpit. In many ways, my relationship with Randy was deeper than most friendships, because I trusted my life to him every time we met.

We all liked to be around him. He filled spaces in our lives that we didn't know we had. When the phone would ring, sometimes he'd bark, "Right rudder!" Pause. He'd cover the phone and explain to me: "Whatever the question is, the answer is probably right rudder." American airplanes tend to spin to the left. Applying the right rudder causes them to recover. People die because they press the wrong pedal. It never entered my mind that it could happen to me.

We sat in his office, and he told me through a cloud of smoke that he had begun counting in 1981 and found that an average of six pilots a year died in this sport. I started flying aerobatics in 1988 and have found Randy's figures to be accurate. "But a lot of them have just had it stamped on their forehead—" and here Randy lifted his fist from the desk to his forehead as if with a rubber stamp: "'I Am Going to Die in an Air Crash.'"

After Randy's death, I called John Morrissey, the coach of the US Aerobatics Team (which competes with all other nations for the world championship every two years) and asked him if he thought I ought to quit. He and I had flown together enough that he should know. He said, "You have to fly eight times a month to be proficient at this. Otherwise, you're taking an unnecessary risk." Randy would fly eight times in a matter of days. What happened to him?

Morrissey's wife, Ann Marie, was a fine pilot, a terrific instructor, and a friend of mine. She died inexplicably on a perfectly clear day while giving a lesson in a perfectly good airplane. We never learned why. "When Ann Marie went in," Morrissey told me, "I thought of three hundred people I'd known who had died since I started flying."

I've lost count. Jan Jones and I started at the same time, and she's dead. Flip Philips. Miles Meritt. Ken Haddon. Rick Massagee. It becomes numbing after a while. Aerobatics is not the most fun I've ever had, but at times it has come very close. Yet I'm beginning to think that there's more to life than dying in a fiery crash.

———————

Just a few days before Randy died, Ken Haddon, an official of the International Aerobatics Club, the sanctioning body for our contests, took off from a private airstrip in Ohio. His wife was watching as Ken passed the hangars at around fifty feet. He pulled up to a forty-five-degree climb. He rolled inverted, continued to climb to five hundred feet, and then attempted to do a half loop to return the way he'd come. He pulled the stick to complete the half loop. His nose pointed at the sky, as he hung upside-down in his harness. Looking out, he saw absolute azure blue all around the amniotic bubble of his canopy. With a steady pressure, he pulled. The nose dropped and gravity took over. He pulled the power back. His view passed through the horizon. Blue met green, and then the earth filled the bubble. He pulled harder and harder to recover from his vertical dive, He had intended to go back past the hangars at fifty feet in the opposite direction. The maneuver, called a reverse Cuban eight, would have been quite a show for those on the ground if he'd completed it. But earth would submit to him no longer, and it pulled him in with greedy arms. Ken hit the ground, and the plane exploded while the stick was still in his hand.

Nothing from my childhood brought me so much joy as flying

upside-down over the mountains of California, or doing Cuban eights over Wisconsin farm fields in July, or snap-rolling over the Santa Clara riverbed. And all the while Randy's voice was in my ear. Sometimes when I'd be in a wicked inverted flat spin, my body jammed up against the canopy by the G-forces, watching the world turn to a nasty brown gumbo of colors, Randy would come on the intercom and say, "For a hundred dollars I'll tell you how to get out of this." And we'd laugh and laugh as we spun our way to the warm green earth. I didn't believe it was possible to crash with Randy's voice in my ear. It never crossed my mind that I might get hurt. When people learned of my sport, sometimes they'd say, "Are you crazy? You've got kids."

And I would plead, "You don't understand." But I was the one who didn't understand.

I flew to Florida with Sheree, Randy's widow, to visit Randy's mother and sister. For many days we all sat and talked and pored over pictures of Randy. We celebrated Randy's life and did not much discuss his death. Sheree was a tall vivacious blonde with a British accent, who smoked a lot and wore oversized tinted glasses. At the car rental place, she selected a sporty convertible. She laughed a lot and was high-spirited and somewhat nervous of demeanor. She was considerate beyond reproach. At one point in the trip she said, "I know how hard this must be for you. I know how much you cared about Randy."

Sheree and I spent one afternoon touring Randy's alma mater, Embry-Riddle Aeronautical University, one of the top aviation schools in the nation. We met with the head of the Flight Department to see if a grant could be set up to teach aerobatics in Randy's Pitts, whose registration number is N260AB, affectionately known as Alpha Bravo. (Randy died in a borrowed plane.) Peter Pierpont, chairman of the Department of Technology, agreed that while Embry-Riddle turned out the finest airline pilots in the world, "if they ever got upside-down, they wouldn't know what to do." Aerobatics training would help. It might have saved a number of 737s that crashed because the rudder malfunctioned and forced them into an inverted attitude.

On another day, Sheree wanted to see Saint Augustine, Florida, and we put the top down and drove up there in the sun. I steeled my nerve and asked her about the crash. She told me about that night, when she waited and waited for him to come home for dinner.

"I had some wine. I had some dinner. It was six, then seven, and I was starting to get pissed," she said. "It was just totally out of character for him to be gone like this. Oh, sure, he was always late, but he'd call eventually and have some story." She called the hangar numerous times. She called the cell phone. But she got only Randy's voice. That was all that was left of him for all of us who had listened: that voice. *Right rudder!* (Pause.) *What's the question?*

Sheree watched as much television as she could, and around midnight she drove to the hangar. She found it open. "The Pitts was sitting there, and the door was wide open. The truck was parked in the lot," she said. "So I thought: *Well, he's okay, because there's the airplane. Now where the hell is he?*"

She locked the hangar and went home. "I didn't want to be the hysterical wife," she said. So she didn't call all their friends in search of Randy.

The next morning she called Bob Miller, who had the hangar next door to Randy's. Miller told her that Randy had gone out about four o'clock with Heidi Cayouette, not in the Pitts, but in Miller's Extra 300, a high-performance competition monoplane. Heidi, who died with Randy, had wanted to fly an Extra 300. She was an experienced airline captain, but she hadn't flown aerobatics in six years.

"Then I knew," Sheree said. She knew everything all at once, and something seemed to rupture inside her. The search was on. By about ten in the morning, they had found the Extra stuck in the ground like a dart.

———————

While Sheree and I were in Florida, I went to visit Clint McHenry, Randy's mentor. McHenry is a legend in the world of aerobatics, a former world champion and, at the time of our meeting, one of only nine living members of the Aerobatics Hall of Fame. Thin and tall, he sat in his living room overlooking a golf course in a suburb near New Smyrna Beach, Florida. Since the earliest age, he had wanted nothing more than to fly. And since that time he had wanted to fly aerobatics. He became an airline pilot, so he flew constantly and had an income and security. Clint won every contest he entered, and when I met him, he was seventy-six and had quit aerobatics. He retired from competition after the 1990 World Cup in Switzerland. By then the Russians and French were dominating the sport. No American had placed higher than third since the eighties. McHenry said he didn't think he'd fly anymore. "I bought a Pitts, but it just sat in the hangar, so I sold it."

He was no gypsy pilot. He had control and judgment. I could see it in the neatness and order of his home, his car, even his clothing. His very leanness bespoke a moderation that told me he had good impulse control. The very fact of his quitting was strong testimonial, like someone who has tested drug-free for a very long time. For anyone will tell you that flying aerobatics is addictive.

Clint helped Randy leave the gypsy life and get a real job. "I ran the aerobatics school at Pompano," Clint said, "and we were really, really busy." Pompano Aerobatics Center was the largest aerobatics training school in the nation. "I told the Beckers [the owners] that Randy would be a good man to have if we could get him. We hired him, and he worked for us for years and did a very nice job. He damaged a couple of airplanes, and John Becker would get mad at him, but he was part of the family for four years or so."

I asked him what he thought might have happened to Randy, and he didn't answer right away. He thought for a moment, and then he told me a story. He told it almost as if he'd forgotten the question.

Another fabled pilot, Bill Thomas, along with Bob Schnuerle and Clint himself, were practicing together for the US National Championship. They met on Sundays at the airfield of Curtis Pitts, the inventor of the Pitts Special. One of them would go up and do aerobatics, while the others watched and offered criticism over the radio. Schnuerle was test pilot for Curtis Pitts. He had made the US Aerobatics Team in 1970 and by 1972 was the team trainer when Charlie Hilliard won Best Individual Pilot and the US team won the Nestor Cup—the world championship— in France. That was the height of American domination of the sport. In other words, these were three of the most experienced aerobatic pilots in the world at that moment in 1974 when Schnuerle went up to find his death.

He was practicing inverted flat spins. For many decades, the inverted flat spin was considered a deadly mystery to be avoided at all costs. It was thought that once a pilot was in such a spin, he could not recover. And these guys were doing it *on purpose*. "At that time, you could have counted on one hand the number of pilots who did inverted flat spins," said McHenry. Schnuerle was not merely one of them; he had taught the maneuver (or rather how to get out of it) to another famed aerobatics pilot, Art Scholl. Scholl died doing a television commercial. He spun all the way into the ocean. We never learned why.

On the Sunday that Schnuerle died, Clint was called away by his airline to fly a trip, so he wasn't able to attend the practice session. Bill Thomas went with Schnuerle to Curtis Pitts's field. Thomas was on the ground watching with a radio in hand to offer comments. When Schnuerle kicked his Pitts into an inverted flat spin, Thomas must have said, "Yes, good, that's nice, very nice." For it was. It was perfect. Thomas watched Schnuerle all the way down.

"When it was time to pull out, he was out of altitude," McHenry said. "We had all talked about this. The thing about an inverted flat spin is that it is perfectly flat. You don't have any sensation of losing altitude. It's very confusing. In an upright spin, you see the ground coming up."

The legendary test pilot Sammy Mason, who explored the unknown region of inverted flat spins, wrote, "The dysphoria was so overwhelming that I was unable to function physically or mentally. I said a brief prayer and waited."

McHenry went on. "You get hung up in what you're trying to do, keeping it perfectly flat. I think Schnuerle had become so involved in the maneuver that he just lost his concentration. Bill Thomas wrote an article about it afterward and said that Schnuerle had become "euphoric."

Euphoric. That's why we go up in the first place. Isn't that the whole point? Or is it?

Morrissey said that you have to have a certain attitude to fly a plane. You have to be a certain type of person. You have to have judgment and control. You can't simply say, "What the hell," and go wild. Anyone with poor impulse control, anyone who is disorganized, should not be flying, and especially not upside-down. Flying upside-down is not skiing. It's not baseball. It's either a religion and permeates every corner of your life, or it's a very patient fatal accident waiting for you. Hence the joke: cheated the devil again . . . the devil is our own nature.

Eric Mueller, a researcher who studies accidents, noticed that in cases of those "unvercoverable" spins, when a pilot managed to bail out, the plane recovered to normal flight even as the pilot floated down in his parachute. The pilot was the problem. When he let go of the controls, the plane righted itself. Planes were made to fly by some very capable engineers. It usually takes a pilot to make them crash.

There are only two scores in this sport, perfect and zero. It's a pass/fail exam. Clint McHenry passed. Randy failed. It is not a judgment upon him. It's an irrevocable fact, like gravity.

I still think Randy was a great pilot. I do not believe he died because he screwed up, although surely he was capable of it. Randy was a master of the how-I-almost-bought-it story. The heavy Russian Yak whose seatbelt gave way while he was inverted, smashing him against the canopy. It knocked him senseless, and he was barely able to get the stick back in his hand. The student who froze on the controls while doing aerobatics, and Randy couldn't get this big fellow off. Randy ran Tom Cruise's Pitts into a fuel pump and totaled it. The cowboy who went flying with his boots on, and one of them got jammed in the rudder pedals. The plane was rolled into a ball on landing, but both occupants walked away. Randy had nine lives. I thought he had a million.

I'll never forget the first time I saw him. Patty Wagstaff, the top pilot in the United States, had just landed at Hartford, Wisconsin. (I had arrived while she was practicing, and I landed underneath her.) As I got out of my plane, Randy climbed into a pink and purple Russian Sukhoi SU26 monoplane with *Pink Floyd* painted on the side. (Sukhoi makes MiG fighter planes.) I'd never seen the man before. He wore a single black glove, and he was concentrating hard as he strode across the ramp toward the outrageous-looking plane. The Sukhoi is a huge plane for aerobatics. It has tremendous power and hypersensitive controls. The engine is a mammoth radial, black like the anus of a rocket.

As Randy climbed into *Pink Floyd* and cinched himself in with the help of the ground crew, I made the assumption that he was some hot-shot from the Russian team, come to show the Americans the error of their ways. His block-like head and barrel-like body fit the cliché, and his single black glove completed the picture. As he tested the controls, I could see him looking left and right, back and front. Certainly he was a Russian spy.

The ground crew started the engine with a pneumatic assist, and as *Pink Floyd* roared to life, it unfurled a plume of oily smoke that crawled along the runway, engulfing other planes and clinging to them in toxic adhesion. Most pilots will see an airplane for the first time—any airplane—and they think: *I can fly that.* I looked at the Sukhoi and thought: *No way.*

Almost the moment Randy left the ground, he snap-rolled. Everyone gathered around to see what he'd do with the monster that had dominated the sport since its introduction in the 1980s. *Pink Floyd* climbed away from the Hartford airfield and turned back toward us. The hot pink plane crossed our field of vision. Randy couldn't have been more than three hundred feet up when he rolled left, right, left, right, about ten times in rapid succession. The roll rate of the Sukhoi is about 720 degrees a second, which is to say, unfathomable. Two complete rolls each second. Randy was just warming up, getting the feel of it. Then he uncorked that 360-horsepower engine and screwed the airplane into a perfect blue sky. I'd never seen anything like it. Ordinary airplanes cannot accelerate vertically. I was so moved I laughed out loud.

I didn't meet Randy that day. I was there to talk to Patty Wagstaff. It was only later that I learned that I had just watched him fly a most amazing routine in a plane that not even Patty would fly. Although she was US champion four times in a row, she felt that the Sukhoi was too much airplane for her. I also learned later that Randy was the first American to fly air shows in a Sukhoi. He was the first non-Russian to compete in a Sukhoi. And he was the first American to train with the Russian team. He spoke one word of Russian: *benzine,* which means gasoline. But later, when I was Randy's student, I watched him communicate with them, and it was beautiful, with Randy gesticulating and jabbering in pidgin Russian, and the Russian pilots nodding solemnly and then bursting into laughter as if he'd told a great joke. And of course, he just *looked* Russian.

Another man on the Hartford field that day had bought a Sukhoi recently. Rick Massagee stood on the wing of his black SU26. I remember hearing him talk to the mechanic who was bleeding his brakes. Rick would make the US team that year. Two years later he'd buy a brand-new Sukhoi SU29, a more advanced model. He would take it up for the first practice of the season and pull the wing off it in a routine maneuver, owing to a flaw in the spar. Rick was killed at Galt Airport, my home field, while all my friends watched helplessly as the pieces of the plane fluttered down. The tremendous force of breaking that carbon-fiber-and-titanium composite wing probably killed him in the cockpit before he hit the ground.

When my first wife, Carolyn, was a child and would shiver, her grandmother would say, "A goose walked over your grave." On my last flight with Randy we practiced inverted flat spins over the very spot where he was to die. Randy told me to close my eyes. He put the plane into an inverted flat spin. Then he told me to open my eyes. No one's hands were on the controls when he said, "Your airplane."

My eyeballs rolled around like loose marbles in my head. I was pinned against the canopy by the centrifugal force, the harsh fluttering and the wicked slamming of the plane, rolling and yawing in opposite directions. We were in the jaws of something grizzly. The plane's nose oscillated violently up and down while we went around and around. Randy called it Mr. Toad's Wild Ride. I reached for the stick, but it was pinned forward and out of my reach . This was nothing new. We practiced inverted flat spins all the time. But something was wrong. What I'd always done before wasn't working. Power off. Let go of the stick (as if I had a choice). Full rudder. Nothing. We were going down and down. I saw the ground coming up, brown and green, like a boiling stew. It was getting close. Really close.

Randy said, at last, calm and mellow through the headphones, "Right ruh-derr."

I stepped on the right rudder, and the plane immediately popped out of the spin. We flew away at treetop level. My heart was pounding. I was sweating and panting. I was afraid. The ground was all around us, tree branches reaching up like the fingers of the buried dead. We were nearly inside the orange grove.

NO MORE IMMELMANS

"How much longer were you going to let me go?" I asked, as we climbed away from the trees.

"Oh, not much longer."

Of course, mine was the classic mistake. I thought we were spinning right, so I stepped on the left rudder. But we weren't. We were *rolling* right. We were spinning left. And I wondered what would have happened at the crucial moment if I had frozen instead of doing the one right thing that was left to do. Was there really enough time left for him to save us? I shivered. But the goose had walked over Randy's grave, not mine.

———

I found Sheree slumped on the couch at Randy's hangar. Everything was as it had always been. The Pitts was still, cool, almost sleeping there. I came to the hangar because I wanted to sense that Randy was gone. The hangar was decorated as if by a nine-year-old boy, with whimsical cutouts of airplanes and cartoon pilots, with blue sky and clouds. The couch where Sheree sat gave the place a comfortable atmosphere, and it was, indeed, where we always sat and talked as the sun went down, drinking soft drinks and beer from the refrigerator in back.

Randy's protégé, a young air show pilot named Edan Shalev, had taken Randy's place at his desk in the small upstairs office with the picture window that overlooked the hangar. The clutter had not been removed. All the framed photographs of Randy, hanging upside-down in a Pitts like some sun-freaked incubus, grinned out at us. The plane—our plane, *Alpha Bravo*—sat there, cocked back on its tailwheel, ready for flight. Sheree slouched in her sunglasses, smoking, and a few of Randy's students came and went, sometimes stopping by to chat, sometimes taking the airplane up, disappearing over the Santa Susana Mountains, and returning an hour later with that grin that says, *Yes, we did it again.* I smiled at them, but every time I watched the Pitts vanish over the ridge, I felt a tightness in my chest until I saw it return. I had lost my innocence.

Miller showed up at the hangar after a while. He was one of the last people to see Randy and Heidi alive. He was a tall and thickly built man in his sixties, wearing a serious black Nomex fireproof flight suit and smoking a cigar. He drove up in a Jaguar and pumped my hand and said, "Let's go fly the jet."

"Okay," I said, not even asking, *What jet?* Only an hour before, I felt that my loss of innocence would somehow protect me. Yet the seduction of flight still had its hold on me. *Just one last flight*, I thought. *I'll make this one exception.*

And: *Fly the jet? What jet?*

Soon we were out on the ramp in the California sun, performing a pre-flight check on a Czechoslovakian Delfin L-29 fighter plane from the sixties. It had one big hole in the back and looked like a buff aluminum stovepipe with a canopy and two crude ejection seats, "Experimental" stenciled on the canopy rail. "I'm trying to get ejection seats that work," Miller said, as he went over the procedure for bailing out in case we didn't make it. He said we could fly up to Santa Barbara to have lunch and talk about Randy. This is standard procedure if you want to interview a pilot: you have to fly somewhere first. Miller had a huge knife strapped to his flying boot on the outside of his flight suit. I asked what it was for. "In case I have to cut my parachute lines."

We climbed up the ladder and into the tandem cockpit and put on fighter-pilot helmets. I connected a multitude of straps, clasps, hasps, and wires. The trick when bailing out in flight was to unhook everything *except* the parachute. One pilot I knew actually got out of his crippled plane safely, pulled the rip cord, watched the parachute canopy open nicely above him with a soft pop. Only then did he learn that he had neglected to fasten his leg straps. He shot out of the harness and fell five hundred feet to the ground. He did that the morning after celebrating his appointment to the US Aerobatics Team, and everyone said it was a morning-after kind of thing to do. Lots of toasts the night before. In a hurry to get home.

Miller started the engine. It was deafening. I put the shield down on my helmet, but from roll-out at Van Nuys all the way to Santa Barbara I could scarcely hear. The acceleration was fierce. Within the first few gasps for breath, we were going more than three hundred knots.

We flew out over the ocean and up the coast. It was a clear day and probably 110 degrees inside the bubble canopy. I was soaked to the skin. I had flown a handful of fighters and trainers, including T-38s and F-4 Phantoms, and I much prefer the light, quick, strong (quiet?) Pitts Special. When the engine quits on something like the Delfin, it has the aerodynamic characteristics of a donkey. A fire in the cockpit is even worse. Amos Buetell, a pilot at my home airport, was bringing his new Laser monoplane home. He had bought the plane the day before. He was on approach when the propeller threw a counterweight. The plane vibrated so badly that it broke a fuel line and sprayed Amos with aviation gasoline. He brought the power back to see if he could reduce the vibration, and it backfired, igniting the fuel. Amos was about to make the US team, but he was incinerated. He managed to land the plane, but it flipped over on him. It took him three days to die.

Miller and I landed at Santa Barbara and took on tons of fuel. The one nice thing about landing in a plane like the L-29 is you really get everyone's attention. Everyone was watching the Delfin from the outdoor seating at the little restaurant. Miller looked like a mad sky warrior with the patches sewn on his black outfit and the knife and a mane of receding white hair. But he was merely a retired housing developer, a guy with lots of money who liked airplanes.

"It had to be a foreign object in the cockpit," he said over club sandwiches. He told me a story, well known among competitors, about a man driving a Pitts. On approach his controls locked up. He forced them with all his strength and managed to get the plane on the ground. A nickel had dropped out of someone's pocket and become caught in the controls. He had bent it in half while struggling with the stick. "He wears it around his neck now," Miller said. "Something jammed the controls. What's he got at those speeds? A second, two seconds? There's not enough time."

I had already talked to the NTSB investigator, Richard Parker. The National Transportation Safety Board investigates all air crashes. Parker told me that he'd gone to the crash site, looked at the plane, and had seen Randy and Heidi in the cockpit. "There is no need to dwell unnecessarily on the crash site," he said, "but that is a very robust plane, and the cockpit was intact, and it contained the occupants." Their bodies were too badly damaged to allow for an autopsy. As for the cause of the crash, he said it would never be known. The plane was removed to a hangar and examined minutely. Its maker, Walter Extra, flew in from Germany to aid in the investigation, along with members of the International Aerobatics Club. No one could find anything wrong with the plane. No bent nickel or similar object was found. "When the plane hits going that fast, everything scatters," Miller continued, "He's got a garage sale. No evidence. No cause. I know that's what happened, plain and simple. The Extra is easy to fly. There's no way either Randy or Heidi drove it into the ground unless something was broken."

We thrive on tales of the dead. Paradoxically, it's the lifeblood of our passion. We even subscribe to newsletters that recount the crashes of our fellow pilots in loving detail, and we pore over them obsessively. It would seem morbid to those who do not fly, but the stories embody our own invincibility. And in our meditations we find no augury of our own fate. On the contrary, the detailed technical analyses of fatal crashes bestow on us a completely illogical sense of mastery. We rehearse the drama to avoid taking part in it.

I now had two completely different theories of what happened. Euphoria and the bent nickel. There would be more.

I flew the Delfin home. Miller asked if I wanted to go out over the valley and do some aerobatics. I told him I didn't much feel like it.

––––––––––––

The beer came out at dusk. Edan Shalev sat quietly in Randy's office. He seemed apart, within himself. He had just taken Randy's sister for a ride in Alpha Bravo, and she had come down in tears. After a while I went to sit with him. He was a youthful Israeli, tall and thin and Mediterranean looking. He had wanted to fly aerobatics since he was a child. Like Clint McHenry, Edan got his license with the sole purpose of flying upside-down. He immediately began flying with Randy, and there was no looking back. Randy groomed him for the contest circuit. Some people spend a lifetime trying to become as good as Edan was right out of the chute. Randy, for example. Something in Randy's demeanor suggested that he had been desperately reaching for a goal, the opportunity for which was in all likelihood behind him. That top position in his field. He was like the scientist who longs for the Nobel Prize and at a certain point realizes that it's never going to come.

But Randy had something else. Maybe he didn't even know he had it. He had a voice, a charisma, a personality that had put him in the hearts of a huge number of people. When Tony Bill delivered the eulogy at Randy's memorial service, he said that when he thought of Randy, he didn't see him, he heard him. I understood that. When flying with Randy, we'd sit in the back seat, the pilot-in-command seat. Randy would sit in front, the passenger seat. His respect for us said: you are the captain of this ship. Then his voice came through the headset we wore. It was a deep, friendly, comforting baritone with a slightly rolling southern sound to it. Like the Wizard of Oz, he could grant our wishes, but we could not see him. We could feel his hands and feet on the controls as he demonstrated maneuvers. Once while teaching me, Randy had flown the entire Sportsman sequence blindfolded to prove a point. Flying well involves learning to feel.

Randy flew air shows in twenty-two countries. Canadian by birth, he was a member of the Canadian Aerobatics Team and competed in two world championships, though he didn't win. He was a stunt pilot and stunt coordinator for motion pictures, including *Primary Colors, Ransom,* and *Congo,* and the TV series *Beverly Hills 90210.* But he had other dreams. To win the world championship (he never did). To finish the degree in aeronautical engineering that he had started at Embry-Riddle (not that either). Finally, Randy dreamed of being an astronaut.

Randy's gypsy soul kept him from all that. The very thing that made us love him, the nine-year-old boy with whimsical cutouts of airplanes and cartoon pilots, Peter Pan with blue sky and clouds painted on his hangar. In the 1980s, he lived out of a French aerobatics plane, a Cap-10, occasionally touching base with his trailer in McKinney, Texas. Like the barnstormers of old, Randy traveled from place to place, giving air shows or rides or lessons and making just enough to get him to the next place. He didn't settle down until he met Sheree, big-boned and beautiful, British, wild as a Pitts, and then he began thinking seriously about why he lived and what for. I saw the worry overcome his smile at times, that stolen, outlaw glance to one side, as if asking himself: *Am I a failure?* I could see him wonder: *Does anyone see through this act?*

When Plan A didn't work, he turned to Plan B: he gave it all to Edan. He passed it to a gifted pilot, who also had a dream to fly.

"It was very disappointing," Edan said of the world championships, where he flew as the sole member of the Israeli Aerobatics

Team. "It was basically cliques of people, and whoever had the most friends or the most money scored the highest. I saw that there was nothing for me in world competition. One team scored high because the judges were from their country. Someone else came up and flew just as well and scored low. It was all hot air. I never went back."

Edan joined a commercial team that performed air shows for pay. Four Pitts Specials, all painted the same. They'd do twenty shows a season. Most air shows are in the summer. In most years, June, July, and August offer only thirteen Sundays.

"We'd be flying at night, which is illegal in the Pitts, flying IFR [in the clouds] in formation. You didn't dare lose sight of your wingman, because if you did, you're lost, and there's no way to find you. But we had to get to the next show. Once we flew all night and flew the show without sleep. It was dreadful."

But he was living the life. He was a real air show pilot. Randy really was the Pied Piper. He'd made Edan into a gypsy, too.

"When Randy died," Edan told me, "it just took the heart out of it. Before that I felt like I was flying with all his knowledge. He had imparted to me something that kept me safe. I mean, he had thirteen thousand hours in the Pitts. I just assumed that because Randy had done all the things he'd done and gotten away with it, that he'd passed on to me what he had. I have only twelve-hundred hours in the Pitts." Edan says *only*, but that's a decade or two of aerobatics for most ordinary pilots. "Now I think about Randy every day," he said. That's the trouble with this sport. One day you're having more fun that you've ever had before. You can't believe it. The next day your life lies around you in pieces. And you can't believe it.

Before the crash, Randy and Edan had a full schedule of teaching. They were a team. They had students coming and going all day long, sometimes sleeping on the couch in the hangar (for a true pilot is forever and always a vagabond). Now Edan teaches only on occasional Sundays and accepts only a select few students. Tom Cruise has come back from shooting a movie in England, and Edan is teaching him in Randy's place. Edan had tried to quit the air show business, "but there were five shows this summer for which they couldn't get a replacement, so I'm flying five shows instead of twenty. My heart's just not in it."

Edan has a real job. A day gig. He does computer design for a robotic helicopter, which carries a motion picture camera.

"Do you fly the helicopter?" I asked.

"No," he said. "I don't want the responsibility. It's too easy to kill somebody. The thing has a fifteen-foot wingspan, and it gets really close to the actors. We've lost rotor blades before." So for the time being, he works only with the computer, and he seems more or less in full retreat from the skies. But maybe Edan knows something we don't know. Maybe Edan has learned a secret. Control and judgment. Maybe Edan is about to have his perfect score. Remember, this test is pass/fail.

I asked Edan what he thought happened to Randy. He said that it sounded as if Heidi had been doing a hammerhead when the trouble started. The only witnesses were a Los Angeles County Sheriff's Department homicide detective and his wife. Michael Scott was driving home from Ventura on Highway 126. His wife, Lisa, looked out the window over the orange groves in the Santa Clara River valley just north of the Santa Susan Mountains. She thought she was looking at a radio-controlled model airplane and tried to point it out to her husband. She knew nothing about airplanes or aerobatics, and so she was able to give only a general description of what happened. As she watched, the plane went straight up. As it climbed, it lost speed, and when it stopped climbing, it began spinning down. She said it spun all the way behind the rows of orange trees. That was on a Saturday. Lisa and Michael Scott didn't think anymore about it until Monday, October 27, when Michael saw the crash reported in the *Los Angeles Times*.

"The plane wasn't spinning when it went in," Edan told me. Richard Parker of the NTSB confirmed that.

"When an aircraft spins in," Parker said, "it hits at a relatively low speed, and the wreckage tends to be scattered on the surface. In this crash, the engine was buried up to the accessory case." In other words, the plane was going fast enough to bury a large six-cylinder, horizontally opposed, three-hundred-horsepower aircraft engine. Someone had managed to recover from the spin. But not soon enough.

I asked Edan if he saw the wreckage, and he said, "No. I couldn't go. I didn't want to see. I made the mistake of going to look when a friend of mine crashed out here. I was naive, and I rushed out there.

And even now, sometimes when I close my eyes, that image just appears in front of me. I didn't want to see Randy like that. I can tell you that it was ugly. There wasn't much left."

"So what do you think it was?" I ask.

"Something went wrong. It had to be something stuck. The Extra doesn't really like to spin. It's difficult to spin, so I don't think they could have gotten into an inadvertent spin. And with both Randy and Heidi on board, they weren't going to just forget and drive it into the ground. Something stuck. Something broke. We'll never know why. But it tells you: it can happen. It doesn't matter who you are."

Tony Bill's wife, Helen Bartlett, was a film producer. Helen loved to fly with us. She took flying lessons and even soloed. She would fly across the country at the drop of a hat. She eagerly accompanied us as a passenger during aerobatics practice. Tony proposed to Helen while flying inverted. "We were flying along," Tony told me, "and I rolled the airplane upside-down and asked her to marry me." So she was not the typical nervous pilot's wife. But after Randy's death, she was having dinner with Tony and Treat Williams, and she confronted them about the Big Question.

With a four-month-old baby crying in the background, Helen said to me, "I told Tony and Treat that I just wanted to know when my husband goes up to fly that if he dies, he'll die happy. I wanted to know that it meant that much to them." It is curious that Helen and Tony remember the response differently. Helen recalls that "Treat said, 'We don't fly to die. We fly to live.' Neither one of them could say that they were willing to accept dying in a crash, so I said they had no business doing it anymore."

But Tony said, "I'd argue with her about that. We both said that flying does make us that happy. And we would die happy if we died in an air crash." These are the contradictions inherent in the sport, the very ones that make us say we'll never go up again. Then when we find a fiery red biplane under our nose, we leap in with complete abandon and charge off into the sky with a big grin.

What passion, what power of freedom, drives us back again and

NO MORE IMMELMANS

again to face this hazard? I know from my own experience that it does not feel dangerous. Faust, when he made his deal with the devil, had only three wishes, and one of them was to fly.

About Randy's death, Helen said, "I think he had a heart attack. It's the only explanation that makes sense to me. I can't think that Randy made a mistake." In fact, one of Heidi's friends described her as "maybe one hundred pounds soaking wet." Randy's student that day was tiny. And if Randy had suffered some sort of incapacitation—heart attack, aneurism—and had slumped over the controls, Heidi might have found it difficult to overcome his weight. At the altitude I'd reached on my last flight with Randy, she might have had two seconds or less to try. She might have broken the stick trying.

Mike Goulian, a top competitor, was doing an outside one-and-a-quarter snap-roll when the stick broke off in his hand. He, like Heidi and Randy, was flying an Extra 300. He was able to pull back on the stump of the stick and land the plane. Heidi might not have been that lucky.

I asked myself: could an overweight chain-smoker who had endured thirteen thousand hours of hard G-forces have a heart attack? I asked Parker at the NTSB, too, but he said that the remains were too badly damaged for a conclusion to be drawn about Randy's health at the time of his death.

I flew my last flight in Randy's Pitts with Edan. I took off and climbed away from Van Nuys, heading north toward the Santa Susana Mountains. It was the way I'd always gone with Randy. A few miles from the airport I practiced Dutch rolls, then rolled inverted and practiced them upside-down. I flew around inverted for a while, turning left and right, doing flat turns, just playing with the airplane, limbering up.

As I made my flat turns, Edan said, "Randy loved that maneuver." I heard a voice in the back of my head. What was it saying?

Yes, Randy would have made Heidi perform the coordination exercises I'd just done from force of habit. She hadn't flown aerobatics in six years. Randy would have wanted to see how she was on the stick, to see how rusty she was. He would have said, "Why don't you try some

Dutch rolls?" And when she was done with those, he would have said, "Now do them inverted." First Dutch rolls, then flat turns, both upright and inverted. That's always how Randy liked to do it. He would have wanted to get Heidi limbered up and ready to fly the sequence. Why was this important?

I remembered that once when Randy's plane was in the shop, we had flown a borrowed Pitts. When I rolled inverted and started shaking the wings in a Dutch roll, we found a pencil, an earplug, a pair of sunglasses, and the odd gum wrappers, all raining down on us. The canopy was clear Plexiglas, and the objects fell so that they were visible there against the amazing sight of the entire topsy-turvy world. That was part of the reason for the exercise: it was a good warm-up, but it was also a way to find anything that might be loose in the cockpit. If there had been a foreign object in the plane with Randy and Heidi that day, it would have fallen to the canopy, and they'd have found it. The bent-nickel theory wasn't holding up.

On that last flight with Edan, I flew between two peaks, and the Santa Clara river valley opened up beneath us. It was a rich valley, a beautiful green flood plain. I began doing loops and spins and rolls. Every once in a while, Edan would take the stick and say, "Let me show you how," and I could feel the transformation. It felt as if I'd passed a violin to Heifetz. The difference in the way the plane felt was frightening. I had gone to contests. I'd even come home with a plaque or two. But I clearly didn't know what I was doing. Not compared with him. Edan had that touch, the golden hands. The curious paradox about him was that he truly was the perfect pilot, clear-headed, serious, in control, no fooling around. Randy's genius was that he saw in Edan what he felt he might be missing. Randy was desperately trying to pass everything to Edan before it was too late.

I moved on to Cuban eights, Immelmans, split-S's—more complex combinations of the basic maneuvers. Then I did a few half-hearted inverted spins and stopped. I circled. "Where did Randy go in?" I asked.

Edan pointed it out. "Right in that orange grove down there by the river," he said. It was all green. I saw no sign that anything had gone wrong down there in that placid valley, especially a thing as violent as the complete destruction of an aircraft or so grisly as the way Randy and Heidi died. I wondered how it was for Randy and Heidi then. Was Randy slumped over the controls, incapacitated? Was Heidi all alone, struggling with the stick, with only moments to spare?

I flew parallel to Highway 126, recalling Michael Scott, who said, "I was surprised that no one else saw. There were Chippies [California Highway Patrol officers] all over the place stopping speeders." But he had not seen much. Only the last moments. "The plane was definitely spinning," he told me. "The tail was rotating in a larger circle than the nose. The wings were rotating. Then it went behind those orange trees, maybe a mile off. I said something about they'd have to buy a new plane, and then when I saw the story in the paper, I felt bad. I shouldn't have said that. I had no idea that there were real people in there." I could hear the shock in his voice, the shock of knowing that he'd witnessed the last moments of two lives.

His wife, Lisa, had watched Randy and Heidi for longer before they crashed. "It was quite a distance, but it caught my eye because sun was reflecting on it," she told me. *The way the sun is reflecting on my wings now*, I thought. *That late light.* It really pops when it hits that high-gloss dope they use to paint these show planes. "It was flying normal straight and level," Lisa said, "but as it was doing that, it would tilt to the left, tilt to the right, tilt to the left, tilt to the right." She was describing Dutch rolls. I knew it. Randy always had us do Dutch rolls, especially if we were rusty.

"Was it right-side-up?" I asked.

"Yes," she said. "Right-side-up. It did that for about a minute. Then it went straight up like it was going to go to the moon."

I could just hear Randy saying it: "Why don't you try a hammerhead?" Randy loved hammerheads, because they were simple maneuvers but difficult to do perfectly, easy to screw up. And because the power was full-on, in trying to recover from the maneuver, a ham-fisted pilot could easily throw the plane into an inverted flat spin and never know what had happened.

Lisa again: "I don't know if he was going to—you know in an air show when they go straight back down again? Or was he going into loop? But all of a sudden he started falling, and it was out of control.

It wasn't doing what he was supposed to do. It was turning and twisting, but it didn't look like it was a maneuver to me. It was nose down. The wings were rolling. The tail was going around wider than the nose. It was falling out of the sky." The plane was ahead of them as they drove, and she watched it disappear behind those dense green trees down there along the river and the road. "When we went past the spot, we looked to see if we could see people trying to find it, but there was no one. No smoke. No puff of dust. It was so sad when we heard there were real people in it."

So sad.

I remembered once or twice when I had nearly died, how sad it was for a moment when I thought I'd never see my kids again. I remembered asking my father what he felt, what he thought, as his B-17 spun inverted toward the earth from twenty-seven thousand feet over Germany on January 23, 1945. He was the lead pilot, and moments before, his left wing had been shot off by flak over Dusseldorf. His copilot was already dead, and my father was unable to get out of the plane. He told me how sad he was when he realized that he was going to die. How sad he was that he'd never see my mother or his mother again. "I wasn't scared," he said. "I was just sad. Very sad."

"I'm through," I told Edan. "I'm going back."

"Don't you want to fly some more?" Edan asked. "You're doing okay. It's your flight. We can do whatever you want."

"No, I'm through. I'm heading home."

———————

A few weeks later I was talking to John Morrissey, and we were recounting how many people had died in this sport. And why. Miles Meritt's name came up. "He bought a Sukhoi SU29," John said. "A dentist doing an air show."

"How did it happen?" I asked.

"I don't do dentistry," was all he said.

His son Matthew Morrissey used to fly with the Red Barons, an air show team that uses Stearmans. The first time they took Matthew up to introduce him to the team, "the guy who was giving Matt the ride ran into the guy he was joining up with," John said. "Matthew's first ride! They managed to get the planes on the ground. They put 'em in a hangar and shut the door so no one could see." John's point: there is no Good Housekeeping Seal of Approval on pilots. So don't trust anyone. People who crash in front of a crowd are not having a "tragic accident." They are members of the why-didn't-it-happen-sooner club.

Last month two of the Red Baron team members ran into each other at an air show. They collided nearly head-on in a great orange fireball, killing both pilots in front of a crowd.

At the end of our conversation, John said, "Come out and fly some stunts."

And I did. Because we don't really believe that the devil will ever call us to account.

I called Clint McHenry to check on a fact or two. "How long has it been since you last flew aerobatics, Clint?" I asked. "You said seven years, I think. Is that right?"

"Yes, I think that was about right," he said over the phone. His seventy-six-year-old voice sounded more youthful than it had before, more full of energy somehow. "But actually I've done it again in the last few days. A friend of mine has a Christen Eagle, and we went up and did some rolling 360s and that sort of thing, but no *serious* stuff." A rolling 360—a turn of 360 degrees while continuously rolling the airplane—is about as serious as it gets.

"Clint!" I said. "Do you mean you're getting *back* into aerobatics?"

"Well, I might be . . ." he said somewhat sheepishly. "I dream about it at night. I might as well go play around a bit."

NO ESCAPE:
THE ENDLESS DREAMS OF ELGIN

One morning I was sitting in the dayroom at Kilbourne I, a long-term unit at Elgin Mental Health Center in Elgin, Illinois, when a frail blond girl knelt before me on the terrazzo floor and began praying. Her face was plain and round and pale, like that of a saint in a prayer book. She appeared to be in pain. She wore a faded yellow blouse, slacks of a flimsy dark blue material, and cloth hospital slippers. She knelt about five feet in front of me, clutching her hands together in a beatific attitude. She tilted her head and cast her eyes heavenward. "Holy Mary, mother of God," she muttered, "pray for us sinners, now and at the hour of our death, amen. Hail Mary, full of grace, the Lord is with thee . . ." The room was hot and close with the smell of bodies. It was an all-female unit with thirty-eight beds. I saw perhaps two-dozen women wandering this way and that or sleeping in chairs or simply standing and staring. I could hear the television set in the next room. *Big Valley* was playing loudly, as some of the women put on makeup with the help of a staff member.

The praying girl stood and approached my chair to look at me. She stood close enough so that I could see the dried saliva at the corners of her mouth. Her lips were cracked and caked with spots of blood. "I'm sorry, Pontius Pilate Jim Wolf," she said. She bent down and kissed me on the forehead. "I'm sorry." She bent again and kissed me full on the mouth. "I hate schizophrenia," she said.

"How do you feel?" I asked.

"Tired. And it hurts right here." She drew her fingernail across her forehead from left to right, as if she would cut the top of her head off to show me what was inside.

A black woman with a moon face stepped forward and said, "I think I'm God but I might be Eve." She smiled and disappeared.

A burly woman with tight blue jeans and a 1950s man's haircut stood by my chair, leaning in close, staring at me intently. Her face was six inches from mine. She had been in the other room where the makeup was being applied. Her cheeks were painted bright purple, like melanoma, and her lips were the color of wine. She looked apparitional, holy, mannish. She looked angry, as if she were about to challenge me, but she only stared, her brown eyes clear and wet with fluorescent reflections, and we stayed like that until a scream from somewhere broke our contact.

I crossed over to Kilbourne II, the men's side, and sat in the nurses' station, a glassed-in booth from which we could watch the patients circling like fish in a tank. Most of them were schizophrenic, though some were bipolar, and others were so depressed that they were dangerous. About 70 percent of the 821 patients at the Elgin Mental Health Center resdie there involuntarily. It was one of the last of the old nineteenth-century mental institutions, set on acres and acres of rolling land, rich with gothic buildings of stone and brick that nestled among the ancient trees.

At 11:05 an aide wheeled out a stainless-steel cart with a black plastic garbage bag tied to the side. On the tray were stacks of little paper cups, a white towel, a green plastic pitcher of red fruit punch, and a white plastic cassette of medications. The cassette looked like an oversized ice tray. Each cube contained a small white paper cup with pills in it. The orange ones were Thorazine, the green or white or yellow ones were Haldol, and the funny pastel fuchsia ones were called Big Bombers, two hundred milligrams of Mellaril. Most of the patients lined up to take their medications, rolling the pills like dice from a cup, then washing them down with a paper jigger of punch. It was a chemical crapshoot: if they rolled the right numbers, they got to go home. Even though they were long-term patients, the chronic cases, the program called for rehabilitation through chemistry and behavior modification. The days of warehousing mental patients were, at least theoretically, over.

The ward was operated on a system called the token economy. Put in simple terms, that behavior modification system allowed patients to earn points for acting normal. For example, if the Kilbourne patients participated in a game of bingo, they received points. If they groomed themselves, they received points. The more things they did that looked normal, the more points they accumulated. Then, at certain times each day, during commissary period, they were given the opportunity to exchange points for candy, cigarettes, coffee, pop. The object was to get the patients out of the mental institution and into the world, where they could do what we all do without thinking about it: act normal and spend our tokens on those things that gratify us.

A man in his thirties circled the room, waving his hands over his head as if he were trying to take off. Suddenly his hands stopped flapping and hit him in the stomach. He recoiled from the blows as if he'd become used to attacks by invisible enemies. His behavior was odd, but it was an improvement. His ears were blown up with scar tissue— true cauliflower ears—from a time when he used to box himself in the head all day long. Behavior modification, the token economy, had changed all that. Now his hands flapped beside his head, wanting to hit his ears but stopping just short, until something snapped and they hit him in the stomach instead.

A patient with a lot of teeth missing, his head shaved and his face unshaved, about forty years old, rolled a cup of pills into his mouth, washed them down with punch, dropped the cup into the black garbage bag tied to the cart, and then knocked on the nurses' station window to get my attention. "Am I going to be discharged?" he asked, shouting to be heard through the glass. Because I was taking notes, he thought I was a psychiatrist.

"Probably," I shouted back. I didn't know what else to say. But in the current mental health system, his chances were good if he just kept rolling those pills and playing bingo. He smiled.

I let myself out of the locked nurses' station and went onto the unit to see him. He had a big brown-toothed smile. "I plan to join the Orange Force," he explained. "Air force. It's in Mexico. Is your name Dave?" I told him it wasn't.

"Were you born in France? Second War?" I asked him if he had been in the war. "Vietnam," he said. "Nineteen sixty-nine."

"What did you do?" I asked him.

"Carried bodies. Chu Lai."

"What else happened?" I asked.

"Napalm," he said.

A stigmata of deep burns scarred the fingers of his right hand from forgetting that he was holding a cigarette and then ignoring the smell of burning flesh and the pain. Some of the burns were fresh; others were old and crusted over with scar tissue and scabs.

"Are you an MP?" he asked.

I could smell his breath, like opening a bad oyster. I had a moment to reflect on whether he was going to kiss me or kill me, and then the unit director took my arm and gently led me away. Back in the nurses' station she said, "I could see some things that you probably don't notice. He was becoming very agitated, and I was worried that he'd, you know . . . "

"Get violent?" I asked.

She nodded.

I went to the Elgin Mental Health Center in search of issues to write about. But ten days later I found myself standing in the dayroom on a ward one morning, looking at myself in a full-length mirror— that wavy, unreal funhouse reflection caused by the fact that the mirror was made out of stainless steel (the patients would smash a glass one)—and I asked the unit director why the mirror was there. "So the patients can check their appearance before they go outside," she said. "Just like normal people." I checked my appearance. I was melting. When I moved, my flesh oozed this way and that. I tried to imagine what it would do to a schizophrenic's confidence, just before going outside to greet the world, to find that he was melting.

I went to Elgin to learn about the mental health system, and instead I found one of the deepest human mysteries: madness itself. Medical science has been unable to learn what causes it or how it works. Insane people are given drugs, but next to nothing is known about when they'll work or why they have the effects they do, and everyone agrees that the side effects are devastating, perhaps terminal. The method of treating mentally ill people is not a system; it is a collection of a few dedicated and ill-equipped people throwing their lives against a hopelessness that is scarcely believable. There is too little money, too little time, and too little knowledge.

If you go insane, is it better to be in or to get out? That is the central paradox—the koan, as it were—of the mental health system. If reality has dissolved, is it better to face it or to seek escape? There are groups of well-meaning citizens advocating change in the mental health system. Some advocate keeping patients in the hospital longer because they need treatment. Others advocate releasing patients because the hospitals are inhumane and poorly run.

"There are no answers," said Ed Throw, unit director of Souster, one of the old units on "the hill," as they call it. When I visited, Souster was home to forty-seven chronically ill patients who had very little chance of improving. Some would never see the street again. Others would go out and be back too soon to know what had hit them. Throw, with thirteen years at Elgin, is typical of the staff. He has dedicated his life to working with the impossible cases. Everyone there will tell you: if a staff member makes it beyond the first year, he'll probably be there until they close the facility. Throw's life revolves around trying to get one man to learn to keep his pants on, another to wash his hands, another to participate in a game of catch. "We are the end of the line," he told me. "You learn to take your rewards in exceedingly small increments. Any improvement is cause for celebration." Behind him on the couch a young man displayed the erection emerging from his unbuttoned pants, while a dozen other patients wandered aimlessly this way and that, circling chairs, sliding along the walls of the barn-like room.

Souster was among the last of the unrehabilitated brick and terrazzo barns that set sounds free to roam at will—coughing, muttering, laughter, the whispering of slippers on tile, the occasional ultrahuman bark or scream. The smell was like insects kept too long in a jar, formic acid and dried grass and the penetrating sharpness of raw milk. The yellowing acoustic tile ceiling looked as if it would fall at any moment. Hygiene was a constant struggle. Two patients on the ward had recently been taken to the medical building for amoebic dysentery. "We've got a lot of hand washing going on," Throw said with a thin and bearded grin. I asked how the disease was transmitted. "Fecal matter," he said. "So as long as you don't get into any of those kinds of activities, you're all right."

One slack-jawed, soft-looking man stalked me with his hand outstretched, waiting for some signal of recognition. I figured: how many people will shake hands with him in an average month here? I'd been warned, but I shook his hand anyway and was promptly taken away to wash my hands.

Behavior modification on Ed Throw's ward was even more difficult than on many other wards. He used not only candy and cigarettes as rewards but the old "time-out" room as well, also known as "withdrawal of positive reinforcement," a brick cell about five-by-six feet with a high ceiling and a small window for observation. It gives a "recipient" (as the state calls mental patients) a chance to reflect and to reconsider acting out (as the state calls it when they go berserk).

I stopped to read some of the graffiti:

YOU ARE GOING TO

DEATH OR HELL WE BE 7734 OR DR. DEATH WILL KILL YOU FOR

THE BLOODY KILL YOU ARE IN PAD.

The messages were like instructions from outer space. Like the madmen themselves they seemed cognate with order, meaning, context—they cried out with purpose—and yet they remained just out of reach of cognition.

Waves of smoke, loud rock-and-roll music, human and television voices, and mechanical noise greeted me as I entered ATC-1, the acute ward, where people come in desperate crisis, hearing voices, suicidal, terrified, hallucinating, catatonic. This was the other end of the line, and many of these people would be back on the street within a few weeks, though some could eventually wind up in long-term wards like Ed Throw's. Men and women moved up the long pastel corridor lit by banks of bright fluorescent light. The patients came at me, trailing plumes of smoke like the visible auras of their mingling souls, shuffling, lurching, passing, turning, retreating.

A man approached. "Are you a new patient?" he asked. I was walking the corridor, bent over, writing in a little black notebook cupped in my hand, and before I could answer, he was gone in a whirling cloud of incandescent smoke. A security mirror was mounted by the nurses' station, and silk ferns hung on the tile wall in plastic pots. A young man in blue jeans and a blue T-shirt paced up and down the hall, clinging close to the wall. Hammered into the back of his hand-tooled leather belt were the words "Bad Bob."

Rick Nelson, director of Adult Services, a slim and dapper administrator with a thin smile and a guarded manner, had escorted me in. Standing in the scalding light, wearing a silver-gray suit, he tried to explain the system. "A sense of optimism which turned out to be bloated," he said, and I think he meant that everybody thought somebody else was going to take responsibility for insane people, but no one did. In fact, when no one else wanted them, when they'd fallen through all the cracks in all the social systems, then they finally came to Elgin. When Elgin was through with them, many would be sent back into the world. Three-fourths of them would fall through the cracks once more and return to Elgin.

Some of them had been circling us ever since we arrived on the ward, and now a young, heavyset woman named Joanne approached Rick Nelson, examined his name tag, and began talking. At first he tried to pretend that she wasn't there, but she really was, she was terribly and irrefutably there, and like so many mental patients, she moved in especially close to engage. Her skin was yellow and puffy. She had applied orange lipstick in a haphazard way to the area around her mouth. She bounced very slightly on the balls of her feet, twitching, glaring, grimacing, as if she might cry. The muscles of her mouth were out of control. Her hands made little rhythmic motions as if she were rolling something between her fingers.

"I need to keep moving and doing things," Joanne said. "I think I'd be a good candidate for employment here. If I had a key, I could take people on field trips."

"We don't hire patients," Nelson said flatly.

"I've had experience," she told him. "I've been in these places five times. I can cut hair." She wore a green jacket with a yellow jacket beneath it and shoes the color of her short reddish-blond hair.

Nelson suggested that she hold down a job for a while to prove herself. Bad Bob came out of a cloud of smoke, sliding along the wall, and scowled at us. He had dark hair and deep-set, angry eyes.

"You teach vocation here?" Joanne asked Nelson. "I know lots of secretaries. The best in the West."

A small group of patients had begun to close around us, and it was becoming clear that our theoretical discussion of the mental health system was in immediate danger of being overwhelmed by the very people that system was meant to serve. Mrs. Trenton, a thin and ragged woman with holes in her shoes, shuffled up to Nelson and asked, "Can a fifty-year-old woman with low blood pressure do aerobics?" He told her that it was probably all right if she asked her physician. She had a drawn, animal look about her, hollow blue eyes, and shattered ceramic skin. We stood in the corridor between the nurses' station and the dayroom. A man approached with an unlit cigarette held just before his pursed lips. He picked up a Bic lighter, which was anchored to the counter of the nurses' station by a shoelace, and lit his cigarette. He didn't smoke it, he consumed it, sucking powerfully, pulling a lungful, then pulling again and again until he was lost in a cloud of smoke, his eyes wide, a puzzled look on his face as if he couldn't understand how he'd come to dissolve in that toxic cloud. The state provided tobacco, and cigarettes were rolled for the patients who couldn't afford to buy their own. They weren't allowed to have matches, so they had to light their cigarettes from others or from the lighter at the nurses' station. A few years earlier, a man had emerged from his room and appeared on the dayroom floor in flames. No one knew how it happened. A helicopter took him to the burn unit in Rockford. There's a great fear of open flames at Elgin. It seems that, despite every precaution, people will inevitably catch fire at times.

Joanne and Mrs. Trenton followed us as we wandered into the dayroom, where a number of people were sleeping on the brightly colored leatherette couches and chairs, while others watched the television mounted high on a wall. Throughout the hospital I saw the same boxlike chairs. The frames were wood and so heavy that it would be virtually impossible to pick one up and throw it. Patients liked to curl up and sleep in the chairs. They looked like people in pretty boxes with no lids.

Joanne said, "If you're familiar with a surgical procedure, what about lobotomy?"

Nelson was quick to respond: "We haven't done one in thirty years."

Mrs. Trenton said, "I did a term paper on lobotomies in college, because I thought it was very cruel."

"I had my tonsils out," Joanne said.

Through the windows I could see a rusting silver water tower amid trees and prairie scrub and the medical building, which was designed by the architect of Marina Towers on the Chicago River. Sitting in the middle of the midwestern prairie, the five-story louvered cylinder looked as if it had come from outer space in the middle of the night and disgorged all those automobiles parked around it, like so many little cocoons. But no one was looking out the window. The patients watched TV or stared at the walls or slept off the first devastating blasts of Thorazine, Haldol, Mellaril, the major tranquilizers that had triggered the mass exodus from insane asylums that began in the 1950s, when Elgin did its last lobotomies. There was no point in performing expensive and time-consuming surgery once psychotropic drugs were discovered. Having worked against mental illness for centuries with no sign of progress, doctors embraced the new drugs. They prescribed them by the truckload and began turning patients loose. The sad outcome has been that mental illness has not disappeared. The drugs, far from curing insanity, have in many ways shaped the behavior I saw: the pill-rolling finger motion, the yellow skin, uncontrollable grimacing, puffing cheeks, puckering mouths, lolling tongues, shuffling gait, tremors, cogwheel rigidity, and generalized rhythmic movements of the body. Mrs. Trenton's low blood pressure was probably a side effect of her medication. Nevertheless, in many cases, psychotropic drugs are the only means of allowing certain patients to hold psychosis at bay.

Joanne disappeared during a Sprint telephone commercial, which came roaring out of the television, then suddenly stopped. "Hear a pin drop," the voice said, and an actual pin dropped in dazzling, crack-of-doom, hyper-realistic colors. A young black man with heavy eyelids slumped across two chairs, dreaming in and out of consciousness. Joanne returned, smoking the stub of a cigar. Mrs. Trenton admonished Rick Nelson, "Don't allow these people to sleep so much."

"They may be getting used to their meds," he said. The first two or three weeks can be like that. They're not sleeping, there's a lot going on behind those catatonic eyes. I talked to one schizophrenic who described her initial stay in a mental hospital: "I spent six weeks lying on my bed on Thorazine, hallucinating that my friends were being assassinated and crucified and that there was a war going on between the fascists and the angels."

Mrs. Trenton complained to Nelson, "I can't get people interested in physical fitness. How much water should I drink?" Nelson looked at her as if she were crazy. It did sound like the kind of question a mental patient would ask, except that one PhD candidate at the hospital was doing her dissertation on patients who compulsively drink water. Maybe Mrs. Trenton was the object of such research and had been made self-conscious about drinking water. On the other hand, maybe she was just crazy.

We fought our way through clouds of smoke to the other side of the acute ward, ATC-2, where we found a young man named Dan dancing by himself to radio rock and roll in the activities room in front of high-tech stereo speakers. He had homemade tattoos all over his hands, thin brown hair, a spotty moustache. He wore a black T-shirt, corduroy pants, shoes from which the laces had been removed, and a new, clear plastic ID bracelet. He was obviously coming off a major manic episode, and he couldn't stop moving.

"How are you feeling?" Nelson asked, looking around the room as if to say, why has a boy in this condition been left alone?

"I'm feeling great," Dan said with a steely grin. "I feel great every day. Every day I feel great." Dan whirled around us, dancing and dancing. He could not stop. He sang along with the song, and when a commercial began, he mouthed the announcer's words and even imitated the sound effects, *vroom, vroom, brrrrrddht!* He was at one with his radio and his meds.

"Probably lithium," Nelson said as we left Dan there to dance. It can take up to three weeks for lithium carbonate to stop a bad manic episode, so Dan had a lot of dancing to do before he was through. Like all medications given for insanity, next to nothing is known about why lithium works. And if it didn't work well enough, Dan might end up in the room we visited next, a plain cinder-block enclosure with a view of a dead tree and an abandoned red-brick building. The single bed in that room had leather shackles with chrome latches.

Twenty-five percent of all people who are hospitalized are there for mental disorders. A typical insurance policy will cover a few weeks of hospitalization and even less outpatient care. I spoke with more than one parent who had watched a son or daughter go from a six-hundred-dollar-a-day private institution to Elgin as the money ran out and the disease, rather than being cured, progressed from one nightmare stage to the next. Some parents have been invited by their private hospital to board their children at a rate of twelve thousand to twenty thousand dollars a month. Some do, and then the whole family goes down with the mental patient. Divorce, depression, addiction, and suicide can all grow out of a case of mental illness. If there is a villain in this story, it is the insurance industry.

Research conducted by the American Psychiatric Association showed that fewer than half of insurance policies paid for psychiatric hospitalization at the same rate as for any other medical condition. Only 10 percent covered outpatient mental health care at the same rate. Since most mental hospitals today push patients out the door as quickly as possible, the outcome is obvious. A study by the League of Women Voters concluded that "insurance discriminates against people with mental illness."

"This discrimination," wrote the APA, "is bad for patients, for business, for mental health providers, and, ultimately, for the community and taxpayers."

Sandy (not her real name) is a schizophrenic who started out as middle class and normal as anyone. She was twenty-six when she began hearing voices. "If you can imagine what it would be like if there were really fairies and gnomes," she explained to me, "that's what it was like. I was literally hearing voices. And sometimes I'd also hear the voices of the people I lived with, talking about me behind my back." Of course, after they found out that she was hearing voices, they did talk about her behind her back, and then she couldn't tell when she was hallucinating and when she was eavesdropping.

The next step was the mental hospital. One of her first experiences was a private institution, "where they charged me eighteen hundred dollars for six weeks of Thorazine without ever realizing that the medication was making me worse, not better." Her family had her transferred to another private hospital in Milwaukee, where doctors changed her medication to Stelazine, and she began to calm down. (Medicating mental illness is a process of trial and error.) By that time, her insurance money was nearly gone, and the nightmare started all over. She spent the next fifteen years in and out of state mental institutions, in and out of her mother's house, in and out of outpatient facilities.

If you met Sandy on the street today, you'd see a blond woman with pleasant features who seems a little quiet but is perfectly articulate when she does speak. She takes fifty dollars a month worth of lithium, Stelazine, and Cogentin, one pill to take her up, another to take her down, and the last to put out the fires set by that treacherous chemical rocket ride. Now, at the age of forty, she has finally gotten Medicaid and can check herself into Ravenswood hospital when she loses control. "Ravenswood is nice," she said. She spends a few weeks there about twice a year, usually because she stops taking her medications. The central paradox for many mental patients is choosing between being insane and taking a toxic substance. Put it another way: Is someone more rational if she chooses the poison or if she chooses insanity?

I asked Sandy to describe what it was like when she was at Elgin (which was about a year before I went there), and she wrote this:

> Day after day with absolutely nothing to do, no one to talk to truthfully, no privacy, no control over anything that happens—that's what it's like. Plus an imposed hidden structure that can provide interminable punishment at any infraction of the buried testament. Either out in the cold or strapped to a bed exposed to any harm.
>
> The infractions of legal protections are numerous. Medications are given without identification. You can imagine how frightened you would be, given a pill without any knowledge of its content or effect from a stranger in a bleak, vacant chamber you've been locked into.
>
> There are laws which state medication can be refused—however, the psychiatrist can override this. The nurse will inform you of this. If you still refuse, big burly security guards will surround, possibly assault, you, and you will be strapped down to a bed by the wrists and ankles and given a shot of an, again, undefined substance.

One of the techniques to control a fighting patient is to cover his mouth and nose with a hand or pillow. With the patient fighting for breath, the other staff can strap down his wrists and ankles. Twice I thought I was at the point of death by suffocation. Once, because I was in a strange place, I believed they'd be back to finish the job and I would be absolutely defenseless.

The mental health community will argue that such treatment is necessary to control the uncontrolled client. I argue that such treatment can do little to stabilize an individual. On the contrary, it creates an intense hostility, hatred, and anger, which erupts over and over again, until you learn to be docile and compliant, usually by going in and out of restraints. Any confrontation between staff and patient usually ends in restraints.

The traumatic and redundant restraint scene can be avoided. It is easy to identify someone who is losing control to the point of needing restraint. These people can be talked down. The staff even knows when it's going to happen: They set up the bed and the straps instead of talking to the person. They get the order for the action, draw the shot, et cetera. All this could be avoided, but it's not.

I showed Sandy the pages a few weeks after she'd written them and asked if she wanted to change anything. She said, "It's not Kafkaesque enough."

The overall effect of the dayroom at Burr, a long-term unit at Elgin, was that of a large, surreal grade school classroom. The sixty-foot-long room was plain painted brick with a terrazzo floor. A stainless-steel cafeteria counter about eight feet long dominated one corner, with a mammoth institutional coffee urn behind, pipes and tubes and spigots snaking in every direction. The stainless-steel refrigerator and ice machine were both secured with padlocks. A few colored metal lockers stood against one wall, a white cafeteria garbage can near the exit. Some light came through the six tall windows with blue flowered curtains. Three out of the fifteen fluorescent lights were turned on, producing a pseudo-electric twilight. The background noise was insistent pop music from a local radio station. I'd just come onto Burr after many days of visiting other units, and by that time, when people asked if I was a new patient, I no longer knew what to tell them. Sometimes

I was taking notes so fast that I couldn't stop to answer, and they'd go away, making their own assumptions. At one point, a woman cornered me in the yard. She said she was a social worker and tried to talk me into coming back onto the unit. She couldn't figure out how the unit had received a new admission without her knowing about it. When she found out that I was a reporter, she went into a protracted fit of embarrassed apology, but I assured her that it was all right, that it didn't matter at all. Then I found out that she was a patient, and I knew I had come full circle—one flew east, one flew west.

One afternoon on Burr, a nice-looking young man named Tommy, with a music player in his pocket, headphones around his neck, came in and sat down at a table to play Simon, an electronic game that looked like a black plastic flying saucer with four large lights on top, red, blue, yellow, green. The mechanism inside of the toy played a tune with the lights. Then Tommy was supposed to press the lights in order to repeat the tune. As the game progressed, the tunes became more and more complicated, until either Tommy or the machine went insane. Whoever went insane first lost. Or won, depending upon your point of view.

Theresa caught my attention. She was a dark-eyed, dark-haired twenty-four-year-old, with a plump, pretty face. She looked Latin or Italian. She'd been staring at me from across the room, leaning over the back of a couch, resting her chin on her arm, when I decided to go over and say hello.

"Welcome to Fantasy Island," she said with a signifying smile. "Kukla Fran and Ollie."

Tommy had defeated Simon, which now sat on the table, blinking catatonically. With a smug smile, Tommy went to the table to paint. Rich, one of the aides, was trying to redirect his creative energy to a blank piece of paper. "You silly boy, you're painting over someone else's picture."

"You and I ought to get a six-pack each and go to a Sox game or something," Tommy told Rich. It sounded like such a reasonable suggestion, but of course, under the circumstances, it was insane. The White Sox weren't playing that day.

A black woman appeared out of nowhere, dressed as if she were on her way to church, with a freshly pressed pink dress, a yellow band around her waist-length hair, a yellow bracelet to match. The patients sometimes materialized like that, out of the clouds of smoke that constantly circled the room like spirits looking for someone to become. That was how I first saw Molly, coming out of a cloud. I felt as if I'd seen her before: classic and fair, with high pink cheeks and pale eyebrows over pale sky-blue eyes, she looked like a young woman in a Vermeer painting, a misty countenance in smoky light falling through glass. She was tall and athletic with curly blond hair cut in a short and stylish way. She had on a pink sweat shirt, gray sweat pants, and athletic socks. Her manner was outgoing, energetic, accommodating, and she liked to get in close, staring eye-to-eye, until it seemed that so much electricity was going back and forth that she could no longer stand it; then she would break down and laugh and cry at the same time. She came right up to the program director, who was sitting next to me.

"Hi, what's your name?" Molly asked.

"Fran."

"Hi, Fran. How ya doin', Fran?"

"I'm fine."

"Beautiful," Molly said, and she got down to business at the art table. She began a random scribble with pencil on a piece of gray construction paper. At first it looked like a child's scrawl. But then she started painting red circles with watercolor over the pencil marks. "That's Saturn," she said to no one in particular. "Jupiter, Neptune . . . " Then she switched to brown paint.

Meanwhile, Burr filled with activity. Across the room a black girl was dancing to Elton John, and the staff shouted encouragement at her. A mutton-chopped man paced back and forth, his hands trembling in his back pockets. Tommy and Rich were playing checkers. Tommy was jumping pieces, laughing, so clean-cut with his black hair shining. It seemed almost as if he was making fun of what he was doing. He seemed to know that he was young and vital and intelligent, cocky and self-possessed. Somehow playing those games and coloring with crayons like a child was robbing him of his real life, and he could see it going, but he could do nothing about it. I noticed the faintest hint of crow's feet appear at the corners of his eyes when he laughed.

It was difficult to remember that Burr was a long-term unit. Tommy was just a boy, but he was growing old in mental institutions.

Molly's solar system had developed into a brown and maroon chaos with a dark green mechanical-looking area at the bottom, feeding up into swirling clouds of brown haloed in an orange mist and surrounded by glowing heavenly bodies. Molly showed the picture to Rich. "Hey, great," said the aide.

Molly said, "This is your green pea toilet paper," and she began laughing and crying at the same time. Then Molly tore her picture into strips and reassembled it with tape.

At two-thirty an aide named Tim hollered, "Commissary!" and everybody who could do so lined up for Jolly Good soft drinks and Nestle Crunch and Almond Joy and foil packets of instant coffee. (The giant urn contained hot water.)

Theresa approached me, flashing her Latin eyes and said, "Fran was on *General Hospital*. Or her twin. I feel pretty drunk, don't you?"

While Molly waited in line, I asked what her painting was called. "Pea green factory bubble squirt-outs," she said. "Would you like to have it?" I said I would. "Can I get you something?" she asked, gesturing to the commissary. I told her I was fine.

Theresa told Fran, "You'll be a legend in your time. I know why you're here. Because you're going to be a woman someday. I really do love you all, but I'm not Jesus Christ. I've only got two arms and two legs. We're family. I've got all your sisters in me."

Molly poured her coffee from one Styrofoam cup to another to cool it, then drank it in one continuous swallow and sat down expectantly. But whatever she had expected did not occur, and she turned her attention to her cigarette, working it into a growing blue cloud that enfolded her like a shroud. A gracious smile overtook her face. "Can I get you something? Pop? Coffee? Something cold? Anything? How about some ice water?" She took a long drag from her cigarette and blew smoke rings, watching them crash onto the table top in front of her. She laughed and cried.

Theresa told Fran, "You can stay overnight if you want to."

"She can, she can," Molly said, stubbing out her cigarette and rubbing her hands together as if she were cold. She opened a Three Musketeers bar, breaking it to share with Theresa.

Theresa accepted the candy without comment and began eating it. "And I still hear a baby crying," she said.

"Well, I'm glad you got a painting," Molly told me.

Theresa said, "I hear this noise. A radio." I told her that I could hear a radio, too, playing over in that corner. She said she heard another one as well. "I write songs in my sleep," she said. "I sing better in my sleep."

"You sure you don't want something?" Molly asked.

Thinking about those young people going home to their parents, I remembered Sandy telling me about returning from her first stay in a mental institution. "My mother's house was just beautiful, and I was thinking it should be an ashram, a spiritual center. I was lying on the floor, and I looked out the window, and I saw grapes and apples on my mother's apple tree. David and I, the man I was attached to, were going to have a heaven on earth, a garden of Eden. This, of course, was just in my imagination. I was just in torment because I knew I was supposed to be getting married, I thought I was pregnant with the Messiah, the Christ child, and I thought I was in jeopardy. I had a hallucination that my mother's walls were going to be spattered with blood. I was just really traumatized."

I stood in a sunny room listening to a woman, a white suburban volunteer, strum a guitar and sing "He's Got the Whole World in His Hands" with a black man who was criminally insane and looked like a football player. The mental health professionals don't say "criminally insane" anymore. They say UST (unfit to stand trial) or NGRI (not guilty by reason of insanity).

A thin, fit, handsome man approached me. I knew in the most general way what his problem was, because everyone where I happened to be that day, on the Forensic Unit, was either UST or NGRI. But he was hard to figure, young with fine, curly red hair and green cat eyes. His skin was the color of coffee with milk. He seemed luminous, like an angel. I couldn't tell if it was the late sunlight or my imagination. He said, "I done five and a half solid in Manteno before it closed and I came here to Elgin." Manteno was a state mental hospital. I asked him what he did to get sent there. "I caught a case," he said.

"Isn't this better than jail?"

"Oh, yeah, it's better than jail," he admitted. "But at least in jail you know you're getting out." His case would be reviewed in 1990. He said that, except for four months, he'd been on Haldol for six years. As I said goodbye, I touched him on the arm. Under his new tennis shirt his tricep was as hard as wood.

Leaving the unit, I asked the administrator what the man had done.

"Murder," he said. "NGRI."

"Oh, then he'll never get out," I suggested.

"No, he may get out. The average length of stay is seven years."

—————————

The second time I saw Molly she was at Elgin's social center on a Saturday morning. Any patient with a grounds pass can go there to spend money, eat, drink, listen to music, and circle the room cadging cigarettes and lights from others. Ashes and cigarettes and paper littered the white round tables and the terrazzo floor. Flies landed on the people and their plates of French fries. Movie posters hung on the walls behind sheets of Plexiglas. The dirty windows were heavily screened and overlooked an old horse barn and concrete block shed from the days when the patients at Elgin ran a working farm. The day was overcast, and the dirt on the windows or some imperfection in the glass was turning the outside into a shimmering hallucination like that stainless-steel mirror I'd seen. I moved my head, and the world rippled like wind-blown water. A couple went by arm in arm.

An electric cigarette lighter had been built into the wall by the snack bar. The patients had to hold down a button and put the tip of the cigarette against the little filament in the wall, then suck. It required getting into such a peculiar posture that it made you look crazy, so most people lit their cigarettes from others that were already lit, which resulted in a continuous dance of kissing embers going round and round the room, whipping the smoke clouds into whirling dust devils.

Molly flew around the room, greeting people she knew from other wards, smoking, exchanging lights and laughs. It was like a convention of intergalactic travelers. Haldol of Burr meets Prolixin of Souster. Mellaril of Kilbourne I meets Dilantin of Pinel.

Molly came up to me looking like a college student. She had put on a little makeup and wore a short denim skirt, white socks, and sandals. We made small talk.

"Hi," I said.

"How are you?"

"Fine. What have you been up to?" I asked.

She told me about Brown School near San Marcos, Texas, where she went when she was little. She said she had liked it a lot. Brown is one of the more famous mental hospitals for children, noted for dealing with really difficult cases. She remembered that the school smelled very good, "like earth, and the laundry smelled good like outdoors and medium." She said she'd been in institutions since she was fourteen. She loved San Marcos. She smiled a lot, her eyes shining with excitement. She said she was going to order a seltzer, but she was so excited that she forgot and just kept on smoking, as her cloud merged with the next and the next, and people passed around us in aimless circles. Molly was so sweet, it was almost as if she worked too hard at it, doing battle with a demon inside, and fire was coming off her in the friction.

"Listen," Molly told me in her breathless, eager, attentive way, "if you want to take a plane to either Egypt to see the ruins or to San Marcos—hey, first-class flight would be fine with me."

"Okay," I said. I was caught in the classic dilemma of dealing with those who are mad, and I think it forms the basic paradox of treatment. I didn't want to lead Molly too far along in her delusion. On the other hand, her delusion was as real to her as my reality was to me. And so, when my drab reality encountered Molly's dazzling universe, I was left to respond with a noncommittal answer until the whirlwind passed and she anchored herself once more in my world.

As I was leaving the social center, Molly invited me to a picnic at Burr. She said that her parents were coming and I should drop by, share a sandwich, join in the fun. I said I'd like that. Fran, my escort, called Burr to ask if it was all right for me to come. I thought that if Molly's parents were coming a long way to see her, they might want to see her alone. I didn't want to be in the way. Fran came back from the phone with an odd look on her face. No picnic had been planned. No parents were coming. No plan had been made.

By my last day at Elgin, I had stopped interviewing administrators and psychiatrists. I had even stopped taking notes. All the issues and the politics of insanity, all the rhetoric and syllogism of the system, had fallen away, leaving nothing but the people who'd baffled and thwarted us all by going mad. By then they had taken me in, and I felt that it was all I could do just to be there. I had begun to understand why some will stand in mute amazement without moving, sometimes for hours on end, the way fish stay still where the water is whitest.

Molly came out into the Burr courtyard, which was formed by the two wings of the red-brick building and by a high chain-link fence topped with small, brightly colored, triangular flags. I could tell that something had happened. Her aura of energy seemed to have collapsed. She came out wearing pink jogging pants pulled up to expose her calves, but she wore no shoes, which was against the rules and unlike her. She was neither defiant nor sloppy. Yet her hair was in disarray, and her gaze was turned inward. She looked angry, or perhaps she had been crying. Her hair was wet, which made it look brown instead of blond. It hung in tight ringlets around her ears and on her neck. The unit director chased her back inside to get her shoes, and after a few minutes Molly emerged again wearing a man's black suede shoes from which the laces had been removed. The tongues lolled out as she walked unsteadily into the sunlight and sat at a picnic table under a tree.

Someone she knew walked by outside the gate and said hello. "Hi. I can't come out today," Molly called. "The staff won't let me." Then she called through the fence. "Have a nice day!"

Theresa sat at a picnic table with me. "Hi, Kukla Fran and Ollie." I turned over a magazine that was on the picnic table between me and Theresa: *Esquire* featured cover story called "How to Buy Clothes."

Tommy was lying curled up on his side beneath a tree, wearing a crucifix around his neck. He was pressing the unit director to call his social worker, but she said she wouldn't know where to find him at this hour. Tommy said he was in his office. "That's where he was," Tommy said, "at least before they arranged to kill my mother. My *alleged* mother," he added with a hint of sarcasm, and I had the same sense I'd had before that he was going to get up and laugh, dusting off his pants, and say, "I had you fooled, didn't I? You thought I was really crazy." But he just curled himself into a tighter ball under the tree.

A nurse came out to make sure that the people on Thorazine used sunscreen. "It blisters them if they're out for more than ten or fifteen minutes. Tommy's okay, he's in the shade."

Molly stood beside a steel pole. A red ball was tied to it on a length of cord to play some sort of game. She listlessly batted the ball around the pole, looking abstracted. The courtyard was beginning to fill with people, and now, out in the bright clear sunlight, without their protective auras of smoke, they looked larval and delicate.

Kim, a pretty technician with curly red hair, was trying to coax a patient out into the yard for some exercise. "Dan, you want to think about coming out now? You're so close. You want me to help you over the step? You're smiling, you're teasing me." I could see Kim standing in the sunlight talking, but I couldn't see Dan, who was in a shadow inside the building. Was Kim having hallucinations there, talking to an invisible man? "Come on, Dan, you can do it."

After twenty minutes of coaxing the darkness, Kim succeeded in getting Dan out into the light. He looked gray and shaken, a man in his early thirties, unshaven, six feet tall, with short brown hair. He wore gray woolen bell-bottom slacks and a blue plaid, long-sleeve shirt, and brand-new white tennis shoes. He had a look on his face at once defiant, gleeful, and terrified, as if, for reasons he couldn't fathom, he had decided to walk a tightrope across Niagara Falls. Kim put a Frisbee into his hand, and suddenly a change came over Dan. With a graceful fluid movement, he crouched a little, tucked his wrist in close to his body, and fired the blue disc into the sunlight. The courtyard went wild. Dan had a talent. He must have been a Frisbee player in his home galaxy, because he had the moves.

"Hey, you've found your calling!" Kim shouted as she nabbed the Frisbee out of the air and sent it zinging back. All at once a group of patients became involved in the game, and everyone's technique, as if by the power of suggestion, seemed spot on. The game went on for ten minutes or so, and the Frisbee went over the fence only once. But then Dan froze with the Frisbee in his arms, as if he had suddenly remembered how thin the rope was, how far the drop. Everyone gathered around and talked to him, but he just looked and looked, first at the sky, then at the people, then at the roaring cataract down between his feet.

Tommy uncurled beneath the tree and got up to sit at the picnic table with me. He smiled and squinted in the light, like a man who has just taken a good summer's nap. I thought: Now he will return to normal. Now he will finally make sense. "I didn't play post office when I was a kid," Tommy said. "They wanted me to, but I wouldn't let them. I told them I was going to play it when I grew up." His eyes were slits, and he talked with his mouth almost closed. He yawned and got up to lie down again. I wondered if they had changed his meds. "Zenith, Magnavox, Buster Brown," he said. Across the courtyard Kim was not about to give up on Dan. She talked and talked, coaxing him gradually out of his panic until, just before I went inside, I saw him wearing the Frisbee on his head, laughing, putting everybody on.

I found Molly stacking books, straightening up in the dayroom. "I was thinking about buying that school there in San Marcos," she said. Our voices echoed as if we were in a church.

I asked her what had happened over the weekend that took away her grounds pass.

"I went swimming at the water hole and security caught me," she said. "The river by the trees where the trees are. Security said, 'Don't do it again, people have drowned in there.' I want to have a swimming pool put back there. Hey, it's summer," she said defensively. "I thought I'd go down and take a dip." She said a group of patients went U/A, as it is called, unauthorized absence, in order to go swimming. "Hey, I've got a picture for you, I'll get it, wait right here." She flew out of the dayroom and went to the dorm, returning in a moment with a large sheet of pale purple construction paper with multicolored crayon words on it. I asked her what she called it. She said, "Once three times a lady she is the lady."

She brought out construction paper and crayons and made a picture of the earth, which she labeled with the cardinal directions, N, E, W, S. She titled the picture, "Through the earth I see them shine, I see the earth as a bottle of wine."

She drew clouds, and they reminded her of the time she took an airplane home from the Brown School in San Marcos, Texas. "I had a steak and a glass of wine served to me. It was absolutely beautiful. I was alone. It was the best adventure in my life. My mom and dad met me at the airport: 'Are you bad! Come on, let's get some lunch,' they said." As she spoke, she cut up her earth and clouds with scissors. "Whenever you want to find the north-south-east-west," she said, "you mark north-south-east-west, move them around and transfer them around. Here." She moved the clouds to the top of the earth. "Now it's raining in the north. I want to buy Brown School, do you know if it's for sale? How much do they want for it?"

I said I didn't know, but that I was sure it would cost a great deal even if it were for sale. Millions.

"That's okay, I'll find some money."

"How?"

"I'll just find it."

People were beginning to come in for two-thirty commissary. Tommy came in yawning. Theresa asked a woman, "What is algebra?" The unit director, whose name was Diane, turned the television on loud. *General Hospital* played.

I asked Molly how she liked television. "It's terrible," she said. "It's horrible. Some people staring at you. Soap operas are especially terrible, all this weird stuff between men and women, paranoia and depression and schizophrenia. They're terrible."

I remembered Sandy telling me that when she was at Elgin she used to have to skip dinner just to get away from the television.

Molly turned to Diane. "Can you put on something besides this sad stuff?"

"Well," Diane said, as if speaking to a child, "Linda asked for it, so when it's done, what do you want to watch?"

"A ball game or something," Molly said. "Diane, really, this is horrible."

People lined the walls, smoking and staring, waiting for the clock to say two-thirty so that they could get coffee or a candy bar. A man who looked like a truck driver, in new blue jeans and a neatly pressed plaid shirt, sat down at the table with me and Molly. Bob looked about forty. He was well groomed, big-boned, with a recently trimmed flat-top and an open, friendly face. I hadn't seen him before, so I asked him how long he'd been there, and then remembered when I'd first arrived, being asked if I were a new patient. Maybe Bob was on the staff. "Since this morning," he said.

Maybe Bob was another reporter, I thought. "Where did you come from?"

"I came from Wyoming at nine o'clock a.m." He had an even smile, a steady gaze, and clean fingernails.

"How did you get here?" I asked.

"Astrally," he said. "Through the air. I go about two million miles above the earth at night by levitation. Then I usually have gravitational pull and come back in. I travel astrally about a million times a day. I used to travel astrally in yoga position, but since I've become bigger and gained weight, since I've been farming and ranching and—being an astronaut—I travel by teleportation."

Tommy sat at the next table over and picked up a book. "Ah, *The Cat in the Hat*," he said with a hint of sarcasm. "I remember *The Cat in the Hat*." He began to read aloud, as if to point out the kindergarten atmosphere of the place and hold it up to ridicule.

"I'm going to get in line now," Molly said. The commissary had opened, and people were getting little packets of instant coffee and Reese's peanut butter cups and pop. Molly brought coffee and cranberry juice for us, and now, as she sat drinking, she began to turn inward, her shoulders rocking gently.

"Did you get a chance to attend the Olympics?" Bob asked. I said I hadn't but that I had seen some events on television. "I was a gold medalist in every event at the Los Angeles Olympics," he said. "Five thousand two hundred twenty-four, three million nine hundred thousand eight hundred and thirty-eight . . ."

Molly withdrew into her cigarette, laughing and crying softly. A loud Kraft mayonnaise commercial was blasting us as the screen filled with cumulo-nimbus whorls of creamy white. A giant came up and muttered at me incoherently, taking my hand in his great, soft paw. Bob rattled off numbers, while Tommy read *The Cat in the Hat* and Molly cried. A girl on the couch shouted, "Goddamnit! That's it!" Checkers went rolling across the tile floor as people wandered up and down, eating, smoking, drinking. I don't know whether it was the sugar or the time of day or the excitement of interacting at the commissary, but the room seemed to be reaching a symphonic climax.

Molly pulled herself together and tried to explain her predicament. "These aren't my real teeth," she said, placing her right hand flat on the table, fingers splayed. "They had to put on lots of lotion to get the pin taken out of this finger. They'll straighten up all right."

Tommy shouted, "Electron bombardment!" then resumed reading: "He picked up the cake and the rake and the gown and the milk and the strings and the books and the dish. And the fan, and the cup and the ship and the fish and he put them away. Then he said, 'That's that.' And then he was gone with a tip of his hat."

I asked Molly what she did when she was little.

She said, "Played volleyball, smoked pot, drank Southern Comfort and fruit punch. Say, I know a writer. He wrote di-ographies. He had a good tact. Do you want me to sing for you? Let me get my radio, and I'll sing for you." When she headed for the dorm, Tommy came over with a coloring book and flipped the pages for the unit director, narrating each drawing. Diane, the unit director, was clearly made uncomfortable by Tommy's closeness and perhaps by the sense that he was mocking her, mocking the coloring book, mocking the insanity of their circumstances. "These are ICBMs," he said, pushing the drawings close to her face. "Save the last dance for me. They say the world's been destroyed before. It was a hell of a car, a Nash, you could find it in any Bible." But as before, his speech seemed to have a subtext: *Okay, you want me to be insane? How's this? Is this insane enough for you?*

Molly came back quickly, saying, "There's people in my home now holding me at gunpoint telling me I can't get my radio, so I can't sing for you. I'm sorry." Then she broke into song anyway: "Mine eyes have seen the glory of the coming of the Lord, he was peeling down the alley in a green and yellow Ford, he had one hand on the throttle and the other on a bottle of Pabst Blue Ribbon beer!"

The unit director informed me that someone from the administration building was coming to take me away.

"I've got to go," I told Molly.

"I'm sorry I couldn't get my radio and sing for you," she said.

"It's okay," I said.

"Maybe some other time." Tommy said, "Sorry. Sorry for spoiling your visit."

"You didn't drink your cranberry juice," Molly said.

"You drink it," I told her.

"Okay. Bye-bye."

———————

One day I was walking the grounds, meditating on what I'd seen. Elgin is a beautiful place set on two hundred acres in the Fox River Valley, with lines of trees in hollows and hills, red-tile roofs on yellow brick dorms, and throughout the area I could see patients taking walks, singly or in groups of two or three. Without warning, a storm broke, and when the rain started, it was as if they didn't know what to make of it. Instead of running for shelter, they froze in mid-stride with the rain pouring around them. I stopped, too, fascinated by what I was seeing, and suddenly I couldn't seem to remember which made more sense, stopping to feel the rain or running to avoid it. Then I started laughing: there we all were, standing in the rain, trying to figure out the right thing to do.